Hebrew Glossary

for texts in

J. H. Eaton's

First Studies in Biblical Hebrew
& Readings in Biblical Hebrew I & II

compiled by

Michael Tunnicliffe

תפורחי זהב במשכיות כסף
דבר דבר על אפניו

ISBN   0 7044 0422 2

1980

This work is produced in the University of Birmingham and may be
obtained directly from the Secretary, Department of Theology,
The University of Birmingham, Birmingham B15 2TT.

PREFACE

This glossary is designed as a companion to three study-aids which are likewise produced in the University of Birmingham and available direct from the Department of Theology.   Thus the words included here are those of the Anthology in J.H.Eaton's First Studies in Biblical Hebrew, *and those also of the biblical Hebrew texts treated in* Readings in Biblical Hebrew *vols.I and II (edited by J.H.Eaton).   Except for the most frequent items, all occurrences in these texts are noted, and the chart on p.v shows at a glance where the passage is treated; in addition, references are given to important comments in the study-aids for particular words.   It is hoped that the glossary will thus assist the reviewing of vocabulary and serve as a work-book for collecting and comparing the various forms and meanings in which the words have been met. A list at the end covers additonal words for the title pages, for the Supplementary Readings of* First Studies, *and for the Ten Songs added in the 1980 edition.*

Most verbs are cited with vowels and the meaning given is primarily that of the Qal (attested or presumed); where vowels are omitted, the meaning given will be that of stems to be cited.   The various meanings of homonyms may be cited as I., 2. etc. without implying a connection; e.g. בֶּ֫גֶד is written once and listed as 'I. TREACHERY, 2. GARMENT'. I have cited the following:

Brown, Driver, Briggs: Hebrew & English Lexicon of the O.T. (OUP 1906)
Gesenius-Kautzsch: Hebrew Grammar (OUP 1910)
G.Fohrer: Hebrew & Aramaic Dictionary of the O.T. (SCM 1973)
W.Holladay: Concise Hebrew & Aramaic Lexicon of the O.T. (Brill 1971)
Koehler-Baumgartner, Hebräisches & Aramäisches Lexikon (Brill, 3.ed. 1967-). Langenscheidt's Pocket Hebrew Dictionary (Hodder & Stoughton).

I am grateful to all who have helped: the Rev.H.St.J.Hart for the inspiring title-page (citing Proverbs 25.11); to my wife Kate for so patiently and thoughtfully typing the first draft and for helping with the proof-reading; to Dorothy Stellinga and Anne Bowen in the Department of Theology for completing the laborious typing; to the members of the University printing unit; and to Mr. Eaton who first taught me Hebrew and who in 1976 asked me to undertake the glossary - little did I realize then the extent of the task!   May the work be of help to some who are now taking the path into the field of the Hebrew Bible, and may they go מֵחַ֫יִל אֶל־חָ֫יִל.

1980   MICHAEL TUNNICLIFFE

ABBREVIATIONS

BOOKS OF THE BIBLE

Gn	= Genesis	Is	= Isaiah	Ps	= Psalms
Ex	= Exodus	Je	= Jeremiah	Pr	= Proverbs
Dt	= Deuteronomy	Ez	= Ezekiel	Jb	= Job
1Sm	= 1 Samuel	Hs	= Hosea	Ct	= Song of Songs
2Sm	= 2 Samuel	Ob	= Obadiah	Ru	= Ruth
1Kg	= 1 Kings	Jo	= Jonah	Ec	= Ecclesiastes
		Na	= Nahum	Es	= Esther
		Zp	= Zephaniah	Ne	= Nehemiah

ENGLISH GRAMMAR

abs	= absolute	intra	= intransitive
abst	= abstract	juss	= jussive
adj	= adjective	m	= masculine
adj.gent	= gentilic adjective	n	= noun
adv	= adverb	n.loc	= place name
coh	= cohortative	n.pr	= proper noun
coll	= collective	pass	= passive
conj	= conjunction	pr	= perfect
cs	= construct	pl	= plural
dem	= demonstrative	pll	= parallel
denom	= denominative	prep	= preposition
emph	= emphatic	pro	= pronoun
exclam	= exclamation	ptc	= participle
f	= feminine	s	= singular
ff	= following	sfx	= suffix
imp	= imperfect	subs	= substantive
imv	= imperative	trans	= transitive
inf	= infinitive	vb	= verb
inter	= interrogative	@	= grammatical point in
interj	= interjection		First Studies

HEBREW GRAMMAR

apoc	= apocopated	i.p	= in pause	Po	= Polel
loc	= He Locale	K	= Kethib	Pu	= Pual
Hi	= Hiphil	Ni	= Niphal	Q	= Qere
Hith	= Hithpael	Pi	= Piel	wc	= waw consecutive
Ho	= Hophal	Pil	= Pilpel		

LITERATURE

B.D.B.	= Brown, Driver, Briggs: Lex.	Lang	= Langenscheidt: Pocket Heb.
Foh	= Fohrer: Heb. & Aram. Dict.	N.E.B.	= New English Bible
F.S.	= First Studies in Bib. Heb.	Pent	= Pentateuch
G	= Septuagint	Rl	= Readings in Bib. Heb. Vol 1
G/K	= Gesenius-Kautzsch: Heb.Gram	R2	= " " " " " 2
Holl	= Holladay: Heb. & Aram. Dict.	R.S.V.	= Revised Standard Version
J.B.	= Jerusalem Bible	Vss	= Ancient Versions
K/B	= Koehler-Baumgartner: Lex.		

OTHERS

* = all instances in readings cited	?(English word) = translation uncertain
H.L. = hapax legomenon	(Hebrew word)? = word uncertain

v

LIST OF PASSAGES COVERED AND PAGES IN FIRST STUDIES AND READINGS 1 & 2

Genesis 1-3   R2 pp1-16
   (1- 8; 2.7-8   F.S p120)
    17-19   R2 pp17-28
    24.1-9   F.S p122

Exodus 20   R1 pp9-14

Deuteronomy 8   R1 pp15-20

1 Samuel 4.1b-7.1   R1 pp1-8
    9.3-13   F.S p124

2 Samuel 11-12   R2 pp29-44
    15.1-4   F.S p123

1 Kings 3.5-14   F.S pp121-122

Isaiah 1-2   R1 pp75-83
   5.1-7   R2 pp71-74
   6.1-3   F.S p119
   52.13-53.12 R2 pp105-112

Jeremiah 11.18-12.6;)
   15.10-21;)
   17.14-18;) R2 pp90-99
   18.18-23;)
   20.7-18   )
   31.31-34   F.S pp122-123

Ezekiel 37.1-14   R1 pp97-100

Hosea 1;2;3;11   R1 pp53-74

Obadiah   R2 pp100-104

Jonah 1-4   F.S pp125-128

Nahum 1-3   R2 pp74-89

Zephaniah 1-3   R1 pp83-97

Psalms 1   R2 pp60-61
   2   R1 pp41-42
   6   R1 pp45-46
   8   R1 pp27-28
   19   R2 pp61-64
   22   R1 pp46-50
   23   R1 pp50-52
   24   R1 pp35-36
   29   R1 pp25-26
   48   R1 pp32-35
   81   R1 pp37-39
   82   R1 pp39-40
   84   R2 pp64-66
   93   R1 pp29-31
   96.1-5   F.S p121
   100   R1 pp21-22
   101   R1 pp44-45
   103   R1 pp23-25
   110   R1 pp43-44
   117   F.S p119
   121   F.S pp123-124
   124   R2 p67
   130   R2 pp67-68
   131   R2 pp68-69
   133   R2 pp69-70
   134   F.S p119
   150   R1 pp22-23

Proverbs 8   R2 pp115-119
   9.1-6   R2 pp114-115

Job 19.23-29   R1 pp100-103

Songs of Songs 1-8   R2 pp120-133

Ruth 1.1-6   F.S p121

Ecclesiastes 1   R1 pp104-106
   3.1-8   R2 pp113-114
   11.7-12.8 R1 pp107-113

Esther 2.21-23   F.S pp119-120

Nehemiah 1;2
   3.33-4.17; }R2 pp45-59
   5;6;7.1-4;13)

AN
HEBREW and *ENGLISH*
LEXICON,
Without POINTS:

IN WHICH

The HEBREW and CHALDEE Words of the *Old Teſtament* are explained in their Leading and Derived Senſes,

The DERIVATIVE WORDS are ranged under their reſpective PRIMITIVES,

AND

The MEANINGS aſſigned to each

Authoriſed by References to Paſſages of SCRIPTURE.

To this Work is prefixed
A METHODICAL
HEBREW GRAMMAR,
Without POINTS;

Adapted to the Uſe of Learners, and of thoſe who have not the Benefit of a Maſter:

ALSO,

The HEBREW GRAMMAR, at ONE VIEW.

By *JOHN PARKHURST*, M. A.
Late Fellow of CLARE-HALL, CAMBRIDGE.

The ſame things uttered in Hebrew, and tranſlated into another tongue, have not the ſame Force in them : and not only theſe things, but the Law itſelf, and the Prophets, and the reſt of the Books have no ſmall Difference when they are uttered in their own language.
Prol. to Eccleſiaſticus.

LONDON:
Printed by and for W. FADEN, in Wine-Office-Court, Fleet-Street.
MDCCLXII.

From an enterpriſing study-aid of 1762, which included a fold-out page summarizing Hebrew grammar at one view.

א

אָב = n.m   FATHER   s Ps 103.13

　　s.cs אֲבִ Gn 17.4,5 אֲבִי Gn 19.37,38; 1Sm 9.3
　　s+sfx Gn 2.24;19.31;24.7;Ex 20.12; 1Sm 9.5; 1Kg 3.6; Je 12.6
　　pl Ex 20.5 +sfx Dt 8.1; Je 31.32; Ps 22.5; Ne 2.3;13.18
　　For forms of s.cs, s+sfx, pl, pl+sfx see @33e & G/K 90 1, 96

אֵב = n.m   YOUNG SHOOT, GREENNESS   pl.cs Ct 6.11 *

אָבַד = vb   TO PERISH, DIE   Qal.pf.3m.s Jo 4.10 3f.s Ez 37.11
　　Qal.imp.3f.s Je 18.18; Ps 1.6   3f.pl 1Sm 9.3 = BE LOST
　　Qal.imp.2m.pl Dt 8.19,20; Ps 2.12 1pl Jo 1.6;3.9
　　Qal.coh.pl Jo 1.14   inf.abs Dt 8.19 inf.cs+sfx Ob 12
　　Pi.imp.3m.s.wc Zp 2.13   inf.cs Ec 3.6
　　Hi.pf.1s.wc Ob 8 +sfx Zp 2.5   ptc.s Dt 8.20 *
　　　　N.B. Hi = CAUSE TO PERISH i.e. DESTROY

אָבָה = vb   TO BE WILLING, CONSENT   Qal.pf.3m.s 2Sm 12.17; Ps 81.12
　　Qal.imp.3f.s Gn 24.5,8 2m.pl Is 1.19 *

אֵבוּס = n.m   FEEDING TROUGH   s.cs Is 1.3 *

אֶבְיוֹן = adj   POOR, NEEDY   Je 20.13; Ps 82.4 *

אֲבִיּוֹנָה = n.f   BERRY OF THE CAPER PLANT   Ec 12.5 *

אֲבִימֶלֶךְ = n.pr.m   ABIMELECH   2Sm 11.21 *

אֲבִינָדָב = n.pr.m   ABINADAB   1Sm 7.1 *

אַבִּיר / אָבִיר = adj   1. STRONG   as subs. = STRONG ONE, HERO   cs Is 1.24 *
　　　　　　2. MIGHTY, VALIANT   pl.cs Ps 22.13 *

אָבַל = vb   TO MOURN   Qal.imp.3f.s Je.12.4
　　Hith.imp.1s Ne 1.4 3m.pl 1Sm 6.19 *

אֵבֶל = n.m   TIME OF MOURNING   2Sm 11.27 *

אָבֵל = n.f   WATER COURSE   1Sm 6.18 for emendation see R1 p8 & G *

אֲבָל = adv   NO, BUT   Gn 17.19 *

אֶבֶן = n.f   STONE   s 1Sm 4.1;5.1;6.14; 2Sm 12.30   cs Gn 2.12
　　m.pl Ex 20.25; Ec 3.5; Ne 3.34 +sfx Dt 8.9; Ne 3.35 *

אָבָק = n.m   DUST   s.cs Na 1.3 *

אֲבָקָה = n.f.coll   AROMATIC POWDER   s.cs Ct 3.6 H.L.

אַבְרָהָם = n.pr.m   ABRAHAM   Gn 17.5ff;18.6ff;19.29;24.1ff

אַבְרָם = n.pr.m   ABRAM   Gn 17.1,3,5 *

אַבְשָׁלוֹם = n.pr.m   ABSALOM   2Sm 15.1,2,3,4 *

אֱגוֹז = n.m.coll   NUT, WALNUT TREE   Ct 6.11   H.L.

אַגָּן = n.m   BOWL, BASIN   s.cs Ct 7.3 *

אִגֶּרֶת = n.f   LETTER   s Ne 2.8;6.5

    pl Ne 2.7;6.19   pl.cs Ne 2.9   pl+sfx Ne 6.17 *

אֵד = n.m   SUBTERRANEAN STREAM

    Gn 2.6   This translation (R2 p8, K/B p3) better than MIST

                            (B.D.B. p15, Lang p4) *

אֱדוֹם = n.loc   EDOM   Ob 1,8 *

אָדוֹן = n.m   LORD, MASTER   s Is 1.24   s+sfx Gn 18.12; 2Sm 11.11

    pl Gn 18.3;19.18 see R2 p21   +sfx Gn 19.2; 24.9;   2Sm 11.9; Zp 1.9

אַדִּיר = adj   MAJESTIC,   subs. NOBLES, GODS

    s Ps 8.2,10;93.4   pl Ps 93.4

    As subs.   pl 1Sm 4.8 = GODS   pl+sfx Na 2.6;3.18 = NOBLES *

אָדַם = vb   TO BE RED   Pu.ptc.m.s Na 2.4   Hi.imp.3m.pl Is 1.18 *

אָדֹם = adj   RED   s Ct 5.10 *

אָדָם = n.m   MAN, MANKIND

    Gn 1.26ff; Dt 8.3; Is 2.9; Ez 37.3; Hs 11.4; Jo 3.7; Zp 1.3

אֲדָמָה = n.f   GROUND, LAND

    s Gn 2.7; Ex 20.12,24; 1Sm 4.12; Hs 2.20; Zp 1.2,3

    s.cs Ez 37.12   s+sfx Is 1.7; Ez 37.14; Jo 4.2

אַדְמָה = n.loc   ADMAH   Hs 11.8 *

אֶדֶן = n.m   PEDESTAL   pl.cs Ct 5.15 *

אֲדֹנָי = n.pr   LORD, ADONAY = YAHWEH   @20d

    Gn 18.27; 1Kg 3.10; Is 6.1; Ez 37.3; Ob 1; Zp 1.7; Ps 2.4

    +sfx Ps 8.2,10

אַדֶּרֶת = n.f   CLOAK   s+sfx Jo 3.6 *

אָהֵב = vb   TO LOVE   Qal.pf.3m.s+sfx 2Sm 12.24

    Qal.pf.3f.s Ct 1.7;3.1,2,3,4   pf.3m.pl Pr 8.36   +sfx Ct 1.3,4

    Qal.imp.1.s Pr 8.17   +sfx Hs 11.1   Qal.imv.m.s Hs 3.1

    Qal.ptc.s Is 1.23 pl.cs Hs 3.1 pl+sfx Ex 20.6; Pr 8.17,21;

                                      Ne 1.5

Qal.ptc.pass.m.s Ne 13.26   ptc.pass.f.s.cs Hs 3.1

Pi.ptc.m.pl+sfx Hs 2.7,9,12,14,15 *

אַהֲבָה = n.f   LOVE   Hs 11.4; Ct 2.4,5,7; 3.5,10;5.8;8.4,6,7

personification Ct 7.7   s+sfx Zp 3.17 *

אֹהֶל = n.m   TENT   s Gn 18.1,2,9,10   + ה loc Ps 19.5

pl.cs Ps 84.11; Ct 1.5 @14d   pl+sfx 1Sm 4.10 *

אֲהָל = n.m   ALOE-WOOD   pl @9e Ct 4.14 *

אַהֲרֹן = n.pr.m   AARON   Ps 133.2 *

אוֹ = conj   OR   Ct 2.7,9,17;3.5;8.14 *

אָוָה = vb   TO DESIRE

Ni = BE DESIRABLE, BEAUTIFUL   pf.3m.s Ps 93.5   3m.pl Ct 1.10

For this parsing see R1 p31 and R2 p124, also Holl. p6, Foh. p6
and compare with that given in B.D.B. p610 and Lang. p204 where
Pi˓el of נ א ה is suggested.

Hith. pf.1.s Je 17.16 *

אוֹי = interj   WOE !   1Sm 4.7,8; Je 15.10 *

אוּלַי = adv   PERHAPS

Gn 18.24ff;24.5; 1Sm 6.5;9.6; Je 20.10; Jo 1.6; Zp 2.3

אָוֶן n.m   TROUBLE, MISDEED   Is 1.13; Ps 6.9; 101.8 *

אוֹנוֹ = n.loc   ONO   Ne 6.2 *

אוֹפָן = n.m   WHEEL   s Na 3.2 *

אוּץ = vb   TO HASTEN   Hi = TO URGE (trans)

Qal.pf.1.s Je 17.16   Hi.imp.3m.pl Gn 19.15 *

אוֹצָר = n.m   1. STOREHOUSE, TREASURY   pl Ne 13.12,13   +sfx Pr 8.21 *

             2. TREASURE   pl+sfx Is 2.7; Je 15.13 *

אוֹר = vb   TO BE LIGHT

Hi.inf.cs Gn 1.15,17   Hi.ptc.f.s.cs Ps 19.9 *

אוֹר = n.m   LIGHT, DAYLIGHT,DAWN   s Gn 1.3,4,5,18; Ec 11.7; 12.2

s.cs Is 2.5   s+ ל = AT DAWN Zp 3.5 *

אוּרִיָּה = n.pr.m   URIAH   2Sm 11.3ff;12.9ff

אוֹת = n.m+f   SIGN, PORTENT   m.s.cs Gn 17.11   f.pl Gn 1.14 *

אָז = adv   THEN   1Sm 6.3; Je 11.18; Hs 2.9; Zp 3.9,11; Ps 2.5

+ מִן = TIME PAST, LONG AGO   Ps 93.2; Pr 8.22

4

אֲזַי = adv   THEN, IN THAT CASE

　　　Probably a dialectic of אָז , only in Ps 124.3,4,5 *

אָזַל = vb   TO BE USED UP   Qal.pf.3m.s 1Sm 9.7 *

אֹזֶן = n.f   EAR

　　　s Ec 1.8 +sfx Ne 1.6,11   pl+sfx Ps 130.2   pl.cs Ne 13.1 *

אָזַן = vb denom.   TO GIVE EAR

　　　Hi.imv.m.s Ps 84.9   f.s Is 1.2   m.pl Is 1.10 *

אָזַר = vb   TO GIRD, PUT ON

　　　Hith.pf.3m.s Ps 93.1 = GIRD ONESELF (for battle) *

אָח = n.m   BROTHER   s Ct 8.1

　　　s+sfx Je 31.34; Ob 10,12; Ne 7.2 @33e, G/K96

　　　pl Ps 133.1 +sfx Gn 19.7; Je 12.6; Hs 2.3; Ps 22.23 @33e, G/K96

אֶחָד = adj   ONE @ 24d

　　　m.s Gn 1.9; 1Sm 6.17; Hs 2.2; Jo 3.4; Ne 1.2   as EACH   Is 6.2

　　　m.s as ordinal FIRST Gn 1.5; 2.11

　　　m.s.cs Gn 3.22; 1Sm 9.3; 2Sm 15.2; Ob 11; Ps 82.7; Ct 4.9

　　　f.s אַחַת Gn 2.21; 1Sm 6.4; 2Sm 12.3; Ct 4.9Q; Ru 1.4; Ne 4.11

　　　f.s אֶחָת 1Sm 6.7; 2Sm 12.1

אָחוֹר = n.m   THE BACK PART, used adverbally BACKWARDS   s.Is. 1.4 *

אָחוֹת = n.f   SISTER

　　　s Ct 8.8 +sfx Ct 4.9,10,12;5.1,2;8.8   pl+sfx Hs 2.3 *

אָחַז = vb   TO SEIZE, GRASP

　　　Qal.pf.3f.s+sfx Ps 48.7   1.s+sfx Ct 3.4

　　　Qal.imv.3m.pl Ct 2.15 = CATCH; Ne 7.3 = BAR

　　　Qal.coh.s Ct 7.9   ptc.pass.pl.cs Ct 3.8 G/K50f *

אָחָז = n.pr.m   AHAZ   Is 1.1; Hs 1.1 *

אֲחֻזָּה = n.f   POSSESSION   s.cs Gn 17.8   s+sfx Ps 2.8 *

אַחֵר = adj   OTHER, STRANGE   f.s Gn 19.21

　　　m.pl Ex 20.3; Dt 8.19; Hs 3.1; Ne 5.5 *

אַחַר = prep   AFTER   s Gn 18.5; Hs 3.5; Jb 19.26; Ct 2.9; Ec 12.2

　　　pl.cs @14f Gn 18.12; Dt 8.19; 1Sm 9.13; Je 31.33; Hs 2.7

　　　pl.cs+ מִן 2Sm 15.1; Hs 1.2; Zp 1.6; Ne 4.7   +sfx 1Sm 6.7

　　　pl.cs+sfx Gn 24.5; 2Sm 11.8; 1Kg 3.12; Je 12.6; Ct 1.4; Ne 4.17

אַחֲרוֹן = adj   COMING AFTER, NEXT, LATER   m.s Ps 48.14; Jb 19.25

    f.s used adverbially AFTERWARDS   Ec 1.11   m.pl Ec 1.11 *

אַחֲרִית = n.f   END   s.cs Is 2.2; Hs 3.5   s+sfx Dt 8.16; Je 12.4 *

אֲחֹרַנִּית = adv   BACKWARDS   1Sm 4.18 *

אֲחַשְׁוֵרוֹשׁ = n.pr.m   AHASUERUS   Es 2.21 *

אֵי = inter.   WHERE?   2Sm 15.2; Jo 1.8   +sfx Gn 3.9; Na 3.17 *

אִי = n.m   ISLE, COASTLAND   pl.cs Zp 2.11 *

אִיכָבוֹד = n.pr.m   ICHABOD (No Glory)   1Sm 4.21 *

אֹיֵב = n.m   ENEMY (strictly ptc. of אָיַב)

    s Je 15.11; Na 3.11; Ps 8.3   +sfx Zp 3.15 R1 p96

    pl.cs 2Sm 12.14 R2 p39   pl+sfx 1Kg 3.11; Is 1.24; Na 1.2;3.13

אֵיבָה = n.f   ENMITY   s Gn 3.15 *

אֵיד = n.m   DISTRESS, DISASTER   s+sfx Ob 13 *

אַיֵּה = inter.   WHERE? (lengthened form of אֵי)

    Gn 18.9;19.5; Je 17.15; Na 2.12 *

אֵיךְ = 1. inter.   HOW?   2Sm 12.18; Je 12.5; Hs 11.8 *

    2. exclam.   HOW !   Ob 5,6; Zp 2.15 *

אֵיכָה = 1. inter.   WHERE?   Ct 1.7 *

    2. exclam.   HOW!   Is 1.21 *

אֵיכָכָה = inter.   HOW?   Ct 5.3 *

אַיִל = n.m   1. RAM   pl Is 1.11 *

    2. OAK, TEREBINTH   pl Is 1.29 *

אַיָּל = n.m   STAG,DEER   pl Ct 2.9,17; 8.14 *

אַיָּלָה = n.f   HIND, DOE   s.cs Ps 22.1   pl Ps 29.9 cs Ct 2.7;3.5 *

אֱיָלוּת = n.f   STRENGTH, POWER   s+sfx Ps 22.20   H.L.

אָיֹם = adj   AWESOME   f.s Ct 6.4,10 *

אַיִן = 1. particle of negation   NOTHING, IS NOT, WAS NOT

    abs Gn 2.5; 1Sm 9.4   cs Dt 8.15; 1Sm 9.7; Ez 37.8; Ps 6.6

    s+sfx @33c Is 1.15; Ec 1.7; Ne 2.2;13.24; Ps 103.16 = NO MORE

    2. adv   WHERE?   WHENCE?

    Only in compound with מִן Jo 1.8; Na 3.7; Ps 121.1

אִישׁ = n.m   MAN, HUSBAND

    s Gn 2.23; 2Sm 15.1; 1Kg 3.13; Is 52.14; Ob 9; Ps 22.7; Ru 1.1

    s = HUSBAND Gn 3.16; 1Sm 4.19,21; Ru 1.3

    s.cs Is 5.3,7;53.10; Je 15.10   s+sfx 2Sm 11.26; Hs 2.4; Ru 1.5

    pl אֲנָשִׁים   Is 53.3; Pr 8.4   elsewhere for pl see אֲנוֹשׁ @33e

אַךְ = adv   SURELY, INDEED, ONLY

    Gn 18.32; Je 12.1; Jo 2.5; Zp 1.18;3.7; Ps 23.6 *

אַכְזָב = adj   DECEPTIVE, DECEITFUL m.s Je 15.18 *

אָכַל = vb   TO EAT

Qal.pf	Qal.imp
3m.s.wc Gn 3.22	3m.s Gn 3.6; 1Sm 9.13
3f.s Na 3.13 +sfx Hs 2.14	3f.s 2Sm 11.25 +sfx Na 3.15
2m.s Gn 3.11; Dt 8.10	2m.s Gn 3.19 +sfx Gn 3.17
1s Ct 5.1; Ne 5.14	1.s Gn 3.12 +sfx Je 15.16
3m.pl Ps 22.30 R1 p49	3m.pl Gn 19.3
3m.pl+sfx Ob 18	2m.pl Is 1.19
	1pl Gn 3.2
Qal.inf.abs Gn 2.16	Juss.3m.s Ct 4.16
Qal.inf.cs Gn 3.11; 1Sm 9.13	Juss.2m.s Gn 2.17;3.17
Qal.inf.cs+sfx Gn 2.17;3.5	Juss.2m.pl Gn 3.1,3
Qal.ptc Na 3.12 pl Is 1.7	coh.m.pl Ne 5.2

    Ni.imp.3f.s Zp 1.18;3.8 = BE CONSUMED

    Pu.pf.3m.pl Na 1.10; Ne 2.3,13   imp.2m.pl Is 1.20

    Hi.imp.3m.s+sfx Dt 8.3; Ps 81.17 1s Hs 11.4

    Hi.ptc+sfx Dt 8.16

אׇכְלָה = n.f   FOOD   s Gn 1.29,30 *

אָכֵן = adv   SURELY, YET, BUT   Is 53.4; Zp 3.7; Ps 82.7 *

אַל = adv of negation, prohibition   LET NOT, MAY NOT @13c

    Gn 18.3; Ex 20.19; 2Sm 11.25; Je 12.6; Ob 12; Pr 8.10; Ct 1.6

אֶל = prep   TO, TOWARDS   Ex 20.19; Dt 8.7; 1Kg 3.5; Jo 1.1

    +sfx.pl form @12e Gn 18.1; 1Sm 4.3; Is 1.23; Ez 37.3; Ps 2.5

    1Sm 5.4 = BY   1 Sm 4.19; Ps 2.7 = CONCERNING

    1Sm 4.21 = BECAUSE OF

אֵל = pro.dem   THESE (usually אֵלֶּה)   Gn 19.8,25 *

אֵל = n.m   STRENGTH, POWER s.cs Ne 5.5 *

אֵל = n.m   GOD, MIGHTY ONE, HERO

    s Ex.20.5; Hs 2.1; Jo 4.2; Na 1.2; Ps 29.3; 150.1; Ne 1.5

    s+sfx Ps 22.2,11   pl Ps 29.1

    as divine name EL Ps 19.2; 82.1 אֵל שַׁדַּי Gn 17.1

אֵלֶּה = pro.pl.dem   THESE

    Gn 2.4; Ex 20.1; 1Sm 4.8; Ez 37.3; Ec 11.9; Ne 1.4;5.6

אֵלָה = n.f   OAK, TEREBINTH   s Is 1.30   *

אֱלוֹהַ = n.m   GOD   s Jb 19.26

    pl = GODS Ex 20.3; 1Sm 4.7; Hs 3.1; Na 1.14; Ps 8.6; 82.1; 96.4

    pl = יְהוֹה Gn 1.1; Ex 20.1; 1Sm 4.4; Is 53.4; Je 31.33

    pl+sfx Ex 20.2; Dt 8.2; 1Kg 3.7; Hs 1.7; Zp 2.7; Ps 81.11

    pl.cs Gn 24.3; 1Sm 5.7; 2Sm 12.7; Je 15.16; Zp 2.9; Ps 96.5

    pl+ לְ = superlative GREATEST   Jo 3.3

אֱלוּל = n.pr.m   ELUL (sixth month, August - September)   Ne 6.15 H.L.

אֵלוֹן = n.m   OAK   pl.cs Is 2.3   *

אֵלוֹן = n.m   TEREBINTH   pl.cs Gn 18.1   *

אַלּוּף = adj   TAME, TRUSTING   m.s Je 11.19   *

אֱלִיל = n.m   IDOL, WORTHLESS THING   pl Is 2.8,18; Ps 96.5

    pl.cs Is 2.20   *

אֱלִימֶלֶךְ = n.pr.m   ELIMELECH   Ru 1.2,3   *

אֱלִיעָם = n.pr.m   ELIAM   2Sm 11.3   *

אֶלְיָשִׁיב = n.pr.m   ELIASHIB   Ne 13.4,7,28   *

אָלַם = vb   TO BE DUMB   Ni.pf.3f.s Is 53.7   *

אַלְמָנָה = n.f   WIDOW   s Is 1.17,23   pl Je 18.21   *

אֶלֶף = n.m   1. CATTLE   pl Ps 8.8   *

           2. THOUSAND   s 1Sm 4.10; 6.19; Ps 84.11; Ct 4.4;8.11,12

    pl Ex 20.6; 1Sm 4.2   *

אֶלְקֹשִׁי = adj.gent   ELKOSHITE   Na 1.1 H.L.

אִם = conj   IF, WHEN   Gn 18.3; Dt 8.2; 1Kg 3.14; Ps 131.2 R2 p69

    Expressing desire IF ONLY Ps 81.9 see B.D.B. p50(3)

    With כִּי = EXCEPT 2Sm 12.3; Ps 1.2; Ne 2.2 B.D.B. pp474-475

    With inter. sense Gn 17.17; Jo 3.9

אֵם = n.f   MOTHER   s.cs Gn 3.20   *

s+sfx Gn 2.24; Ex 20.12; Je 15.10; Hs 2.4; Ps 22.10; Ct 1.6

אָמָה = n.f   FEMALE SLAVE   s+sfx Ex 20.10,17   pl+sfx Na 2.8   *

אֻמָּה = n.f   TRIBE, PEOPLE   pl Ps 117.1 @9e   *

אָמוֹן = n.m   1. MASTER WORKMAN   Pr 8.30   R2 pp118-119   *

         n.pr.m   2. AMON (King of Judah)   Zp 1.1   *

                   3. AMON (Egyptian deity)   Na 3.8   *

אֱמוּנָה = n.f   STEADFASTNESS   s Hs 2.22   +sfx Ps 100.5   *

אָמוֹץ = n.pr.m   AMOZ   Is 1.1;2.1   *

אמל = vb   TO LANGUISH   Pulal pf.3m.s Na 1.4   R2 p77   *

אֻמְלַל = adj   FEEBLE, WEAK m.s Ps 6.3   H.L.

אֲמֵלָל = adj   FEEBLE   m.pl Ne 3.34   H.L.

אָמָּן = n.m   MASTER WORKMAN   s Ct 7.2   H.L.   cf אָמוֹן   1.

אמן = vb   TO BE FIRM, RELIABLE   Ni.pf.3m.pl Je 15.18; Ps 93.5
    Ni.ptc.f.s Is 1.21,26; Ps 19.8   m.pl Ne 13.13   m.pl.cs Ps 101.6
    Hi = TO TRUST   pf.3m.s Is 53.1   imp.3m.pl Jo 3.5
    Hi.juss.2m.s Je 12.6   *

אָמֵן = adv VERILY, TRULY, AMEN   Ne 5.13   *

אֻמְנָה = adv TRULY, REALLY   Gn 18.13   *

אֲמָנָה = n.loc AMANA (in Antilebanon area)   Ct 4.8   *

אָמֵץ = vb   TO BE STRONG   Pi.imv.m.s Na 2.2   inf.cs+sfx Pr 8.28   *

אָמַר = vb   TO SAY, SPEAK

Qal.pf	Qal.imp
3m.s Ez 37.5; Zp 3.20; Ec 1.2	3m.s Ex. 20.20; Jo 1.6; Ne 2.2
3f.s Hs 2.7; Pr 9.4	3f.s Gn 3.2; 2Sm 11.5; Es 2.22
2m.s Dt 8.17; 2Sm 11.21	2m.s Ex 20.22; 2Sm 11.25
1s Jo 2.5; Ps 82.6; Ne 4.16	1s Ez 37.3; Hs 3.3; Ne 1.5
3m.pl 1Sm 4.7; Is 2.3; Je 12.4	3m.pl Gn 18.5; 2Sm 12.19
	3f.pl 1Sm 9.12
Qal.imv.m.pl Hs 2.3	2m.pl Jb 19.28
Qal.inf.cs Je 31.34; Ec 1.16	1pl 2Sm 12.18
Qal.ptc.m.s Ob 3; Ps 29.9	juss.3m.s Ps 124.1
Qal.ptc.f.s Zp 2.15	
Qal.ptc.m.pl Je 17.15; Ne 5.2	Ni.imp.3m.s Hs 2.1; Zp 3.16

9

אֹמֶר = n.m   WORD, UTTERANCE   s Ps 19.3,4

pl.cs Ps 19.15; Pr 8.8 (K/B suggests form אֵמֶר) *

אֲמַרְיָה = n.pr.m AMARIAH   Zp 1.1 *

אֶמֶשׁ = adv   YESTERDAY   Gn 19.34 *

אֱמֶת = n.f   TRUTH, FAITHFULNESS

s 1Kg 3.6; Ps 19.10; Pr 8.9; Ne 7.2   s.cs Ps 117.2 *

אֲמִתַּי = n.pr.m   AMITTAI   Jo 1.1 *

אָן = adv   WHERE?   + ה loc Ct 6.1; Ne 2.16 *

אָנָּא/אָנָּה = interj, particle of entreaty   OH PLEASE! I PRAY!

Jo 1.14;4.2; Ne 1.5,11 *

אֱנוֹשׁ = n.m MAN, HUMAN BEING   s Ps 8.5;103.15 s.cs Je 20.10

pl @33e Gn 18.2; 1Sm 4.9; Is 2.11; Jo 1.10 +sfx Je 18.21

pl.cs Gn 17.23; 1Sm 5.7; 2Sm 11.16; Je 11.21; Ob 7; Jo 3.5

אֲנָחָה = n.f SIGHING, LAMENT   s+sfx Ps 6.7 *

אֲנַחְנוּ = pro WE   Gn 19.13; Is 53.4; Ps 100.3;103.14; Ne 2.17

אֲנִי = pro I   Gn 17.1; 2Sm 11.11; Ez 37.5; Jo 1.9; Ps 82.6

pleonastic Ec 1.16 see R1 p106, B.D.B. p59, G/K 135b

אֳנִיָּה = n.f SHIP   s Jo 1.3,4,5   pl.cs Is 2.16; Ps 48.8 *

אָנֹכִי = pro I   Gn 24.3; Ex 20.2; 1Kg 3.7; Je 31.32; Jo 1.9

אָנַף = vb TO BE ANGRY   Qal.imp.3m.s Ps 2.12 @ 15c *

אָנַשׁ = vb TO BE WEAK, SICK   Qal.ptc.pass.m.s Je 17.16

Qal.ptc.pass.f.s Je 15.18   Ni.imp.3m.s 2Sm 12.15 *

אָסַף = vb TO GATHER, TAKE AWAY   Qal.pf.1s Zp 3.18

Qal.imp.3m.s 2Sm 12.29 +sfx 2Sm 11.27   3m.pl 1Sm 5.8,11

Qal.imv.m.s 2Sm 12.28   inf.abs Zp 1.2 R1 p84   inf.cs Zp 3.8 *

אָסָף = n.pr.m   ASAPH   Ps 81.1;82.1; Ne 2.8 *

אָסַר = vb TO TIE, BIND   Qal.pf.2m.pl 1Sm 6.7

Qal.imp.3m.pl+sfx 1Sm 6.10   ptc.pass.m.s Ct 7.6   m.pl Ne 4.12 *

אֶסְתֵּר = n.pr.f ESTHER   Es 2.22 *

אַף = conj INDEED, YEA, ALSO   Ps 93.1; Pr 9.2; Ct 1.16; Ne 2.18

in question Gn 3.1;18.13,23,24

אַף = n.m 1. NOSTRIL, ANGER   s.cs 2Sm 12.5; Zp 2.2,3

s+sfx Is 2.22; Je 15.14; Hs 11.9; Jo 3.9; Na 1.6; Ps 124.3

dual Jo 4.2; Na 1.3; Ps 103.8; Gn 19.1 = FACE   +sfx Gn 2.7;3.19

    2. NIPPLE   dual?+sfx Ct 7.9 R2 p132   *

אָפָה = vb   TO BAKE   Qal.pf.3m.s Gn 19.3   *

אֵפוֹ = adv   THEN, THEREFORE   Jb 19.23   *

אֵפוֹד = n.m   EPHOD   s Hs 3.4   *

אָפִיק = n.m   WADI, CHANNEL   pl.cs Ct 5.12   *

אֲפֵלָה = n.f   THICK DARKNESS   s Zp 1.15   *

אֶפֶס = n.m   END, NOTHING   s Zp 2.15 R1 p93   pl.cs Ps 2.8;22.28

as adv. of limitation ONLY, HOWEVER   2Sm 12.14   *

אָפַף = vb   TO SURROUND   Qal.pf.3m.pl+sfx Jo 2.6   *

אֲפֵק = n.loc   APHEK   1Sm 4.1   *

אֵפֶר = n.m   ASHES   s Gn 18.27; Jo 3.6   *

אֶפְרֹחַ = n.m   YOUNG BIRD   pl+sfx Ps 84.4   *

אַפִּרְיוֹן = n.m   LITTER, SEDAN   s Ct 3.9   R2 p127 for etymology H.L.

אֶפְרַיִם = n.pr.m   EPHRAIM   1Sm 9.4; Hs 11.3,8,9; Ob 19   *

אֶפְרָתִי = adj.gent   EPHRATHITE   pl Ru 1.2   *

אֶצְבַּע = n.f   FINGER   pl+sfx Is 2.8; Ps 8.4; Ct 5.5   *

אֵצֶל = subs. used as prep   BESIDE

s 1Sm 5.2   +sfx Pr 8.30; Ne 2.6;3.35;4.6,12   *

אָצַר = vb   TO STORE UP   Hi.imp.1s Ne 13.13 R2 p58   *

אַרְבֶּה = n.m   TYPE OF LOCUST   s Na 3.15,17   *

אֲרֻבָּה = n.f   WINDOW   pl Ec 12.3   R1 p111 for interpretation   *

אַרְבַּע = n   FOUR @25d   m.s Ez 37.9; Ne 6.4   f.s Gn 2.10

f.s.cs 1Sm 4.2   f+dual ending = FOURFOLD   2Sm 12.6   *

אַרְבָּעִים = n.pl   FORTY   Gn 18.28; Dt 8.2; 1Sm 4.18; Jo 3.4; Ne 5.15

אַרְגָּז = n.m   CHEST, BOX   s 1Sm 6.8,11,15   *

אַרְגָּמָן = n.m   PURPLE, PURPLE CLOTH   s Ct 3.10;7.6   *

אָרָה = vb   TO PLUCK   Qal.pf.1s Ct 5.1   *

אֲרוּכָה = n.f   RESTORATION   s Ne 4.1   *

אָ ר ו ן = n.m   ARK, CHEST   s 1Sm 6.13; 2Sm 11.11

    s.cs+ בְּ רִ ית   1Sm 4.3,4,5   +   יהוה   1Sm 4.6;5.3

    s.cs+ אֱלֹהִים   1Sm 4.11;5.1

אֶרֶז = n.m   CEDAR, PINE TREE   s.ip Ct 8.9

    pl Ps 29.5; Ct 1.17;5.15   pl.cs Is 2.13; Ps 29.5   *

אַרְזָה = n.f.coll   CEDAR PANELLING   Zp 2.14 H.L.

אָרַח = vb   TO WANDER   Qal.ptc.m.s 2Sm 12.4   *

אֹרַח = n.m   PATH, WAY   s Ps 19.6   s.cs Gn 18.11; Pr 8.20

    pl+sfx Is 2.3   pl.cs Ps 8.9   *

אָרַח = n.pr.m   ARAH   Ne 6.18   *

אֲרִי = n.m   LION   s Ps 22.17 R1 p48, K/B p473 for alternative

    pl @9e Na 2.12; Zp 3.3; Ct 4.8   *

אַרְיֵה = n.m   LION   s Hs 11.10; Na 2.12,13; Ps 22.14,22   *

אָרֵךְ = vb   TO BE LONG

    Hi.pf.1s 1Kg 3.14   imp.3m.s Is 53.10   3m.pl Ex 20.12   *

אָרֵךְ = adj   LONG SUFFERING   m.s.cs Je 15.15; Jo 4.2; Na 1.3;

                           Ps 103.8   *

אֹרֶךְ = n.m   LENGTH (of time)   s.cs Ps 23.6;93.5   *

אַרְמוֹן = n.m   CITADEL, FORTIFIED PALACE   pl+sfx @9e Ps 48.4,11   *

אֶרֶץ = n.f   EARTH, LAND

    s Gn 1.1;24.3; Dt 8.1; 2Sm 15.4; Hs 1.2; Jo 2.7; Ps 100.1

    s.cs Ex 20.2; 1Sm 9.4; Is 53.8; Je 31.32; Ru 1.1

    s+sfx Gn 24.4; 1Sm 6.5; Is 1.7; Jo 1.8; Na 3.13; Pr 8.31

    s+ ה loc Gn 18.2;19.1; 1Sm 5.3,4; 2Sm 12.16

אָרַר = vb   TO CURSE

    Qal.ptc.pass.m.s Gn 3.14; Je 20.14,15   f.s Gn 3.17   *

אָרַשׂ = vb   TO BETROTH   Pi.pf.1s+sfx Hs 2.21,22   *

אַרְתַּחְשַׁשְׂתְּא = n.pr.m   ARTAXERXES   Ne 2.1;5.14;13.6   *

אֵשׁ = n.f   FIRE   s Gn 19.24; Je 15.14; Ob 18; Na 1.6; Ps 29.7

    s.cs Na 2.4; Zp 1.18

אַשְׁדּוֹד = n.loc   ASHDOD   1Sm 5.5,6,7;6.17; Zp 2.4   + ה loc 1Sm 5.1   *

אַשְׁדּוֹדִי = adj.gent   ASHDODITE   m.pl 1Sm 5.3,6; Ne 4.1

    f.pl Ne 13.23   *

אִשָּׁה = n.f   WOMAN, WIFE   s Gn 2.22;24.3; 2Sm 11.2; Hs 3.1; Ru 1.5

s.cs Ex 20.17; 1Sm 4.19; 2Sm 11.3;12.10; Hs 1.2

s+sfx Gn 2.24;17.15; 2Sm 11.11;12.9; Hs 2.4; Ru 1.1

pl נָשִׁים @33e Gn 18.11; Na 3.13; Ct 1.8; Ru 1.4; Ne 13.23

pl+sfx 2Sm 12.11; Je 18.21; Ne 4.8;5.1   pl.cs 2Sm 12.8

אַשּׁוּר = n.loc   ASSYRIA, ASSHUR   Gn 2.14; Hs 11.5,11; Na 3.18
                                                          Zp 2.13   *

אֲשִׁישָׁה = n.f   RAISIN CAKE   pl Ct 2.5   pl.cs Hs 3.1   *

אֶשְׁכּוֹל = n.m   CLUSTER   s.cs Ct 1.4   pl Ct 7.8   pl.cs Ct 7.9   *

אָשָׁם = n.m   GUILT OFFERING   s 1Sm 6.3,4,8,17; Is 53.10   *

אַשְׁפֹּת = n.f   DUNG HEAP   s Ne 2.13   *

אַשְׁקְלוֹן = n.loc   ASHKELON   1Sm 6.17; Zp 2.4,7   *

אֲשֶׁר = relative pro   WHO, WHICH

Gn 24.2; Dt 8.1; 1Sm 9.5; 1Kg 3.6; Je 31.32; Hs 1.1; Jo 1.5

אָשַׁר = vb   TO GO STRAIGHT   Qal.imv.m.pl Pr 9.6

Pi.imp.3m.pl+sfx Ct 6.9 = PRONOUNCE HAPPY

Pi.imv.m.pl Is 1.17 = SET RIGHT   *

אֹשֶׁר = n.m   HAPPINESS, BLESSEDNESS   only in pl.cs אַשְׁרֵי R1 p42

Ps 1.1;2.12;84.5,6,13; Pr 8.32,34   *

אַתְּ = pro.2f.s   YOU   Na 3.11; Ct 6.4   *

אֵת/אֶת־ = particle denoting object of verb @6c

Gn 1.1; Ex 20.1; 1Sm 9.3; Is 1.4; Jo 1.5; Ps 134.1; Ec 1.13

+sfx @16f Gn 17.2; Dt 8.6; 2Sm 12.9; Je 31.34; Ez 37.12; Ct 2.7

with מִן Ps 24.5

אֵת/אֶת־ = prep   WITH   2Sm 11.9; Is 53.9; Je 12.5; Zp 3.19; Ne 6.16

+ מִן 2Sm 15.3 B.D.B. p86

+sfx Gn 17.3; Ex 20.23; 1Sm 9.3; 2Sm 12.17; Je 12.1(G/K 103b)

אֵת = n.m   MATTOCK, PLOUGHSHARE   pl Is 2.4   *

אַתָּה/אַתָּ = pro.2m.s   YOU   Ex 20.10; 2Sm 15.2; 1Kg 3.6; Ob 8; Jo 1.8

אָתוֹן = n.f   SHE-ASS   pl 1Sm 9.3,5   *

אַתֶּם = pro.2m.pl   YOU   Ex 20.22; Hs 1.9; Zp 2.12; Ps 82.6; Ne 1.8

אֶתְמוֹל = adv   FORMERLY   1Sm 4.7   *

אֶתְנָה = n.f   HIRE OF A PROSTITUTE   s Hs 2.14   *

בְּ

בְּ = prep   IN   s+sfx Dt 8.9; 1Sm 6.15; Jc 31.32; Jo 1.3; Ps 24.1

= AGAINST   Ex 20.16; 1Sm 5.9;6.9; Is 1.2

= AS   Is 2.2 G/K 119i = FOR   Gn 18.28 R2 p24

= FROM   Ps 84.6   of price Is 2.22 G/K 119p

בְּאֵר = n.f   WELL   s.cs Ct 4.15   *

בְּאֵרִי = n.pr.m   BEERI   Hs 1.1   *

בְּאֻשִׁים = n.m.pl   WILD GRAPES   Is 5.2,4   *

בָּבֶל = n.loc   BABEL, BABYLON   Ne 13.6   *

בָּגַד = vb   TO ACT TREACHEROUSLY

Qal.pf.3m.pl Je 12.6   ptc.pl.cs Je 12.1   *

בֶּגֶד = n.m   1 TREACHERY   s.ip Je 12.1   *

2 GARMENT   pl+sfx Ps 22.19; Ne 4.17   *

בִּגְדוֹת = n.f.pl.abst   TREACHERY, FAITHLESSNESS   Zp 3.4 H.L.

בִּגְתָן = n.pr.m   BIGTHAN   Es 2.21   *

בַּד = n.m   PART, SEPARATION

s+sfx = ALONE   Gn 2.18; Dt 8.3; Is 2.11,17

pl Hs 11.6 see R1 p72, B.D.B. p94, K/B p105   *

בָּדָא = vb   TO DEVISE   Qal.ptc m.s+sfx Ne 6.8 R2 p55   *

בָּדָד = n.m   ISOLATION   s Je 15.17   *

בְּדִיל = n.m   DROSS (from refining process)   pl+sfx Is 1.25   *

בָּדַל = vb   TO SEPARATE   Hi.imp.3m.s Gn 1.4,7   3m.pl Ne 13.3

Hi.inf.cs Gn 1.14,18   ptc.m.s Gn 1.6   *

בְּדֹלַח = n.m   BDELLIUM   s Gn 2.12   *

בֹּהוּ = n.m   EMPTINESS, VOID   s Gn 1.2   *

בָּהַל = vb   TO BE TERRIFIED   Ni.pf.3f.s Ps 6.4   3m.pl Ps 6.3;48.6

Ni.imp.3m.pl Ps 6.11   ptc.f.s = SUDDEN DESTRUCTION Zp 1.18 R1 p88

Pi.imp.3m.s+sfx Ps 2.5   *

בְּהֵמָה = n.f   CATTLE   s Gn 1.24;2.20; Jo 3.7;4.11; Zp 1.3; Ne 2.12

s+sfx Ex 20.10   pl Je 12.4

בּוֹא = vb   TO COME, GO   @30b

Qal.pf

    3m.s Ex 20.20; 1Sm 9.12

    3f.s Gn 18.21 R2 p33; 1Sm 6.14

    1.s Ct 5.1; Ne 6.10

    3m.pl 1Sm 9.5; Is 2.19

    2m.pl Dt 8.1

    imv.m.s Is 2.10

    imv.f.s Ez 37.9; Na 3.14

    imv.m.pl Ps 100.2,4

    inf.cs 1Kg 3.7; Jo 1.3   +sfx 1Sm 9.13; Ps 121.8

    ptc.m.s 2Sm 11.10; Ec 1.4   f.s Jo 1.3

    ptc.m.pl Gn 18.11; Je 31.31   f.pl Ne 6.17

Hi.pf

    3m.s+sfx Ct 1.4;2.4

    1.s Ez 37.12   +sfx Ne 1.9

    3m.pl Ne 13.12

    inf.cs Is 1.13; Na 2.12

    imv.m.s Je 17.18

    ptc.m.s Ez 37.5 +sfx Dt 8.7   pl Ne 13.15,16

Qal.imp

    3m.s 2Sm 15.4; Ps 121.1

    3f.s Gn 19.33; Jo 2.8

    2m.s Jo 1.8; Ps 101.2

    1.s 2Sm 11.11; Hs 11.9

    3m.pl 1Sm 7.1; Ps 22.32

    2m.pl Is 1.12

    1.pl Ne 4.5

    juss.3m.s Je 17.15; Ct 4.16

    juss.2m.s Ob 13

    juss.2f.s Ct 4.8

Hi.imp

    3m.s Gn 2.19   +sfx Ec 11.9

    2m.s Je 18.22

    1.s Zp 3.20   +sfx Ct 8.2

    3m.pl Gn 19.10   +sfx 1Sm 5.1

    1.pl 1Sm 9.7

בּוּז = vb TO DESPISE   Qal.imp.3m.pl Ct 8.1,7   inf.abs Ct 8.7   *

בּוּזָה = n.f CONTEMPT   s Ne 3.36   H.L.

בּוּקָה = n.f EMPTINESS, DESOLATION   s Na 2.11   H.L.

בּוֹר = n.m CISTERN, PIT   s Ec 12.6   *

בּוֹשׁ = vb TO BE ASHAMED   @30d   Qal.pf.3m.pl Je 20.11; Ps 22.6

    Qal.imp.2f.s Zp 3.11   3m.pl Is 1.29; Ps 6.11

    Qal.juss.3m.pl Je 17.18   coh.m.s Je 17.18

    Hi.pf.3f.s Hs 2.7   Hith.imp.3m.pl Gn 2.25   *

בּוּשָׁה = n.f SHAME   s Ob 10   *

בַּז = n.m BOOTY, PLUNDER   s Je 15.13   *

בָּזָה = vb TO DESPISE   @32   Qal.pf.3m.s Ps 22.25

    Qal.pf.2m.s 2Sm 12.9   +sfx 2Sm 12.10   imp.3m.pl Ne 2.19

    Qal.ptc.pass.m.s   בָּזוּי Ob 2   s.cs Ps 22.7

    Ni.ptc.m.s Is 53.3   *

בִּזָּה = n.f   BOOTY, PLUNDER   s Ne 3.36   *

בָּזַז = vb   TO PLUNDER   Qal.imp.3m.pl+sfx Zp 2.9   imv.m.pl Na 2.10 *

בָּחוּר = n.m   YOUNG MAN   s Ec 11.9   pl Je 11.22   +sfx Je 18.21   *

בְּחוּרוֹת = n.f.pl.abst AGE OF YOUTH   +sfx Ec 11.9;12.1   *

בָּחַן = vb   TO TEST   Qal.pf.2m.s Je 12.3

        Qal.imp.1.s+sfx Ps 81.8   ptc.m.s Je 11.20;20.12   *

בָּחַר = vb   TO CHOOSE

        Qal.pf.2m.s 1Kg 3.8   1.s Ps 84.11; Ne 1.9   2m.pl Is 1.29

        Qal.ptc.pass.m.s Ct 5.15   Ni.ptc.m.s Pr 8.10,19   *

בָּטַח = vb   TO TRUST   Qal.pf.3f.s Zp 3.2   3m.pl Ps 22.5,6

        Qal.ptc Je 12.5; Ps 84.13   Hi.ptc+sfx   MAKE ME SECURE Ps 22.10   *

בֶּטַח = n.m   SECURITY, SAFETY   s Hs 2.20; Zp 2.15   *

בָּטֵל = vb   TO CEASE, BE IDLE   Qal.pf.3m.pl Ec 12.3   H.L.

בֶּטֶן = n.f   WOMB, BELLY   s Ps 22.10,11   s.cs Jo 2.3   s+sfx Ct 7.3 *

בִּין = vb   TO UNDERSTAND, PAY ATTENTION   @30

        Qal.imp.3m.s Ps 19.13; 2Sm 12.19   1.s Ne 13.7   3m.pl Ps 82.5

        Ni.ptc.m.s 1Kg 3.12

        Hi.imv.m.pl Pr 8.5   inf.cs 1Kg 3.9,11   ptc.m.s Pr 8.9

        Hithpolel.pf.3m.s Is 1.3   3m.pl Is 52.15   *

בֵּין = prep   BETWEEN   s.cs Gn 1.4; 1Kg 3.9; Is 5.3; Ob 4; Jo 4.11

        s+sfx Gn 3.15;17.2ff; Is 5.3

        time reference Ne 5.18 (rare, see B.D.B. p 107d)

בִּינָה = n.f   UNDERSTANDING, INSIGHT   s Pr 8.14;9.6   *

בִּירָה = n.f   FORTIFIED CITY, CITADEL   s Ne 1.1;2.8;7.2   *

בֵּית = prep   BETWEEN   f of בֵּין s.cs Pr 8.2   *

בַּיִת = n.m   HOUSE   @33e   s Gn 17.12; Ps 84.4; Ec 12.3; Ne 2.8

        s.cs Ex 20.2; Dt 8.14; Is 5.7   s+sfx Gn 24.2; Ps 93.5; Pr 9.1

        pl Dt 8.12; Ne 7.4   pl.cs Zp 2.7   pl+sfx Je 18.22; Hs 11.11

        + ה loc Gn 19.10; 1Sm 6.7

        of animals 1Sm 6.7,10   of birds Ps 84.4

בֵּית־הַשִּׁמְשִׁי = adj.gent BETHSHEMESHITE   1Sm 6.14,18   *

בֵּית־לֶחֶם = n.loc BETHLEHEM   Ru 1.1,2   *

בֵּית־שֶׁמֶשׁ = n.loc BETHSHEMESH   1Sm 6.9ff

בָּכָא = n.m ?WATERLESS PLACE   ?BALSALM TREE   B.D.B. p113, Lang p 40

    s Ps 84.7 in phrase עֵמֶק הַבָּכָא R2 p65   *

בָּכָה = vb   TO WEEP   Qal.imp.2m.s.wc 2Sm 12.21

    Qal.imp.1.s 2Sm 12.22; Ne 1.4   inf.cs Ec 3.4   *

בִּכּוּרִים = n.m.pl   FIRST FRUITS   Na 3.12; Ne 13.31   *

בְּכִי = n.m   WEEPING   s+sfx Ps 6.9   *

בְּכִירָה = n.f   FIRST BORN   Gn 19.31,33,34,37   *

בַּל = particle of negation   NOT (poetic equivalent of לֹא)   Ps 93.1 *

בָּלָה = vb   TO WEAR OUT   @32   Qal.pf.3f.s Dt 8.4

    Qal.inf.cs+sfx Gn 18.12   *

בְּלִי = particle of negation   NOT, WITHOUT   Ps 19.4   + מִן Zp 3.6   *

בְּלִיַּעַל = n.m   WORTHLESSNESS   s Ps 101.3

    almost as a name BELIAL   Na 1.11;2.1   R2 p78   *

בָּלַע = vb   TO SWALLOW   Qal.pf.3m.pl+sfx Ps 124.3

    Qal.inf.cs Jo 2.1   *

בִּלְעָם = n.pr.m   BALAAM   Ne 13.2   *

בָּלַק = vb   TO DEVASTATE, LAY WASTE   Pu.ptc.f.s Na 2.11   *

בִּלְתִּי = conj   SO AS NOT, IN ORDER NOT

    with לְ +inf Gn 3.11;19.21; Dt 8.11   לְ +imp Ex 20.20   *

בָּמָה = n.f   HIGH PLACE   s 1Sm 9.12   + ה loc 1Sm 9.13   *

בֵּן = n.m   SON   s Gn 17.16; 1Sm 4.20; 1Kg 3.6; Je 20.15; Hs 1.3

    s.cs בֶּן Gn 17.12; Is 1.1; Ez 37.9; Jo 1.1   בֶּן Jo 4.10

    pl Gn 3.16; Ex 20.5; Hs 11.10; Ps 103.13; Pr 8.32; Ct 2.3

    pl+sfx Gn 18.19; 2Sm 12.3; Je 11.22; Hs 2.6; Ru 1.1; Ne 4.8

    pl.cs Ex 20.22; 2Sm 11.1; Is 53.14; Ob 12; Pr 8.4; Ec 1.13

    young of animals Gn 18.7,8; 1Sm 6.7,10

    with time reference = DAYS/YEARS OLD   Gn 17.1ff; 1Sm 4.15; Jo 4.10

בָּנָה = vb   TO BUILD   Qal.pf.3f.s Pr 9.1   1.s Ne 6.1   3m.pl Zp 1.13

    Qal.pf.1.pl Ne 2.18,20   imp.3m.s.apoc Gn 2.22; Is 5.2

    Qal.imp.2m.s Dt 8.12   1.pl Ct 8.9; Ne 3.38

    Qal.juss.2m.s Ex 20.25   coh.s+sfx Ne 2.5 pl Ne 2.17

    Qal.ptc.m.s Ne 6.6   m.pl Ne 3.33,35,37;4.11,12

    Qal.ptc.pass.m.s. Ct 4.4   m.pl Ne 7.4

    Qal.inf.cs Ec 3.3; Ne 4.4   Ni.pf.3f.s Ne 7.1   *

בִּנְיָמִין = n.pr.m   BENJAMIN   1Sm 4.12;9.1; Ob 19   *

בֶּן־יְמִינִי = adj.gent   BENJAMINITE   1Sm 9.4   lacks ־בֶּן   *

בַּעַד = subs used as prep   BEHIND, THROUGH, AWAY FROM
    s Ct 4.1,3;6.7   s.cs 1Sm 4.18; 2Sm 12.16   s+sfx Jo 2.7   *

בָּעָה = vb   TO ENQUIRE, SEARCH OUT   Ni.pf.3m.pl Ob 6   *

בָּעַל = vb   TO MARRY, BE HUSBAND TO   Qal.pf.1.s Je 31.32   *

בַּעַל = n.m   OWNER, LORD   & n.pr.m   BAAL in Hs 2.10; Zp 1.4
    s.cs Na 1.2   s+sfx 2Sm 11.26; Hs 2.18   pl Hs 2.15,19;11.2
    pl.cs Ne 6.18   pl(of honour)+sfx Is 1.3 G/K 124i   *

בַּעֲלָה = n.f   MISTRESS   s.cs Na 3.4   *

בַּעַל־הָמוֹן = n.loc   BAAL-HAMON (site unknown)   Ct 8.11   H.L.

בָּעַר = vb   TO BURN, CONSUME   Qal.pf.3m.pl.wc Is 1.31
    Qal.imp.3m.s Ps 2.12   ptc.f.s. Je 20.9
    Pi.inf.cs Is 5.5   Hi.pf.1.s.wc Na 2.14   *

בָּצֵק = vb   TO SWELL UP   Qal.pf.3f.s Dt 8.4   *

בָּצַר = vb   TO FORTIFY, MAKE IMPREGNABLE   Qal.ptc.m.pl Ob 5
    Qal.ptc.pass.f.s Is 2.15; Je 15.20   f.pl Zp 1.16   *

בָּקַע = vb   TO BREAK OPEN   Pi.imp.3m.pl 1Sm 6.14   *

בִּקְעָה = n.f   VALLEY, PLAIN   s Dt 8.7; Ez 37.1,2   s.cs Ne 6.2   *

בָּקַק = vb   TO EMPTY   Qal.imp.3m.pl+sfx Na 2.3   ptc.pl Na 2.3   *

בָּקָר = n.m   CATTLE, HERD   s Gn 18.7,8; 2Sm 12.2; Jo 3.7
    s+sfx Ex 20.24; Dt 8.13; 2Sm 12.14   *

בֹּקֶר = n.m   MORNING   s Gn 1.5;19.27; 1Sm 5.4; Je 20.16; Zp 3.3
    pl Ps 101.8   Ps 130.6   *

בָּקַשׁ = vb   TO SEEK
Pi.pf   Pi.imp
3m.s Is 1.12   3m.s.wc 2Sm 12.16
3f.s+sfx Hs 2.9   2f.s Na 3.11
1.s Ct 3.1; Ne 5.18   1.s Na 3.7
1.s+sfx Ct 3.1b,2; 5.6   3m.pl Es 2.21
3m.pl Hs 3.5; Zp 1.6   1.pl Ne 5.12   +sfx Ct 6.1

Pi.imv.m.s 1Sm 9.3   m.pl Zp 2.3   coh.s Ct 3.2

Pi.ptc.m.s Ne 2.4   m.pl Je 11.21   m.pl.cs Ps 24.6

Pi.inf.cs Ec 3.6; Ne 2.10   Pu.imp.3m.s.wc Es 2.23   *

בַּר = adj   PURE   m.s.cs Ps 24.4   f.s Ps 19.9; Ct 6.9,10

Ps 2.12 is perhaps used adverbially.
Could be Aramaic form בַּר = SON.   Text may need emendation.
See RSV and R1 p42 for full discussion   *

בֹּר = n.m   POTASH (used in smelting process)   s Is 1.25   H.L.

בָּרָא = vb   TO CREATE   Qal.pf.3m.s Gn 1.1,27;2.3

Qal.imp.3m.s Gn 1.21,27   ptc.pl+sfx Ec 12.1

Ni.inf.cs+sfx Gn 2.4   *

בָּרָה = vb   TO EAT   Qal.3m.s בָּרָא 2Sm 12.17 for spelling see R2 p40 *

בְּרוֹשׁ = n.m   CYPRESS or FIR TREE   pl Na 2.4   meaning spears? R2 p81 *

בְּרוֹת = dialectical form of above   m.pl Ct 1.17   H.L.

בַּרְזֶל = n.m   IRON   s Dt 8.9; 2Sm 12.31; Je 15.12; Ps 2.9; Jb 19.24   *

בָּרַח = vb   TO FLEE, HASTEN   Qal.imp.3m.s Ne 6.11   3m.pl Ne 13.10

Qal.imv.m.s Ct 8.14   inf.cs Jo 1.3;4.2   ptc.m.s Jo 1.10

Hi.imp.1.s+sfx Ne 13.28   *

בְּרִיחַ = n.m   BAR   pl+sfx Jo 2.7; Na 3.13   *

בְּרִית = n.f   COVENANT   s Gn 17.7; 1Sm 4.3; Je 31.31; Hs 2.20; Ne 1.5

s.cs Ne 13.29   s+sfx Gn 17.2; Dt 8.18; Je 31.32; Ob 7; Ps 103.18

בָּרַךְ = vb   TO BLESS   Qal only in ptc.pass Je 20.14; Ps 124.6

Ni.pf.3m.pl Gn 18.18 is reflexive R2 p20

Pi.pf.3m.s Gn 24.1; Ex 20.11   2m.s Dt 8.10

Pi.pf.1.s Gn 17.16,20   +sfx Gn 17.16; Ex 20.24

Pi.imp.3m.s Gn 1.22,28;2.3; 1Sm 9.13; Ps 29.11   +sfx Ps 134.3

Pi.imv.3f.s Ps 103.1,2,22   3m.pl Ps 96.2;100.4;103.20,21,22
                                                    134.1,2   *

בֶּרֶךְ = n.f   KNEE   dual Na 2.11   *

בְּרָכָה = n.f   BLESSING   s Ps 24.5;133.3; Ne 12.2   pl Ps 84.7   *

בְּרֵכָה = n.f   POOL   s.cs Na 2.9; Ne 2.14   pl Ct 7.5   *

בֶּרֶכְיָה = n.pr.m   BERECHIAH   Ne 6.18   *

בָּרָק = n.m   LIGHTNING   s.cs Na 3.3   pl Na 2.5   *

בָּרַר = vb   TO PURIFY   Qal.ptc.pass.f.s Zp 3.9   f.pl Ne 5.18   *

בֶּשֶׂם = n.m   SPICE   s Ct 5.13;6.2   +sfx Ct 5.1

pl Ct 4.10,14;8.14   +sfx Ct 4.16   *

בָּשַׂר = vb   TO BRING NEWS, BEAR TIDINGS   Pi.pf.3m.s Je 20.15

Pi.imv.m.pl Ps 96.2   ptc.m.s 1Sm 4.17; Ne.2.1   *

בָּשָׂר = n.m   FLESH   s Gn 2.21ff; Ez 37.6,8   s.cs Gn 17.11ff; Ne 5.5

s+sfx Gn 2.23;17.13; Ps 84.3; Jb 19.26; Ec 11.10; Ne 5.5

בָּשָׁן = n.loc   BASHAN   Is 2.13; Na 1.4; Ps 22.13   *

בֹּשֶׁת = n.f   SHAME   s Je 20.18; Zp 3.5   +sfx Zp 3.19   *

בַּת = n.f   DAUGHTER   s 2Sm 12.3; Is 1.8; Hs 1.6; Zp 3.14 R1 p95 - 96

s.cs 2Sm 11.3; Hs 1.3; Ne 6.18   s+sfx@33e Ex 20.10

pl @33e Gn 19.8; Ct 2.2;6.9   +sfx Gn 19.12; Je 11.22; Ne 4.8

pl.cs Gn 24.3; Ps 48.12; Ct 1.5; Ec 12.4

with time reference = YEARS OLD   Gn 17.17

בָּתָה = n.f   RUIN, DEVASTATION   s Is 5.6   H.L.

בֶּתֶר = n.m   PORTION or n.pr.m.   BETHER

Ct 2.17   so either CLOVEN MOUNTAINS,   or MOUNTAINS OF BETHER   *

בַּת־רַבִּים = n.loc   BATH-RABBIM   Ct 7.5   H.L.

בַּת־שֶׁבַע = n.pr.f   BATHSHEBA   2Sm 11.3;12.24   *

ג

גֵּאָה = n.f   PRIDE   s Pr 8.13   H.L.

גֵּאֶה = adj   PROUD   m.s Is 2.12   *

גַּאֲוָה = n.f   PRIDE   s+sfx Zp 3.11   *

גָּאוֹן = n.m   ARROGANCE   s Pr 8.13   +sfx Is 2.10,19,21; Zp 2.10

s.cs Je 12.5   R2 p93; Na 2.3   *

גֵּאוּת = n.f   MAJESTY   s Ps 93.1   *

= vb   1. TO REDEEM   Qal.ptc.m.s Ps 103.4   +sfx Jb 19.25   *

2. TO DEFILE   Ni.ptc.f.s Zp 3.1   *

גֹּאֶל = n.m   POLLUTION   pl.cs Ne 13.29   H.L.

גָּבַה = vb   TO BE HIGH, EXALTED   Qal.pf.3m.s Is 52.13; Ps 131.1

Qal.inf.cs Ps 103.11   f ending @15d Zp 3.11   Hi.imp.2m.s Ob 4   *

גָּבֹהַ = adj   HIGH, EXALTED   m.s. Is 2.15; Ec 12.5   m.s.cs Ps 101.5
      f.pl Zp 1.16   *

גַּבְהוּת = n.f   HAUGHTINESS   s Is 2.11,17   *

גְּבוּל = n.m   BORDER, TERRITORY   s Ob 7   s.cs 1Sm 6.12
      s+sfx 1Sm 6.9; Zp 2.8   pl+sfx 1Sm 5.6; Je 15.13   *

גִּבּוֹר = 1. adj   STRONG   Ps 24.8   *
      2. n.m   STRONG ONE, HERO   s Je 20.11; Zp 1.14;3.17; Ps 19.6
      m.pl Ct 3.7;4.4   +sfx Ob 9; Na 2.4   pl.cs Ps 103.20; Ct 3.7   *

גְּבוּרָה = n.f   STRENGTH   s Pr 8.14   pl+sfx Ps 150.2 = MIGHTY DEEDS   *

גִּבְעָה = n.f   HILL   s 1Sm 7.1   s.cs Ct 4.6
      pl Is 2.2,14; Na 1.5; Zp 1.10; Pr 8.25; Ct 2.8   *

גִּבְעוֹן = n.loc   GIBEON   1Kg 3.5   *

גָּבַר = vb   TO BE STRONG   Qal.pf.3m.s Ps 103.11;117.2
      Qal.pf.3m.pl 2Sm 11.23   *

גָּג = n.m   ROOF   s 2Sm 11.2   s.cs 2Sm 11.2   pl @9e Zp 1.5   *

גְּדוּד = n.m   MARAUDING BAND   s Je 18.22   *

גָּדוֹל = adj   GREAT   m.s Dt 8.15; 1Kg 3.6; Jo 1.4; Zp 1.10; Ps 96.4
      m.s.cs Na 1.3   m.s+sfx Je 31.34; Jo 3.5   f.s 1Sm 4.5; Jo 1.2
      m.pl Gn 1.16,21   +sfx Jo 3.7; Na 3.10   f.pl Ps 131.1

גִּדּוּפִים = n.m.pl   REVILINGS   cs Zp 2.8   *

גְּדִיָּה = n.f   KID   pl+sfx Ct 1.8   H.L.

גָּדֵל = vb   TO BECOME GREAT   Qal.pf.3f.s Gn 19.13   imp.3f.s 2Sm 12.3
      Pi.pf.2m.s+sfx Jo 4.10   1.s Is 1.2   ptc.f.pl Ct 5.13 R2 pl30
      Hi.pf.1.s Ec 1.16   imp.2m.s Gn 19.19   3m.pl Zp 2.8,10
      Hi.juss.2m.s Ob 12   *

גֹּדֶל = n.m   GREATNESS   s+sfx Ps 150.2   *

גְּדַלְיָה = n.pr.m   GEDALIAH   Zp 1.1   *

גָּדַר = vb   TO BUILD A WALL   Qal.pf.1.s Hs 2.8   *

גָּדֵר = n.m   WALL   s+sfx Is 5.5; Hs 2.8   *

גְּדֵרָה = n.f   WALL   pl Na 3.17   pl.cs Zp 2.6   *

גּוֹב/גֹּבַי = n.m.coll   LOCUST SWARM   both Na 3.17 R2 p88   *

גּוֹי = n.m   NATION   s Gn 17.20;18.18; Is 1.4;2.4; Zp 2.1,14 s.cs Zp 2.5   s+sfx Zp 2.9   pl.cs Gn 18.18

pl Dt 8.20; Is 52.15; Ob 1; Na 3.4; Ps 2.1;96.3; Ne 5.8

גְּוִיָּה = n.f   BODY, CORPSE   s Na 3.3   +sfx Na 3.3   pl Ps 110.6   *

גּוּף = vb   TO SHUT, CLOSE   Hi.juss.3m.pl Ne 7.3   H.L.

גּוּר = vb   1. TO RESIDE AS AN ALIEN   Qal.inf.cs Gn 19.9; Ru 1.1   *

              2. TO DREAD, FEAR   Qal.imv.m.pl Ps 22.24; Jb 19.29   *

גּוּר = n.m   CUB, WHELP (of lion)   s.cs Na 2.12   *

גֹּר = n.m   CUB, WHELP (of lion)   pl+sfx Na 2.13   *

גּוֹרָל = n.m   LOT   s Ob 11; Jo 1.7; Na 3.10; Ps 22.19

        pl @9e Jo 1.7   *

גָּזַל = vb   TO CUT OFF   Qal.ptc.pl+sfx Is 53.7

Ni.pf.3m.pl Na 1.12   *

גָּזִית = n.f   HEWN STONE   s Ex 20.25   *

גָּזַר = vb   TO CUT   Ni.pf.3m.s Is 53.8   1.pl Ez 37.11   *

גָּחָה = vb   TO DRAW OUT   Qal.ptc+sfx Ps 22.10   *

This parsing in K/B and Foh. In Lang listed under גּוּחַ, also
B.D.B. p161 though here alternative is suggested.

גָּחוֹן = n.m   BELLY   s+sfx Gn 3.14   *

גַּיְא = n.m   VALLEY   s Ne 2.13,15   s.cs Ps 23.4   *

גִּיד = n.m   SINEW   pl Ez 37.6,8   *

גִּיחוֹן = n.pr   GIHON (one of the rivers of Eden)   Gn 2.13   *

גִּיל = vb   TO REJOICE   Qal.imp.3m.s Zp 3.17   juss.3f.s Ps 48.12

        Qal.coh.pl Ct 1.4   imv.m.pl Ps 2.11   *

גַּל = n.m   WAVE,FOUNTAIN   s Ct 4.12   pl+sfx Jo 2.4   *

גַּלְגַּל = n.m   WHEEL   s Ec 12.6   *

גָּלָה = vb   TO UNCOVER, EXPOSE   Qal.pf.3m.s 1Sm 4.21,22

Ni.pf.3f.s Is 53.1   juss.2m.s Ex 20.26

Pi.pf.1.s Je 11.20;20.12; Na 3.5   imp.1.s Hs 2.12

Pu.pf.3f.s Na 2.8   *

גֻּלָּה = n.f   BASIN, BOWL   s.cs Ec 12.6   *

גֹּלָה = n.f   EXILE   s Na 3.10   *

גָּלוּת = n.m.coll   EXILES   s.cs Ob 20   *

גָּלִיל = n.m   PEG, ROD, CYLINDER   pl.cs Ct 5.14   *

גָּלַל = vb   TO ROLL AWAY   Qal.imv.m.s Ps 22.9   R1 p47 for meaning   *

גָּלָל = n.m   DUNG   pl Zp 1.17   *

גִּלְעָד = n.loc   GILEAD   Ob 19; Ct 4.1; 6.5   *

גָּלַשׁ = vb   TO STREAM DOWN   Qal.pf.3m.pl Ct 4.1;6.5   R2 p128   *

גַּם = adv   EVEN, ALSO   Gn 3.6; 2Sm 11.12; 1Kg 3.13; Is 1.15; Ru 1.5
   Zp 1.18 = NEITHER / NOR   Ne 3.35 = YES   Ne 6.1 = ALTHOUGH

גְּמוּל = n.m   BENEFIT, REWARD   s+sfx Ob 15   pl+sfx Ps 103.2   *

גָּמַל = vb   1. TO DEAL WITH   Qal.pf.3m.s Ps 103.10   *
               2. TO WEAN   Qal.imp.3f.s Hs 1.8   ptc.pass.m.s Ps 131.2 *

גֹּמֶר = n.pr.f   GOMER   Hs 1.3   *

גַּן = n.m   GARDEN   s Gn 2.8;3.1; Ct 4.12   s.cs Gn 2.15;3.23,24
   s+sfx Ct 4.16;5.1;6.2   pl Ct 4.15;6.2;8.13

גָּנַב = vb   TO STEAL   Qal.imp.3m.pl Ob 5   juss.2m.s Ex 20.15   *

גַּנָּב = n.m   THIEF   pl Is 1.23; Ob 5   *

גַּנָּה = n.f   GARDEN   s Is 1.30   s.cs Ct 6.11   pl Is 1.29   *

גָּעָה = vb   TO LOW (of cattle)   Qal.pf.3m.pl 1Sm 6.12   *

גָּעַר = vb   TO REBUKE   Qal.ptc.m.s Na 1.4   *

גַּף = n.m   HEIGHT, TOP   pl.cs Pr 9.3   *

גֶּפֶן = n.f   VINE   s Dt 8.8; Ct 6.11;7.9,13   +sfx Hs 2.14
   pl Ct 2.13   *

גָּפְרִית = n.f   BRIMSTONE, SULPHUR   s Gn 19.24   *

גֵּר = n.m   ALIEN, SOJOURNER   s+sfx Ex 20.10   *

גָּרֵם = vb   TO GNAW so Holl.   p64 rather than B.D.B. p175 TO LEAVE
   Qal.pf.3m.pl Zp 3.3   R1 p93   *

גָּרַשׁ = vb   TO DRIVE OUT   Ni.pf.1.s Jo 2.5
   Pi.imp.3m.s.wc Gn 3.24   3m.pl+sfx Zp 2.4   *

גֶּשֶׁם = 1. n.m   RAIN   s Ct 2.11; Ec 12.2   *
           2. n.pr.m   GESHEM   Ne 2.19;6.1,2   וְגַשְׁמוּ Ne 6.6   *

גַּת = 1. n.f   WINE PRESS   pl Ne 13.15   *
        2. n.loc   GATH   1Sm 5.8;6.17   *

גִּתִּית = n.f   GITTITE   Ps 8.1;81.1;84.1   *

Name of a musical instrument (lyre ?) or of a tune. Found only in these 3 Psalm headings. For other possibilities see R1 p27.

ד

דָּאַג = vb   TO BE ANXIOUS   Qal.pf.3m.s 1Sm 9.5   *

דָּבַב = vb   ? TO GLIDE   Qal.ptc.m.s Ct 7.10   H.L.

דִּבָּה = n.f   WHISPERING, SLANDER   s.cs Je 20.10   *

דִּבְלַיִם = n.pr.m   DIBLAIM   Hs 1.3   *

דָּבַק = vb   TO CLING   Qal.pf.3m.s.wc Gn 2.24
Qal.imp.3m.s Ps 101.3   3f.s+sfx Gn 19.9   Ho.ptc.m.s Ps 22.16   *

דָּבַר = vb   TO SPEAK   Qal.ptc.m.s Jo 3.2; Ps 101.7
Pi.pf.3m.s Gn 17.23;24.7; Is 1.2; Hs 1.2; Ob 18; Jo 3.10; Ne 6.12
Pi.pf.2m.s Gn 18.5;19.21   1.s Ex 20.22; Ez 37.4   1.pl 2Sm 12.18
Pi.imp.3m.s Gn 17.3; Ex 20.1; 1Sm 9.6   1.s Je 12.1;20.8; Pr 8.6
Pi.imp.3m.pl Je 12.6; Zp 3.13   3f.pl 1Sm 4.20   juss.3m.s Ex 20.19
Pi.coh.s Gn 18.30,32   imv.m.s Ex 20.19   ptc.m.s Ne 13.24
Pi.inf.cs Gn 17.22; 2Sm 11.19; Je 18.20; Ec 1.8   +sfx Ct 5.6
Pu.imp.3m.s Ct 8.8

דָּבָר = n.m   WORD, MATTER   s Gn 24.9; 1Kg 3.10; Jo 3.6; Es 2.22; Ne 1.8
s+sfx 1Sm 9.10; Jo 4.2; Ps 103.20;130.5
s.cs 2Sm 12.9; Is 1.10; Je 17.15; Jo 1.1; Zp 2.5; Ps 101.3
pl Ex 20.1; Ps 19.4; Ec 1.8; Ne 1.4;5.6;6.6ff
pl+sfx 2Sm 15.3; 1Kg 3.12; Je 15.16;18.18; Ne 6.19
pl.cs 2Sm 11.18; Ps 22.2; Ec 1.1; Es 2.23; Ne 1.1;2.18

דִּבְרָה = n.f   MANNER   s.cs+archaic ending Ps 110.4 R1 p43   *

דְּבַשׁ = n.m   HONEY   s Dt 8.8; Ps 19.11;81.17; Ct 4.11   +sfx Ct 5.1 *

דָּג = n.m   FISH   s Jo 2.1,11; Ne 13.16Q
pl Zp 1.10   pl.cs Zp 1.3; Ps 8.9   *

דָּגָה = n.f   FISH   s Jo 2.2   s.cs Gn 1.26,28   *

דָּגוֹן = n.pr.m   DAGON   1Sm 5.2,3,4,5   *

דָּגַל = vb   1. TO LOOK   Qal.ptc.pass Ct 5.10 = BE DISTINGUISHED H.L.
2. TO SET UP A BANNER   Ni.ptc.f.pl Ct 6.4,10 R2 p130   *

דֶּגֶל = n.m   BANNER, SIGN   s+sfx Ct 2.4   R2 pp125-126   *

דָּגָן = n.m   GRAIN   s Hs 2.10,24; Ne 5.2;13.5   +sfx Hs 2.11

דָּהַר = vb   TO RUSH, GALLOP   Qal.ptc.m.s Na 3.2   H.L.

דּוֹד = n.m   BELOVED   s+sfx Is 5.1; Ct 1.13;2.3;4.16;5.2;6.1;7.10;8.5
    pl+sfx = LOVE Ct 1.2,4;4.10;7.13

דּוּד = n.m   POT, BASKET   s Ps 81.7   *

דָּוִד = n.pr.m   DAVID   2Sm 11.1; 1Kg 3.6; Hs 3.5; Ps 6.1; Ct 4.4

דּוּדָאִים = n.m.pl   MANDRAKES   Ct 7.14   *

דַּוָּי = adj   SICK, SEVERELY ILL   m.s Is 1.5   *

דּוּמִיָּה = n.f   SILENCE, REST   s Ps 22.3   *

דּוֹנַג = n.m   WAX   s.ip Ps 22.15   *

דּוּר = vb   TO DWELL   Qal.inf.cs Ps 84.11   *

דֹּר/דּוֹר = n.m   GENERATION   s Ps 22.31;24.6 (R1 pp35-36);48.14;100.5;
    s+sfx Is 53.8   R2 p110   pl+sfx Gn 17.9,10,12   *   Ec 1.4

דַּי = n.m   ENOUGH   s.cs+בּ Na 2.13   + כּ Ne 5.8   + מִן Je 20.8
    s+sfx Ob 5   *

דִּין = vb   TO JUDGE   Qal.imp.3m.s Ps 110.6   *

דִּין = n.m   JUDGEMENT   s Jb 19.29K   difficult   see R1 p103   *

דָּכָא = vb   TO CRUSH   Pi.inf.cs+sfx Is 53.10   Pu.ptc.m.s Is 53.5   *

דֳּכִי = n.m   CRASHING (of waves)   s+sfx Ps 93.3   R1 pp31-32   H.L.

דַּל = adj   POOR, WRETCHED   m.s Zp 3.12; Ps 82.3,4   *

דָּלַג = vb   TO LEAP   Qal.ptc.m.s Zp 1.9   Pi.ptc.m.s Ct 2.8   *

דַּלָּה = n.f.coll   HAIR   s.cs Ct 7.6   *

דְּלָיָה = n.pr.m   DELAIAH   Ne 6.10   *

דָּלַק = vb   TO BURN   Qal.pf.3m.pl.wc Ob 18   *

דֶּלֶת = n.f   DOOR   s Gn 19.6,9,10; Ct 8.9   dual Ec 12.4
    pl Ne 6.1;7.1,3;13.19   +sfx Pr 8.34   pl.cs Ne 6.10   *

דָּם = n.m   BLOOD   s Jo 1.14   +sfx Zp 1.17   s.cs Is 1.11
    pl Is 1.15; Na 3.1   pl.cs Hs 1.4   *

דָּמָה = vb   1. TO RESEMBLE   Qal.pf.3f.s Ct 7.8   1.pl Is 1.9
    Qal.imv.m.s Ct 2.17;8.14   ptc.m.s Ct 2.9

Pi.pf.1.s+sfx Ct 1.9   1.pl Ps 48.10   R1 pp33-34 for implication *

     2. TO DESTROY   K/B p216   Holl p 72

Ni.pf.3m.s Zp 1.11   2m.s Ob 5   *

דְמוּת = n.f   LIKENESS   s+sfx Gn 1.26   *

דָמַם = vb   TO BE STILL   Po'el.pf.1.s Ps 131.2   *

דִמְעָה = n.f.coll   TEARS   s+sfx Ps 6.7   *

דַּמֶּשֶׂק = n.loc   DAMASCUS   Ct 7.5   *

דַעַת = n.f   KNOWLEDGE   s Ps 19.3; Pr 8.9,10,12; Ec 1.16,17,18

    s+sfx Is 53.11   s.cs Gn 2.9,17   *

דָּפַק = vb   TO KNOCK   Qal.ptc.m.s Ct 5.2   *

דַּרְדַּר = n.m.coll   THISTLES   s Gn 3.18   *

דָּרוֹם = n.m   SOUTH   s Ec 1.6   *

דְּרוֹר = n.f   SWALLOW   s Ps 84.4   *

דָּרַךְ = vb   TO TREAD   Qal.imp.3m.pl 1Sm 5.5   ptc.m.pl Ne 13.15   *

דֶּרֶךְ = n.m+f   PATH, WAY   m.s Dt 8.2; 1Sm 4.13; Na 2.2; Ps 2.12; Pr 8.2

    m.s.cs Gn 3.24;18.19; 1Sm 6.9; 2Sm 15.2; Ps 1.1; Pr 8.13;9.6

    m.s+sfx Gn 19.2; Is 53.6; Hs 2.8; Jo 3.8,10; Na 1.3; Pr 8.22

    f.s Je 12.1   +sfx 1Sm 9.6   m.pl.cs Ec 11.9

    m.pl+sfx Dt 8.6; 1Kg 3.14; Is 2.3; Ps 81.14;103.7; Pr 8.32

דָּרַשׁ = vb   TO SEEK, INQUIRE   Qal.pf.3m.pl+sfx Zp 1.6

    Qal.imp.3m.s 2Sm 11.3   imv.m.pl Is 1.17

    Qal.inf.cs 1Sm 9.9; Ec 1.13   ptc.m.pl+sfx Ps 22.27;24.6Q   *

דָּשָׁא = vb   TO SPROUT, BE GREEN   Hi.juss.3f.s Gn 1.11   *

דֶּשֶׁא = n.m   FRESH GRASS   s Gn 1.11,12; Ps 23.2   *

דָּשֵׁן = vb   TO BE FAT   Pi.pf.2m.s Ps 23.5 = ANOINT   *

דָּשֵׁן = adj   FAT, WELL FED   m.pl.cs Ps 22.30   *

ה

הַ/הֲ/הֶ = inter.particle used as a prefix   @29e

    Gn 24.5; 2Sm 11.3; Je 15.12; Ob 5; Jo 4.2; Na 3.8; Pr 8.1   R2 p115

הֶבֶל = n.m   VAPOUR, TRANSITORY THING, VANITY

26

          s Ec 1.2,14;11.8,10;12.8   s.cs Ec 1.2;12.8

          pl Ec 1.2;12.8   pl.cs Jo 2.9 *

הָגָה = vb TO MURMUR, MUSE   Qal.imp.3m.s Ps 1.2; Pr 8.7

          Qal.imp.3m.pl Ps 2.1 *

הִגָּיוֹן = n.m MEDITATION, THINKING   s.cs Ps 19.15   *

הֲדֹם = n.m FOOTSTOOL   s Ps 110.1   *

הָדָר = n.m SPLENDOUR   s Is 53.2; Ps 8.6; 29.4

          s.cs Is 2.10,19,21   pl.cs Ps 110.3   *

הֲדָרָה = n.f SPLENDOUR or ATTIRE   s.cs Ps 29.2 Rl p25   *

הוּא = pro.3m.s HE, HIMSELF, THAT

          Gn 24.7; Dt 8.18; 1Sm 4.12; Hs 1.5; Jo 1.10; Ps 24.2; Ru 1.1; Ec 1.5

הוֹד = n.m MAJESTY   s+sfx Ps 8.2 *

הָוָה = vb TO BECOME (= הָיָה) Qal.ptc.m.s Ne 6.6   *

הוֹי = interj WOE!   Is 1.4,24; Na 3.1; Zp 2.5;3.1   *

הוֹלֵלוֹת = n.f.pl MADNESS (only in Ec)   Ec 1.17   *

הוּם = vb TO BE IN UPROAR   Ni.imp.3f.s 1Sm 4.5   *

הוֹן = n.m WEALTH   s Pr 8.18   s.cs Ct 8.7   *

הוֹשֵׁעַ = n.pr.m HOSEA   Hs 1.1,2   *

הִיא = pro.3f.s SHE, HERSELF, THAT

          2Sm 11.4; Is 1.13; Ez 37.1; Na 3.10; Ct 6.9; Ru 1.3; Ne 2.18

          Only rarely appears in Pent. where הוּא is common gender and so is

          repointed הִוא (as a Q perpetuum) B.D.B pp214-215 see

          Gn 2.12;3.12,20;17.14;19.20,38

הָיָה = vb TO BE, HAPPEN, BECOME @32h

          Qal.pf   Qal.imp

          3m.s 1Kg 3.12; Jo 4.10   3m.s Ec 1.9; apoc Ru 1.1

          3f.s Gn 1.2; Ez 37.1   3f.s Zp 2.4; apoc 1Sm 4.10

          2m.s Gn 17.4   2m.s Je 15.18; apoc Na 3.11

          1.s Je 31.33; Ec 1.12   2f.s Hs 3.3

          3m.pl Je 18.23K; Ne 4.16   1.s Pr 8.30; apoc Ne 1.4

          2m.pl Gn 3.5; 1Sm 4.9   3m.pl Je 31.33; Ru 1.2

          1.pl Is 1.9; Ne 3.36   2m.pl Is 1.30

                                   1.pl 2Sm 11.23; Ne 2.17

Qal.juss.3m.s.apoc Gn 1.3   3f.s.apoc Ne 1.6,11   2m.s Je 17.17

Qal.juss.3m.pl Je 18.21; Ps 19.15   3f.pl Je 18.21; Ps 130.2

Qal.imv.m.s Gn 17.1   m.pl 1Sm 4.9   inf.abs Gn 18.18; Je 15.18

Qal.inf.cs 2Sm 12.10; Jo 4.6   +sfx Jo 4.2   Ni.pf.3m.s Ne 6.8

הֵיכָל = n.m   TEMPLE, PALACE   s Is 6.1; Na 2.7; Ne 6.10,11

s+sfx Ps 29.9;48.10   s.cs Jo 2.5,8   *

הָלְאָה = adv   FARTHER, THITHER   Gn 19.9   *

הֲלִיכָה = n.f   WAY   +sfx Na 2.6 (pl in K, s in Q)   *

הָלַךְ = vb   TO WALK   @28b

Qal.pf	Qal.imp
3m.s 1Kg 3.6; Ps 1.1	3m.s Jo 3.3; Ru 1.1
3f.s Na 3.10	3f.s Hs 2.15
2m.s Dt 8.19	2m.s Gn 24.4; 1Kg 3.14
1.s Ne 2.16	1.s Ps 23.4; Ct 4.6
3m.pl 1Sm 6.12	3m.pl 1Sm 6.6; Ps 81.3
2m.pl Gn 19.2	2m.pl Ne 5.9
1.pl 1Sm 9.6	1.pl 1Sm 9.7

inf.abs 1Sm 6.12	coh.s Hs 2.7,9
inf.cs Gn 24.5; Dt 8.6	coh.pl 1Sm 9.6; Is 2.3
inf.cs+sfx 1Sm 9.9	imv.m.s 1Sm 9.3; Jo 1.2
ptc.m.s Jo 1.11; Ec 1.4	imv+emph Gn 19.32; Ne 6.2
ptc.m.pl 1Sm 6.12; Ps 84.12	imv.f.s Ct 2.10,13
ptc.f.pl Ne 6.17	imv.m.pl 1Sm 9.9; Is 2.3

Pi	Hi	Hith
pf.1.s Ps 131.1	pf.3m.s+sfx Dt 8.2	imp.3m.s 2Sm 11.2
imp.1.s Pr 8.20	pf.1.s+sfx Hs 2.16	imp.1.s Ps 101.2
imp.3m.pl Ps 81.14	ptc.m.s+sfx Dt 8.15	imp.3m.pl Ps 82.5
imv.m.s Ec 11.9		imv.m.s Gn 17.1
		ptc.m.s Gn 3.8

הֵלֶךְ = n.m   TRAVELLER   s 2Sm 12.4   H.L.

הָלַל = vb   1. TO PRAISE   Pi.imp.1.s+sfx Ps 22.23

Pi.imp.3m.pl Ps 22.27; Ne 5.13   +sfx Ps 84.5; Ct 6.9

Pi.juss.3f.s Ps 150.6   imv.m.pl Je 20.13; Ps 117.1,2;150.1,6

Pi.imv.m.pl+sfx Ps 22.24;150.2ff   Pu.ptc.m.s Ps 48.2;96.4

2. TO HURTLE ABOUT   Hithpo'el.imp.3m.pl Na 2.5   *

For this root see R2 p81, Holl p81, Foh p65

הֵם/הֵמָּה = pro.3m.pl   THEY   Gn 3.7; 1Sm 9.5; Je 31.32; Es 2.21; Ne 1.10
+בְּ Ob 18; Ec 12.1   +לְ Gn 3.7; Ru 1.4   +מִן Ob 11; Ct 3.4
As emphatic copula   1Sm 4.8   Rl p2

הָמָה = vb   TO MURMUR   Qal.pf.3m.pl Ct 5.4   *

הָמוֹן = n.m   1. SOUND   s 1Sm 4.14   *   2. CROWD   s.cs Gn 17.4,5 *

הֵן/הֵנָּה = pro.3f.pl   THEY   +בְּ Gn 19.29   +כְּ 2Sm 12.8
+לְ 1Sm 9.11   *

הֵן = interj   BEHOLD!   Gn 3.22;19.34   *

הִנֵּה = interj   BEHOLD!   Gn 1.29; 1Sm 9.6; 1Kg 3.12; Je 31.31;   Ez 37.2
+sfx @33c 2Sm 12.11; Je 11.22; Hs 2.8; Na 2.14; Zp 3.19; Ct 1.15

הֵנָּה = adv   HERE, HITHER   Pr 9.4   *

הַס = interj   HUSH   Zp 1.7   *

הָפַךְ = vb   TO TURN, OVERTURN   Qal.pf.3m.s Je 20.16
Qal.imp.3m.s Gn 19.25; Ne 13.2   1.s Zp 3.9
Qal.inf.cs Gn 19.29   +sfx Gn 19.21
Ni.pf.3m.s Hs 11.8   3m.pl 1Sm 4.19   ptc.f.s Jo 3.4
Hith.ptc.f.s Gn 3.24   *

הֲפֵכָה = n.f   OVERTHROW, DESTRUCTION   s Gn 19.29   H.L.

הַר = n.m   MOUNTAIN   s Ex 20.18; Dt 8.7; Ob 8; Ps 48.3,12
s.cs 1Sm 9.4; Is 2.2; Zp 3.11; Ps 2.6   s+הָ loc Gn 19.17,19
pl Is 2.2; Jo 2.7; Na 1.5;2.1;3.18; Ps 121.1; Pr 8.25; Ct 2.8
pl.cs הָרֵי Ct 2.17;8.14   הַרְרֵי Ps 133.3; Ct 4.8
pl+sfx Dt 8.9

הָרַג = vb   TO KILL   Qal.pf.2m.s 2Sm 12.9   1.pl+sfx Ne 4.5
Qal.inf.cs Ec 3.3   +sfx Ne 6.10
Qal.ptc.pass.m.pl Ez 37.9   m.pl.cs Je 18.21   *

הֲרֵגָה = n.f   SLAUGHTER   s Je 12.3   *

הָרָה = vb   TO CONCEIVE, BE PREGNANT
Qal.imp.3f.s.apoc 2Sm 11.5; Hs 1.3,6,8   3f.pl Gn 19.36
Qal.ptc.f.s+sfx Hs 2.7; Ct 3.4   *

הָרָה = adj.f   PREGNANT   s 1Sm 4.19; 2Sm 11.5   s.cs Je 20.17   *

הֵרָיוֹן = n.m   PREGNANCY   הֵרֹנֵךְ = s+sfx Gn 3.16

spelling due to contraction or error B.D.B. p248, R2 p14   *

הָרֵס = vb   TO TEAR DOWN   Qal.imv.m.s+sfx 2Sm 11.25   *

ז

זְאֵב = n.m   WOLF   pl.cs Zp 3.3   *

זָבַח = vb   TO SACRIFICE   Qal.pf.2m.s Ex 20.24
     Qal.imp.3m.pl 1Sm 6.15; Jo 1.16; Ne 3.34   coh.s Jo 2.10
     Pi.imp.3m.pl Hs 11.2   *

זֶבַח = n.m   SACRIFICE   s 1Sm 9.12,13; Hs 3.4; Jo 1.16; Zp 1.7,8
     pl 1Sm 6.15   +sfx Is 1.11   *

זֵד = adj   INSOLENT, PRESUMPTUOUS   m.pl Ps 19.14   *

זָדוֹן = n.m   INSOLENCE, PRESUMPTUOUSNESS   s.cs Ob 3   *

זֶה = pro.dem   THIS   Gn 24.9; Dt 8.2; 1Kg 3.6; Is 6.3; Ps 48.15
     +בְ 1Sm 9.11; 2Sm 11.12   +כְ 2Sm 11.25   +מִן Jo 1.8
     f.s = זֹאת 1Sm 9.6; Is 1.12; Jo 1.7; Jb 19.26; Ct 3.6
     f.s = זֹה B.D.B. p262   +כְ 2Sm 11.25

זָהָב = n.m   GOLD   s Gn 2.11; Ex 20.23; 1Sm 6.4; Hs 2.10; Na 2.10
     s.cs Gn 2.12   s+sfx Is 2.20; Zp 1.18

זָהַר = vb   TO SHINE   Ni.ptc.m.s Ps 19.12   R2 p63   *

זוּעַ = vb   TO TREMBLE   Qal.imp.3m.pl Ec 12.3   *

זוּר = vb   1. TO BE A STRANGER   Qal.ptc.m.s Ps 81.10; Jb 19.27
     Qal.ptc.m.pl Is 1.7; Ob 11   Ni.pf.3m.pl Is 1.4   *
                2. TO PRESS OUT   Qal.pf.3m.pl Is 1.6   R1 p76   *

זֵידוֹן = adj   RAGING, SEETHING   m.pl Ps 124.5   H.L.

זַיִת = n.m   OLIVE TREE   s.cs Dt 8.8   pl+sfx Ne 5.11   *

זָכָה = vb   TO BE CLEAR, PURE   Hith.imv.m.pl Is 1.16   *

זַכּוּר = n.pr.m   ZACCUR   Ne 13.13   *

זָכַר = vb   TO REMEMBER   Qal.pf.2m.s Dt 8.2,18   1.s Jo 2.8
     Qal.imp.3m.s Gn 19.29; Na 2.6   2m.s+sfx @21e Ps 8.5
     Qal.imp.1.s Je 31.34   +sfx Je 20.9   3m.pl Ps 22.28
     Qal.juss.3m.s Ec 11.8   imv.m.s Je 18.20; Ne 1.8   +sfx Je 15.15
     Qal.imv.m.s+הָ @13a Ne 5.19   m.pl Ne 4.8

Qal.inf.abs Ex 20.8 used as imv   G/K 113bb

Qal.ptc.m.pl.cs Ps 103.18   ptc.pass.m.s Ps 103.14   G/K 50f

Ni.imp.3m.s Je 11.19   3m.pl Hs 2.19

Hi.imp.1.s Ex 20.24   coh.pl Ct 1.4   inf.cs+sfx 1Sm 4.18

זָכָר = n.m   MALE   s Gn 1.27;17.10ff; Je 20.15

זֵכֶר = n.m   REMEMBRANCE   s+ sfx Ps 6.6   *

זִכָּרוֹן = n.m   REMEMBRANCE   s Ec 1.11; Ne 2.20   s.cs Ec 1.11   *

זָלַל = vb   TO BE WORTHLESS   Qal.ptc.m.s Je 15.19   *

זְמוֹרָה = n.f   BRANCH   pl+sfx @9e Na 2.3   *

זָמִיר = n.m   PRUNING   s Ct 2.12   R2 p126   H.L.

זמן = vb.denom   TO BE FIXED, APPOINTED (of time)
       Pu.ptc.f.pl Ne 13.31   *

זְמָן = n.m   TIME, APPOINTED TIME   s Ec 3.1; Ne 2.6   *

זָמַר = vb   1.   TO PRUNE   Ni.imp.3m.s Is 5.6   *
             2.   TO MAKE MUSIC   Pi.imp.1.s Ps 101.1   *

זִמְרָה = n.f   SONG, MELODY   s Ps 81.3   *

זָנָה = vb   TO ACT AS HARLOT, BE UNFAITHFUL   Qal.pf.3f.s Hs 2.7
       Qal.imp.3f.s Hs 1.2   2f.s Hs 3.3   inf.abs Hs 1.2
       Qal.ptc.f.s Is 1.21; Na 3.4   *

זְנוּנִים = n.m.pl.abst PROSTITUTION, UNFAITHFULNESS   Hs 1.2;2.6
       +sfx Hs 2.4; Na 3.4   cs Na 3.4   *

זֵעָה = n.f   SWEAT   s.cs Gn 3.19   H.L.

זַעַם = n.m   CURSE, WRATH   s Je 15.17   +sfx Na 1.6; Zp 3.8   *

זַעַף = n.m   RAGING (of sea)   s+sfx Jo 1.15   *

זָעַק = vb   TO CRY OUT   Qal.pf.3m.pl Ps 22.6
       Qal.imp.3f.s 1Sm 4.13   1.s Je 20.8   3m.pl 1Sm 5.10; Jo 1.5
       Hi.imp.3m.s Jo 3.7 = ISSUE A PROCLAMATION   *

זְעָקָה = n.f   OUTCRY   s Je 18.22;20.16   +sfx Ne 5.6   s.cs Gn 18.20 *

זֵק = n.m   FETTER, CHAIN   pl Na 3.10   *

זָקֵן = vb   TO BE OR BECOME OLD   Qal.pf.3m.s Gn 18.12;19.31;24.1
       Qal.pf.1.s Gn 18.13   ptc.s.cs Gn 24.2   *

זָקָן = n.m   BEARD   s Ps 133.2   s.cs Ps 133.2   *

זָקֵן } = adj   OLD   subs   OLD MAN   m.s Gn 19.4; 1Sm 4.18
m.pl Gn 18.11   m.pl.cs 1Sm 4.3; 2Sm 12.17   *

זְרוֹעַ = n.f   ARM   s.cs Is 53.1   s+sfx Ct 8.6   pl+sfx Hs 11.3   *

זָרַח = vb   TO RISE (of sun)   Qal.pf.3m.s Ec 1.5   3f.s Na 3.17
Qal.inf.cs Jo 4.8   ptc.m.s Ec 1.5   *

זָרַע = vb   TO SOW   Qal.pf.1.s+sfx Hs 2.25   ptc.m.s Gn 1.29
Ni.juss.3m.s Na 1.14   Hi.ptc.m.s Gn 1.11,12   *

זֶרַע = n.m   SEED, OFFSPRING   s Gn 1.11; Is 1.4;53.10; Ps 22.24
i.p Gn 1.29;19.32,34   s+sfx Gn 1.11;17.7;24.7

זָרַר = vb   TO PRESS OUT   Qal.pf.3m.pl Is 1.6   H.L.
So K/B p272, Holl p93, Lang p88. B.D.B. suggests root זוּר p266

ח

חָבָא = vb   TO HIDE   Ni.imp.1.s Gn 3.10   Hith.imp.3m.s Gn 3.8   *

חַבּוּרָה = n.f   WOUND, STRIPE   s Is 1.6   +sfx Is 53.5 (coll)   *

חָבַל = vb   1. TO ACT CORRUPTLY   Qal.pf.1.pl Ne 1.7
Qal.inf.cs Ne 1.7 (used as abs R2 p47)   Pi.ptc.m.pl Ct 2.15   *
2. TO BE IN LABOUR   Pi.pf.3f.s Ct 8.5   +sfx Ct 8.5   *

חֶבֶל = n.m   1. CORD   s Ec 12.6   pl.cs Hs 11.4   *
2. REGION, DISTRICT   s.cs Zp 2.5,6   *

חֹבֵל = n.m   SAILOR (rope-puller)   s.coll Jo 1.6   *

חֲבַצֶּלֶת = n.f   CROCUS, ASPHODEL (NEB)   s.cs Ct 2.1   *

חָבַק = vb   TO EMBRACE   Qal.inf.cs Ec 3.5
Pi.imp.3f.s+sfx Ct 2.6;8.3   inf.cs Ec 3.5   *

חָבֵר = n.m   COMPANION   pl Ct 8.13   +sfx Ct 1.7   pl.cs Is 1.23   *

חָבַשׁ = vb   TO BIND UP   Qal.ptc.pass.m.s Jo 2.6
Pu.pf.3m.pl Is 1.6   *

חַג = n.f   FESTIVAL   s+sfx Hs 2.13; Ps 81.4   pl+sfx Na 2.1   *

חָגָב = n.m   LOCUST, GRASSHOPPER   s Ec 12.5   *

חָגַג = vb   TO KEEP A PILGRIMAGE FESTIVAL   Qal.imv.f.s. Na 2.1   *

חֲגָוִים = n.m.pl   CLEFTS   cs Ob 3; Ct 2.14   *

חֲגוֹרָה = n.f   LOINCLOTH   pl Gn 3.7   *

חָדַל = vb   TO CEASE   Qal.pf.3m.s Gn 18.11

　　　Qal.imp.3m.s 1Sm 9.5   imv.m.pl Is 1.16;2.22   *

חָדֵל = adj   HOLDING BACK   m.s.cs Is 53.3 R2 p107   *

חִדֶּקֶל = n.pr   RIVER TIGRIS   Gn 2.14   *

חֶדֶר = n.m   CHAMBER, INNER ROOM   s.cs Ct 3.4   pl+sfx Ct 1.4   *

חָדַשׁ = vb   TO RENEW   Hith.pf.3f.s Ps 103.5   *

חָדָשׁ = adj   NEW   m.s Ps 96.1; Ec 1.9,10

　　　f.s 1Sm 6.7; Je 31.31   m.pl Ct 7.14   *

חֹדֶשׁ = n.m   NEW MOON, MONTH   s Is 1.13; Ps 81.4   +sfx Hs 2.13

　　　s.cs Ne 1.1;2.1   pl 1Sm 6.1   +sfx Is 1.14   *

חוּג = n.m   CIRCLE   s Pr 8.27   R2 p118   *

חָוָה = vb   1. TO BOW DOWN, MAKE OBEISANCE   (some explain from שׁחה)

　　　Hištapel.pf.2m.s Dt 8.19   imp.3m.s Gn 18.2;19.1; 2Sm 12.20

　　　Hištapel.imp.3m.pl Is 2.8; Zp 2.11; Ps 22.28,30

　　　Hištapel.juss.2m.s Ex 20.5; Ps 81.10   imv.m.pl Ps 29.2

　　　Hištapel.inf.cs Is 2.20   ptc.m.pl Zp 1.5

　　　For this unusual form see explanation in R1 p11 R2 p21   *

　　　2. TO DECLARE   Pi.imp.3m.s Ps 19.3   *

חַוָּה = n.pr.f   EVE   Gn 3.20   *

חוֹחַ = n.m   BRAMBLE   pl Ct 2.2   *

חוּט = n.m   THREAD   s.cs Ct 4.3   *

חֲוִילָה = n.loc   HAVILAH   Gn 2.11   B.D.B p296 for possible location   *

חוּל/חִיל = vb   TO DANCE, WRITHE   Qal.pf.3f.s Hs 11.6

　　　Polel.imp.3m.s Ps 29.9   Polal.pf.1.s Pr 8.24,25 ⌣ BE BORN

　　　Hi.imp.3m.s Ps 29.8   *

חוֹל = n.m   SAND   s.cs Hs 2.1   *

חוֹמָה = n.f   WALL   s 2Sm 11.20; Is 2.15; Ne 2.15   +sfx Na 2.6;3.8

　　　s.cs Je 15.20; Ne 1.3   pl Ct 5.7   pl.cs Ne 2.13

חוּס = vb   TO PITY   Qal.pf.2m.s Jo 4.10   imp.1.s Jo 4.11

　　　Qal.imv.m.s+ הָ @13a Ne 13.22   *

חוּץ = n.m   STREET, OPEN SPACE   s Gn 19.16; Ct 8.1; Ne 13.8,20

　　　s+ ה loc Gn 19.17   pl @9e Na 2.5;3.10; Pr 8.26   +sfx Zp 3.6 *

חוּשׁ = vb   TO HURRY   Qal.imv.m.s+הָ @13a Ps 22.20   *

חוֹתָם = n.m   SEAL   s Ct 8.6   *

חָזָה = vb   TO SEE, PERCEIVE   Qal.pf.3m.s Is 1.1;2.1
   Qal.imp.1.s Jb 19.26,27   2m.pl Ct 7.1   1.pl Ct 7.1   *

חָזוֹן = n.m   VISION   s.cs Is 1.1; Ob 1.1; Na 1.1   *

חָזַק = vb   TO BE STRONG, FIRM, TO GRASP(Hi)
   Qal.pf.2m.s+sfx Je 20.7   Pi.imp.3m.pl Ne 2.18
   Pi.imv.m.s Na 2.2; Ne 6.9   +sfx 2Sm 11.25   f.s Na 3.14
   Hi.pf.1.s Ne 5.16   imp.3m.pl Gn 19.16   inf.cs+sfx Je 31.32
   Hi.imv.m.s 2Sm 11.25   f.s Na 3.14   ptc.f.s Ne 4.11
   Hi.ptc.m.pl Ne 4.10,15   Hith.imv.m.pl 1Sm 4.9   *

חָזָק = adj   STRONG   f.s Ne 1.10; as superlative 2Sm 11.15   *

חָזְקָה = n.f   STRENGTH, FORCE   s Jo 3.8   *

חִזְקִיָּה = n.pr.m   HEZEKIAH   Zp 1.1   *

חָטָא = vb   TO SIN, MISS (a goal)   Qal.pf.3m.s Ne 13.26
   Qal.pf.1.s 1Sm 12.13; Ne 6.13   3m.pl Zp 1.17   1.pl Ne 1.6
   Qal.imp.2m.pl Ex 20.20   ptc.m.s Is 1.4   +sfx Pr 8.36
   Hi.pf.3m.pl Ne 13.26   *

חֵטְא = n.m   SIN   s.cs Is 53.12   pl+sfx Is 1.18; Ps 103.10   *

חַטָּא = n.m   SINNER   pl Is 1.28; Ps 1.1,5   *

חַטָּאת = n.f   SIN   s+sfx Gn 18.20; 2Sm 12.13; Je 18.23;31.34; Ne 3.37
   pl.cs Ne 1.6   pl+sfx Je 15.13   *

חִטָּה = n.f   WHEAT   s Dt 8.8; Ps 81.17   pl @9e 1Sm 6.13; Ct 7.3 *

חַי = adj   LIVING   m.s Gn 3.20; 2Sm 12.18; Hs 2.1; Jb 19.25
   Formula in oath 2Sm 11.11 (R2 p32);12.5; Zp 2.9   +sfx 2Sm 11.11
   f.s Gn 1.20ff   m.pl Is 53.8; Je 11.19; Ps 124.3; Ct 4.15
   כָּעֵת חַיָּה = NEXT YEAR or SPRING   Gn 18.10,14   R2 p22

חָיָה = vb   TO LIVE   Qal.pf.3m.s חָיָה Gn 3.22
   Qal.pf.3m.s חַי 2Sm 12.22; Ne 6.11   2m.pl Ez 37.5,6,14
   Qal.imp.3m.s Dt 8.3; Ec 11.8   3f.s.apoc Gn 19.20
   Qal.imp.3m.pl Ez 37.10   3f.pl Ez 37.3   2m.pl Dt 8.1   1.pl Ne 5.2
   Qal.juss.3m.s Ne 2.3   3m.pl Ez 37.9   imv.m.pl Pr 9.6
   Pi.pf.3m.s Ps 22.30   imp.3m.s+sfx 2Sm 12.3   3m.pl Ne 3.34
   Pi.imp.1.pl Gn 19.32,34   Hi.inf.cs Gn 19.19   *

חַיָּה = n.f ANIMAL, LIVING THING s Gn 1.28; Zp 2.15
s.cs Gn 1.25;2.19; Hs 2.14 +archaic ending G/K 90n Gn 1.24; Zp 2.14

חַיִּים = n.m.pl.abst LIFE Gn 2.7; Ps 133.3; Pr 8.35
+sfx Gn 3.14; Jo 2.7; Ps 23.6;133.4 R1 p24

חַיִל = n.m 1. WEALTH, STRENGTH s Dt 8.17,18; 2Sm 11.16; Na 2.4
s+sfx Je 15.13; Ob 11; Zp 1.13; Ps 110.3
2. ARMY s Ez 37.10; Ne 2.9; s.cs Ne 3.34 R2 p50 *

חֵיל/חֵל = n.m RAMPART, FORTRESS s Ob 20; Na 3.8 +sfx Ps 48.14 R1 p34 *

חִיל = n.m ANGUISH, PAIN s Ps 48.7 *

חֵיק/חֵק = n.m BOSOM s+sfx 2Sm 12.3,8; Jb 19.27 *

חֵךְ = n.m PALATE s+sfx Pr 8.7; Ct 2.3;5.16;7.10 *

חכה = vb TO WAIT FOR Pi.imv.m.pl Zp 3.8 *

חֲכַלְיָה = n.pr.m HACALIAH Ne 1.1 *

חכם = vb TO BE WISE Qal.imv.m.pl Pr 8.33
Hi.ptc.m.s.cs Ps 19.8 *

חָכָם = adj WISE, EXPERT m.s 1Kg 3.12; Je 18.18 m.pl Ob 8 *

חָכְמָה = n.f WISDOM s Pr 8.1ff; Ec 1.13ff ?pl Pr 9.1 R2 p114

חָלָב = n.m MILK s Gn 18.8; Ct 4.11;5.12 +sfx Ct 5.1 *

חֵלֶב = n.m FAT s.cs Is 1.11 (of beasts); Ps 81.17 (of wheat) *

חלה = vb TO BE SICK, WEAK Qal.ptc.m.s Ne 2.2 f.s.cs Ct 2.5;5.8
Ni.ptc.m.s Na 3.19 = SORE Hi.pf.3m.s Is 53.10 *

חֲלוֹם = n.m DREAM s 1Kg 3.5 *

חַלּוֹן = n.m/f WINDOW m.s Zp 2.14 f.pl Ct 2.9 *

חַלְחָלָה = n.f ANGUISH, WRITHING s Na 2.11 *

חֳלִי = n.m SICKNESS s Is 1.5;53.3 pl+sfx Is 53.4 *

חֲלִי = n.m ORNAMENT pl Ct 7.2 *

חֶלְיָה = n.f NECKLACE s+sfx Hs 2.15 H.L.

חָלִילָה = exclam FAR BE IT! GOD FORBID! Gn 18.25 *

חלל = vb 1. TO POLLUTE, PROFANE Pi.pf.3m.pl Zp 3.4
Pi.imp.2m.s+sfx Ex 20.25 inf.cs Ne 13.18 ptc.m.pl Ne 13.17
Hi = TO BEGIN pf.3m.pl Ne 4.1 imp.3m.s Jo 3.4 *

2. TO PIERCE   Po'al.ptc.m.s Is 53.5   *

חָלָל = n.m   PIERCED ONE, SLAIN   s Na 3.3   pl.cs Zp 2.12   *

חַלָּמִישׁ = n.m   FLINT   s Dt 8.15   *

חָלַף = vb   TO PASS AWAY, CHANGE   Qal.pf.3m.s Ct 2.11
Qal.imp.3m.s Is 2.18   Pi.imp.3m.s 2Sm 12.20   *

חָלַץ = vb   TO DELIVER, SAVE   Pi.imp.1.s+sfx Ps 81.8
Pi.imv.m.s+ה @13a Ps 6.5   *

חָלַק = vb   TO DIVIDE, SHARE OUT   Qal.inf.cs Ne 13.13
Pi.imp.3m.s Is 53.12   1.s Is 53.12   3m.pl Ps 22.19   *

חֵלֶק = n.m   PORTION   s Ne 2.20   *

חָם = n.m   FATHER-IN-LAW   s+sfx 1Sm 4.19,21   *

חֹם = n.m   HEAT   s.cs Gn 18.1   *

חֶמְאָה = n.f   CURD   s Gn 18.8   *

חָמַד = vb   TO DESIRE, DELIGHT IN   Qal.pf.2m.pl Is 1.29
Qal.imp.1.pl+sfx Is 53.2   juss.2m.s Ex 20.17
Ni.ptc.m.s Gn 2.9;3.6   m.pl Ps 19.11   Pi.pf.1.s Ct 2.3   *

חֶמְדָּה = n.f   DESIRE   s Is 2.16; Na 2.10   *

חַמָּה = n.f   1. HEAT   s+sfx Ps 19.7   *   2. SUN   s Ct 6.10   *

חֵמָה = n.f   ANGER   s Na 1.2; Jb 19.29   s.cs 2Sm 11.20
s+sfx Je 18.20; Na 1.6; Ps 6.2   *

חָמוֹץ = n.m.?coll   THE RUTHLESS   s Is 1.17   H.L.

חַמּוּק = n.m   CURVE   pl.cs Ct 7.2   H.L.

חֲמוֹר = n.m   ASS   s Is 1.3   +sfx Ex 20.17   pl Ne 13.15   *

חֲמִישִׁי = ordinal number   FIFTH   m.s Gn 1.23   f.s Ne 6.5   *

חָמַל = vb   TO SPARE, HAVE PITY   Qal.pf.3m.s 2Sm 12.6
Qal.imp.3m.s 2Sm 12.4   inf.cs Gn 19.16   *

חָמַם = vb   TO BE WARM   Qal.inf.cs Ne 7.3   *

חָמַס = vb   TO TREAT VIOLENTLY   Qal.pf.3m.pl Zp 3.4   ptc.m.s Pr 8.36   *

חָמָס = n.m   VIOLENCE   s Is 53.9; Je 20.8; Jo 3.8; Zp 1.9   s.cs Ob 10*

חָמַק = vb   TO TURN ASIDE   Qal.pf.3m.s Ct 5.6   *

חֹמֶר = n.m   1. MORTAR, CLAY   s Na 3.14   *

חֹמֶר = 2. HOMER (a dry measure)   s.cs Hs 3.2   *

חֲמִשָּׁה = number FIVE   @25d
　　　　f.s Gn 18.28; 1Sm 6.4,16; Hs 3.2; Ne 6.15   f.s.cs 1Sm 6.18   *

חֲמִשִּׁים = number FIFTY   m.pl Gn 18.24ff; 1Sm 6.19; 2Sm 15.1; Ne 5.17

חֵן = n.m FAVOUR   s Gn 18.3;19.19; Na 3.4; Ps 84.12   *

חָנָה = vb TO ENCAMP   Qal.pf.3m.pl 1Sm 4.1   imp.3m.pl 1Sm 4.1
　　　Qal.imv.m.s 2Sm 12.28   ptc.m.pl 2Sm 11.11; Na 3.17   *

חַנּוּן = adj GRACIOUS   m.s Jo 4.2; Ps 103.8   *

חָנַט = vb TO RIPEN   Qal.pf.3f.s Ct 2.13 R2 pl26 H.L.

חֲנִית = n.f SPEAR   s Na 3.3   pl+sfx Is 2.4   *

חָנַן = vb TO BE GRACIOUS, SHOW FAVOUR   Qal.pf.3m.s+sfx 2Sm 12.22Q
　　　Qal.imp.3m.s+sfx 2Sm 12.22K   imv.m.s+sfx Ps 6.3   *

חָנָן = n.pr.m HANAN   Ne 13.13   *

חֲנָנִי = n.pr.m HANANI   Ne 1.2;7.2   *

חֲנַנְיָה = n.pr.m HANANIAH   Ne 7.2   *

חָנַק = vb TO STRANGLE   Pi.ptc.m.s Na 2.13   *

חֶסֶד = n.m STEADFAST LOVE   s Ex 20.6; 1Kg 3.6; Jo 4.2; Ps 103.4
　　　s+sfx Gn 19.19; Jo 2.9; Ps 100.5; Ne 13.22   pl+sfx Ne 13.14

חָסָה = vb TO SEEK REFUGE   Qal.pf.3m.pl Zp 3.12
　　　Qal.ptc.m.pl.cs Na 1.7; Ps 2.12   *

חָסִין = adj STRONG   m.s Is 1.31   *

חָסֵר = vb TO LACK, BE IN NEED   Qal.imp.3m.s Ct 7.3
　　　Qal.imp.2m.s Dt 8.9   1.s Ps 23.1   3m.pl Gn 18.28
　　　Pi.imp.2m.s+sfx Ps 8.6   *

חָסֵר = adj LACKING   m.s Pr 9.4   *

חֶסְרוֹן = n.m DEFICIT, WHAT IS LACKING   s Ec 1.15 H.L.

חֻפָּה = n.f CANOPY, BRIDAL CHAMBER   s+sfx Ps 19.6   *

חָפַז = vb TO BE PANIC STRICKEN   Ni.pf.3m.pl Ps 48.6   *

חָפְנִי = n.pr.m HOPHNI   1Sm 4.4,11,17   *

חָפֵץ = vb TO DELIGHT IN, DESIRE   Qal.pf.3m.s Is 53.10; Ps 22.9
　　　Qal.pf.2m.s Jo 1.14   1.s Is 1.11   imp.3f.s Ct 2.7;3.5;8.4

חֵפֶץ = n.m   DELIGHT, PLEASURE, BUSINESS   s Ec 3.1;12.1
   s.cs Is 53.10   s+sfx Ps 1.2   pl Pr 8.11   *

חָפֵר = vb   TO BE ASHAMED   Qal.imp.2m.pl Is 1.29   *

חֲפַרְפָּרָה = n.f   ?MOLE (R.S.V.),?DUNG BEETLE (N.E.B.)   pl Is 2.20   H.L.
   read לחפר פֵּרוֹת as one word, as in Qumran ms.   Context suggests
   some kind of digging creature derived from root חָפַר TO DIG.

חָפַשׂ = vb   TO SEARCH   Ni.pf.3m.pl Ob 6   Pi.imp.1.s Zp 1.12   *

חָצַב = vb   TO HEW OUT, CLEAVE   Qal.pf.3m.s Is 5.2   3f.s Pr 9.1
   Qal.imp.2m.s Dt 8.9   ptc.m.s Ps 29.7   Ni.imp.3m.pl Jb 19.24   *

חֵצִי = n.m   HALF   s Ne 13.24   s.cs Ne 4.10   s+sfx Ne 3.38;
                                                                    4.10,15   *

חָצִיר = n.m   GREEN GRASS   s Ps 103.15   *

חֹצֶן = n.m   BOSOM   s+sfx Ne 5.13   *

חָצֵר = n.m/f   COURT, ENCLOSURE   m.pl+sfx Is 1.12; Ps 84.11
   m.pl.cs Ne 13.7   f.pl+sfx Ps 100.4   f.pl.cs Ps 84.3   *

חֹק = n.m   SOMETHING PRESCRIBED, STATUTE   s Zp 2.2 R1 p89; Ps 81.5
   s.cs Ps 2.7   s+sfx Pr 8.29   pl Ne 1.7   +sfx 1Kg 3.14   *

חֻקָּה = n.f   STATUTE, DECREE   pl+sfx Dt 8.11   *

חָקַק = vb   TO INSCRIBE, DECREE   Qal.inf.cs+sfx Pr 8.27,29
   Po'el.imp.3m.pl Pr 8.15   Ho.imp.3m.pl Jb 19.23   *

חֹר/חוֹר = n.m   HOLE   s Ct 5.4 R2 p129   pl+sfx Na 2.13   *

חֹר = n.m   NOBLE   (late Hebrew especially Ne)
   pl Ne 2.16;4.8,13;5.7   pl.cs Ne 6.17;13.17   *

חָרֵב = vb   TO BE DRIED UP, LAID WASTE   Hi.pf.3m.s Na 1.4   1.s Zp 3.6   *
   B.D.B. has 2 separate roots but recent commentaries combine them.

חָרֵב = adj   WASTE, DESOLATE   f.s Ne 2.3,17   *

חֶרֶב = n.f   SWORD   s Gn 3.24; Je 11.22; Hs 1.7; Ps 22.21; Jb 19.29
   s.cs 2Sm 12.9   s+sfx Zp 2.12; Ct 3.8; Ne 4.12
   pl+sfx Is 2.4; Ne 4.7
   tool used in hewing stone   s+sfx Ex 20.25

חָרְבָּה = n.f   DRYNESS, DESOLATION   s Zp 2.14   R1 p92   *

חָרַד = vb   TO TREMBLE   Qal.imp.3m.pl Hs 11.10,11
   Hi.ptc.m.s Na 2.12; Zp 3.13   *

38

חָרֵד = adj   TREMBLING, FEARFUL   m.s 1Sm 4.13   *

חָרָה = vb   TO BURN (of anger)   Qal.pf.3m.s Jo 4.4,9
      Qal.imp.3m.s Gn 18.30; 2Sm 12.5; Jo 4.1; Ne 3.33;4.1;5.6
      Qal.inf.cs Ps 124.3   Ni.pf.3m.pl Ct 1.6
      Tip'el (G/K 55h)imp.2m.s =   TO COMPETE   Je 12.5 R2 p93
      this form is disputed and may be denom. of תחרה K/B p337   *

חֲרוּזִים = n.m.pl   STRING OF BEADS   Ct 1.10   H.L.

חָרוּל = n.m   CHICKLING, WEED   s Zp 2.9   *

חָרוֹן = n.m   ANGER, BURNING   s Ne 13.18   +sfx Ps 2.5
      s.cs Hs 11.9; Jo 3.9; Na 1.6; Zp 2.2;3.8   *

חָרוּץ = n.m   GOLD   s Pr 8.10,19   *

חָרִיץ = n.m   TOOL   pl.cs 2Sm 12.31   *

חֲרִישִׁי = adj ?SULTRY, ?AUTUMNAL   f.s Jo 4.8   see B.D.B. p362   H.L.

חֲרַכִּים = n.m.pl   LATTICE WINDOW   Ct 2.9   H.L.

חֶרְמוֹן = n.loc   HERMON   Ps 133.3; Ct 4.8   *

חֹרֹנִי = adj.gent   HORONITE   m.s Ne 2.10,19;13.28   *

חָרַף = vb   TO REPROACH   Pi.pf.3m.pl Zp 2.8,10
      Pi.imp.3m.pl+sfx Ne 6.13   *

חֶרְפָּה = n.f   REPROACH, TAUNT, SHAME
      s Je 15.15;20.8; Zp 3.18; Ne 1.3;2.17   +sfx Ne 3.36
      s.cs Zp 2.8; Ps 22.7; Ne 5.9   *

חֶרֶשׂ = n.m   EARTHEN VESSEL, POTSHERD   s Ps 22.16   *

חָרַשׁ = vb   TO BE SILENT   Hi.imp.3m.s Zp 3.17   3m.pl Ne 5.8   *

חָשַׂךְ = vb   TO WITHOLD, REFRAIN   Qal.imv.m.s Ps 19.14   *

חָשַׂף = vb   TO STRIP, MAKE BARE   Qal.imp.3m.s Ps 29.9   *

חָשַׁב = vb   TO THINK, PLAN, DEVISE   Qal.pf.3m.pl Je 11.19
      Qal.pf.1.pl+sfx Is 53.3,4   coh.pl Je 18.18
      Qal.ptc.m.s Na 1.11   m.pl Ne 6.2,6
      Ni.pf.3m.pl Ne 13.13   ptc.m.s Is 2.22
      Pi.pf.3f.s Jo 1.4 = ABOUT TO   imp.2m.pl Na 1.9   *

חֶשְׁבּוֹן = n.loc   HESHBON   Ct 7.5   *

חָשָׁה = vb   TO BE SILENT   Qal.inf.cs Ec 3.7   *

חָשֵׁךְ = vb   TO BE, GROW DARK   Qal.pf.3m.pl Ec 12.3

Qal.imp.3f.s Ec 12.2   *

חֹשֶׁךְ = n.m   DARKNESS   s Gn 1.2ff; Na 1.8; Zp 1.15; Ec 11.8

חֲשֵׁכָה = n.f   DARKNESS   s Ps 82.5   *

חֲתַחַת = n.m   TERROR   pl Ec 12.5   H.L.

חִתִּי = adj.gent   HITTITE   2Sm 11.3ff;12.9,10

חָתַם = vb   TO SEAL   Qal.ptc.pass.m.s Ct 4.12   *

חָתָן = n.m   SON-IN-LAW, BRIDEGROOM

s Gn 19.12; Ps 19.6; Ne 6.18;13.28   pl+sfx Gn 19.14   *

חֲתֻנָּה = n.f   WEDDING, MARRIAGE   s+sfx Ct 3.11   H.L.

חָתַר = vb   TO DIG, ROW   Qal.imp.3m.pl Jo 1.13   *

חָתַת = vb   TO BE DISMAYED   Qal.pf.3m.pl Ob 9

Qal.juss.3m.pl Je 17.18   coh.s Je 17.18   *

ט

שָׁבַח = vb   TO SLAUGHTER   Qal.pf.3f.s Pr 9.2   inf.cs Je 11.19   *

שֶׁבַח = n.m   SLAUGHTER   s Is 53.7   +sfx Pr 9.2   *

שִׁבְחָה = n.f   SLAUGHTER   s Je 12.3   *

שָׁבַע = vb   TO SINK   Ho.pf.3m.pl Pr 8.25   *

שָׁהוֹר = adj   PURE, CLEAN   f.s Ps 19.10   *

שָׁהֵר = vb   TO BE PURE   Pi.pf.1.s+sfx Ne 13.30

Pi.imp.3m.pl Ne 13.9   Hith.ptc.m.pl Ne 13.22   *

שׁוֹב = vb   TO BE PLEASING, GOOD   Qal.pf.3m.pl Ct 4.10   *

שׁוֹב = 1. adj   GOOD, PLEASANT   m.s Gn 1.10; Hs 2.9; Jo 4.3; Ps 100.5

f.s Dt 8.7,10; Ne 2.8,18b   f.s.cs 2Sm 11.2; Na 3.4

m.pl Dt 8.12; 2Sm 15.3   as superlative   m.s Ps 84.11   f.s Pr 8.11

2. n.m   A GOOD THING, WELFARE

s Gn 2.9b,17;3.5,22; 1Kg 3.9; Je 15.11; Ps 23.6;84.12;103.5   *

שׁוּב = n.m   GOODNESS, WELL-BEING   s.cs Is 1.19   s+sfx Hs 3.5   *

שׁוֹבָה = n.f   WELFARE   s Je 18.20; Ne 2.10,18;5.19;13.31

pl Je 12.6   +sfx Ne 6.19   *

טוֹבִיָּה = n.pr.m   TOBIAH   Ne 2.10;3.35;4.1;6.1;13.4

טוּל = vb   TO HURL   Hi.pf.3m.s Jo 1.4

Hi.imp.3m.pl Jo 1.5   +sfx Jo 1.15   imv.m.pl+sfx Jo 1.12   *

טְהוֹר = n.m   TUMOUR   Mostly Q for K עפלים in 1Sm 5 and 6

Also twice in K   pl.cs 1Sm 6.17   pl+sfx 1Sm 6.11   *

טָחַן = vb   TO GRIND   Qal.ptc.f.pl Ec 12.3   *

טַחֲנָה = n.f   MILL   s Ec 12.4   *

טִיט = n.m   MUD, CLAY   s Na 3.14   *

טִירָה = n.f   BATTLEMENT   s.cs Ct 8.9   *

טַל = n.m   DEW   s Ps 110.3; Ct 5.2   s.cs Ps 133.3   *

טֻמְאָה = n.f   UNCLEANNESS   s+sfx 2Sm 11.4   *

טָמַן = vb   TO HIDE   Qal.pf.3m.pl Je 18.22   Ni.imv.m.s Is 2.10   *

טָנַף = vb   TO SOIL, DEFILE   Pi.imp.1.s+sfx Ct 5.3   H.L.

טָעַם = vb   TO TASTE   Qal.juss.3m.pl Jo 3.7   *

טַעַם = n.m   DECREE, WILL   s.cs Jo 3.7   *

טִפְסָר = n.m   SCRIBE (Akkadian loan-word)   pl+sfx Na 3.17   *

טֹרַה = n.m   BURDEN   s Is 1.14   *

טָרִי = adj   FRESH   f.s Is 1.6   *

טֶרֶם = adv   BEFORE   Gn 2.5;19.4; 1Sm 9.13; Zp 2.2; Pr 8.25   *

טָרַף = vb   TO TEAR   Qal.ptc.m.s Na 2.13; Ps 22.14   *

טֶרֶף = n.m   PREY   s Na 2.13;3.1; Ps 124.6   +sfx Na 2.14   *

טְרֵפָה = n.f   TORN FLESH   s Na 2.13   *

 י

יָאַל = vb   TO UNDERTAKE, RESOLVE   Hi.pf.1.s Gn 18.27,31   *

יְאֹר = n.m   CANAL OF R. NILE   pl Na 3.8   *

יֹאשִׁיָּהוּ = n.pr.m   JOSIAH   Zp 1.1   *

יָבַל = vb   TO BRING, BEAR ALONG   Hi.imp.3m.pl Zp 3.10

Ho.imp.3m.s Is 53.7; Je 11.19   *

רָבֵשׁ = 1. vb   TO BE DRIED UP   Qal.pf.3m.s Ps 22.16   3m.pl Ez 37.11

Qal.imp.3m.s Je 12.4; Jo 4.7   Pi.imp.3m.s+sfx Na 1.4   *

2.adj   DRY   m.s Na 1.10   f.pl Ez 37.2,4   *

יַבָּשָׁה = n.f   DRY LAND   s Gn 1.9,10; Jo 1.9,13;2.11   *

יָגָה = vb   TO AFFLICT (Hi)?Ni.ptc.m.pl.cs Zp 3.18   Rl p96   *

יָגוֹן = n.m   GRIEF, SORROW   s Je 20.18   *

יְגִיעַ = n.m   TOIL, LABOUR   s+sfx Ne 5.13   *

יָגַע = vb   TO TOIL, BE WEARY   Qal.pf.1.s Ps 6.7   *

יָגֵעַ = adj   WEARISOME   m.pl Ec 1.8   *

יָד = n.f   HAND   s Es 2.21; Ne 13.21

s.cs Gn 19.16; 2Sm 15.2; Je 15.21; Ez 37.1; Ps 121.5; Ne 2.8

s+sfx Gn 24.2; Dt 8.17; 1Sm 9.8; Je 31.32; Zp 1.4; Ps 81.15

dual Ne 7.4   dual.cs Je 18.21; Ct 7.2

dual+sfx 1Sm 5.4; Is 1.15; Ps 8.7;19.2;134.2; Ne 2.18

   BY THE SIDE OF   1Sm 4.13,18; Pr 8.3

יָדָד = vb   TO THROW   Qal.pf.3m.pl Ob 11; Na 3.10   *

יָדָה = vb   TO PRAISE, CONFESS   Hi.imp.3m.s Ps 6.6

Hi.imv.m.pl Ps 100.4   Hith.ptc.m.s Ne 1.6   *

יָדִיד = adj   BELOVED   m.s+sfx Is 5.1   f.pl Ps 84.2   *

יְדִידְיָה = n.pr.m   JEDIDIAH (= Solomon)   2Sm 12.25   H.L.

יָדַע = vb   TO KNOW   @28b

Qal.pf	Qal.imp
3m.s Jo 4.11; Ps 103.14	2f.s Ct 1.8
3f.s Hs 2.10	1.s 1Kg 3.7; Ps 101.4
2m.s Dt 8.3 +sfx Je 12.3	3m.pl Gn 3.7; Je 31.34
1.s Jo 4.2 +sfx Gn 18.19	2m.pl Jb 19.29
3m.pl Jo 1.10; Ps 82.5	
2m.pl 2Sm 11.20; Ez 37.6	coh.s Gn 18.21; Je 11.18
1.pl 1Sm 6.9	coh.pl Gn 19.5; Jo 1.7

Qal.imv.m.s Je 15.15; Ec 11.9   m.pl Je 31.34; Ps 100.3

Qal.inf.cs   @28c Gn 3.22; Dt 8.2; Ec 1.17

Qal.ptc.m.s Jo 1.12; Zp 3.5   m.pl.cs Gn 3.5b   pass.m.s.cs Is 53.3

Ni.pf.3m.s 1Sm 6.3; Na 3.17; Ps 48.4   imp.3m.s Es 2.22

Hi.pf.3m.s+sfx Dt 8.3; Je 11.8   imp.3m.s Ps 103.7

Hi.coh.s Is 5.5   imv.m.pl+sfx 1Sm 6.2

יָהַב = vb   TO GIVE   Qal.imv.m.pl 2Sm 11.15   R2 p33; Ps 29.1,2   *

יֵהוּא = n.pr.m   JEHU   Hs 1.4   *

יְהוּדָה = n.loc   JUDAH   Is 5.3; Je 31.31; Ob 12; Ps 48.12; Ru 1.1

יְהוּדִי = adj.gent   JEWISH   m.pl Ne 1.2;2.16;3.33 etc.

יְהוּדִית = adv   JEWISH LANGUAGE   Ne 13.24   *

יהוה = n.pr   YAHWEH   @20d   1Kg 3.5; Je 31.31; Jo 1.1; Ru 1.6 etc.

name of God of Israel with vowels of אֲדֹנָי etc in Q

יְהוֹחָנָן = n.pr.m   JEHOHANAN   Ne 6.18   *

יְהוֹסֵף/יוֹסֵף = n.pr.m   JOSEPH   Ob 18; Ps 81.6   *

יְהוֹשֻׁעַ = n.pr.m   JOSHUA (a Bethshemeshite)   1Sm 6.14,18   *

יוֹאָב = n.pr.m   JOAB   2Sm 11.1ff;12.26,27

יוֹאָשׁ = n.pr.m   JOASH   Hs 1.1   *

יוֹיָדָע = n.pr.m   JOIADA   Ne 13.28   *

יוֹם = n.m   DAY   s Gn 1.5; 1Sm 5.5; Is 2.12; Jo 3.4; Ps 19.3

s.cs Je 17.16,18; Zp 1.7ff

TODAY   Gn 19.37; 1Sm 4.3; 2Sm 11.12; Ps 2.7; Ne 1.11

pl @33e Gn 24.1; 1Kg 3.11; Je 31.31; Jo 2.1; Es 2.21

pl.cs Gn 3.14; Is 1.1; Hs 1.1; Ps 23.6; Ru 1.1; Ec 11.8

pl+sfx Ex 20.12; 1Kg 3.13,14; Je 20.18; Ps 103.15

יוֹמָם = adv   BY DAY   Ps 1.2;22.3;121.6; Ne 1.6;4.3   *

יוֹנָה = 1. n.f   DOVE   s Hs 11.11   +sfx Ct 2.14;5.2;6.9

pl @9e Na 2.8; Ct 1.15;4.1;5.12   *

2. n.pr.m   JONAH   Jo 1.1ff;2.1ff;3.1ff;4.1ff

יוֹתָם = n.pr.m   JOTHAM   Is 1.1; Hs 1.1   *

יִזְרְעֶאל = n.loc/n.pr.m   JEZREEL   Hs 1.4,5;2.2,24   *

יַחַד = adv   TOGETHER   Hs 11.7,8; Ps 2.2;133.1   *

יַחְדָּו = adv   TOGETHER   2Sm 12.3; Is 1.28; Hs 2.2; Ps 48.5; Ne 4.2

יְחִזְקִיָּהוּ = n.pr.m   HEZEKIAH   Is 1.1; Hs 1.1   *

יָחִיד = adj   ONLY   f.s+sfx Ps 22.21 = MY LIFE R1 p48   *

יָחַל = vb   TO WAIT HOPEFULLY   Pi.imv.m.s Ps 130.7;131.3

Hi.pf.1.s Ps 130.5   *

יָטַב = vb   TO BE WELL PLEASING, DO GOOD (Hi)

Qal.imp.3m.s 1Kg 3.10; Ne 2.5,6   2f.s Na 3.8 G/K 70e

Hi.juss.3m.s+sfx Ec 11.9   inf.abs Is 1.17 G/K 113d; Jo 4.4,9

Hi.inf.cs+sfx Dt 8.16   imv.m.s Zp 1.12   *

יַיִן = n.m   WINE   s Gn 19.32; Pr 9.5; Ct 1.2; Ne 2.1;5.15;13.15

s.cs Ct 7.10;8.2   s+sfx Zp 1.13; Pr 9.2; Ct 5.1

יַד = K error for יַד BY SIDE OF   1 Sm 4.13   *

יָכַח = vb   TO DECIDE, JUDGE   Ni.coh.pl Is 1.18

Hi.pf.3m.s Is 2.4   juss.2m.s+sfx Ps 6.2   *

יָכֹל = vb   TO BE ABLE, OVERCOME @15b, 29d

Qal.pf.3m.s 1Sm 4.15   3m.pl Ob 7; Jo 1.13

Qal.imp.3m.s 1Sm 6.20; 1Kg 3.9; Zp 1.18; Ec 1.8,15   2m.s Je 20.7

Qal.imp.1.s Gn 19.19; 2Sm 12.23; Is 1.13; Je 20.9; Ps 101.5; Ne 6.3

Qal.imp.3m.pl Je 15.20;20.11; Ct 8.7   1.pl Ne 4.4

Qal.coh.pl Je 20.10   *

יָלַד = vb   TO BEAR, GIVE BIRTH TO, BEGET   @ 28b

Qal.pf.3f.s Gn 19.38; 2Sm 12.15   +sfx Je 20.14; Ct 8.5

Qal.pf.2f.s 1Sm 4.20   +sfx Je 15.10   1.s+sfx Ps 2.7 G/K 27s

Qal.imp.3f.s Gn 17.17; 1Sm 4.19; Hs 1.3   2f.s Gn 3.16   1.s Gn 18.13

Qal.inf.cs 1Sm 4.19 Rl p3; Zp 2.2; Ec 3.2

Qal.ptc.f.s Gn 17.19; Ps 48.7   +sfx Ct 6.9

Ni.imp.3m.s Gn 17.17   inf.cs+sfx Hs 2.5   ptc.m.s Ps 22.32

Pu.pf.3m.s Je 20.15   1.s Je 20.14   Hi.imp.3m.s Gn 17.20

יֶלֶד = n.m   CHILD   s 2Sm 12.15ff   pl.cs Is 2.6; Hs 1.2

pl+sfx Ru 1.5

יַלְדוּת = n.m   CHILDHOOD   s Ec 11.10   +sfx Ps 110.3; Ec 11.9   *

יִלּוֹד = adj   BORN   m.s 2Sm 12.14   *

יָלִיד = adj   BORN   m.s.cs Gn 17.12,13,27   m.pl.cs Gn 17.23   *

יָלַל = vb   TO HOWL, WAIL   Hi.imv.m.pl Zp 1.11   *

יְלָלָה = n.f   HOWLING, WAILING   s Zp 1.10   *

יֶלֶק = n.m   FORM OF LOCUST   s Na 3.15,16   *

יָם = n.m   SEA   s Gn 1.26; Ex 20.11; Hs 2.1; Jo 1.4; Ec 1.7

יָמִין‎ s = Mediterranean יָם‎ = FROM THE WEST   Hs 11.10   Rl p74

pl Gn 1.10,22; Jo 2.4; Ps 8.9;24.2

יָמִין‎ = n.f   RIGHT HAND   s 1Sm 6.12

s+sfx Jo 4.11; Ps 48.11;110.1,5;121.5; Ct 2.6;8.3   *

יָנָה‎ = vb   TO OPPRESS   Qal.ptc.f.s Zp 3.1   *

יָבַק‎ = vb   TO SUCK   Qal.ptc.m.s Is 53.2; Ct 8.1   m.pl Ps 8.3   *

יָסַד‎ = vb   TO ESTABLISH, FOUND   Qal.pf.3m.s+sfx Ps 24.2

Ni.pf.3m.pl Ps 2.2 Rl p41   Pi.pf.2m.s Ps 8.3

Pu. ptc.m.pl Ct 5.15   *

יָסַף‎ = vb   TO ADD, INCREASE, DO AGAIN   Hi.pf.1.s Ec 1.16

Hi.imp.3m.s Gn 18.29; 1Sm 9.8; Na 2.1; Ec 1.18   2f.s Zp 3.11

Hi.imp.1.s Hs 1.6; Jo 2.5   2m.pl Is 1.5   juss.2m.pl Is 1.13

Hi.coh.s 2Sm 12.8   ptc.m.pl Ne 13.18   *

יָסַר‎ = vb   TO DISCIPLINE, ADMONISH   Ni.imv.m.pl Ps 2.10

Pi.imp.3m.s Dt 8.5   2m.s+sfx Ps 6.2   ptc.m.s+sfx Dt 8.5   *

יָעַד‎ = vb   TO GATHER TOGETHER, ASSEMBLE   Ni.pf.3m.pl Ps 48.5

Ni.imp.1.pl Ne 6.10   coh.pl Ne 6.2   *

יַעַן‎ = conj   BECAUSE   + אֲשֶׁר‎ 1Kg 3.11   *

יָעַץ‎ = vb   TO ADVISE, COUNSEL

Qal.ptc.m.s Na 1.11   as title COUNSELLOR rather than as in B.D.B. p419

Qal.ptc.m.pl+sfx Is 1.26   Ni.coh.pl Ne 6.7   *

יַעֲקֹב‎ = n.pr.m   JACOB   Is 2.3; Ob 10; Na 2.3; Ps 22.24;24.6;81.2

יַעַר‎ = n.m   1. HONEYCOMB   s+sfx Ct 5.1   *

                  2. WOOD, FOREST   s Hs 2.14; Ct 2.3   pl Ps 29.9   *

יָפָה‎ = vb   TO BE BEAUTIFUL   Qal.pf.2f.s Ct 7.7   3m.pl Ct 4.10;7.2 *

יָפֶה‎ = adj   BEAUTIFUL, FAIR   m.s Ct 1.16   m.s.cs Ps 48.3

f.s Ct 1.15;4.1,7;6.4,10

subs = FAIR ONE Ct 1.8;5.9;6.1   +sfx Ct 2.10,13   *

יָפוֹ‎ = n.loc   JOPPA   Jo 1.3   *

יָצָא‎ = vb   TO GO, COME OUT @28b

Qal.pf	Qal.imp
3m.s Gn 19.23; Ps 19.5	3m.s 1Sm 4.1; Jo 4.5
3f.s Ct 5.6	3f.s 2Sm 11.8b; Is 2.3
2m.s Gn 24.5	3m.pl Gn 17.6; 2Sm 11.17
1.s Je 20.18	1.pl Ct 7.12

Qal.coh.s Ne 2.13   imv.f.s Ct 1.8   m.pl Gn 19.14   f.pl Ct 3.11

Qal.inf.cs @28c 2Sm 11.1; 1Kg 3.7; Ne 4.15   +sfx Ps 121.8

Qal.ptc.m.s Gn 2.10; Ps 19.6   m.pl Dt 8.7   f.pl 1Sm 9.11

Hi.pf.3m.s 2Sm 12.30,31   1.s+sfx Ex 20.2

Hi.imp.3m.s+sfx Ez 37.1   3f.s Gn 1.12   2m.s Je 15.19

Hi.imp.3m.pl+sfx Gn 19.16   juss.3f.s Gn 1.24   coh.s Gn 19.8

Hi.imv.m.s Gn 19.12   +sfx Gn 19.5   inf.cs+sfx Gn 19.17; Je 31.32

Hi.ptc.m.s Dt 8.15   +sfx Dt 8.14   m.pl Ne 6.19

יצב = vb   TO TAKE ONE'S STAND   Hith.imp.3m.pl Ps 2.2   *

יצג = vb   TO SET, PLACE   Hi.pf.1.s+sfx Hs 2.5   imp.3m.pl 1Sm 5.2 *

יִצְהָר = n.m   OIL   s Hs 2.10,24; Ne 5.11;13.5,12   *

יִצְחָק = n.pr.m   ISAAC   Gn 17.19,21;24.4   *

יָצַר = vb   TO FORM, FASHION   Qal.pf.3m.s Gn 2.8

Qal.imp.3m.s Gn 2.7,19   ptc.m.s = POTTER Ps 2.9   *

יֵצֶר = n.m   FORM   s+sfx Ps 103.14   *

יָצַת = vb   TO BURN   Ni.pf.3m.pl Ne 1.3;2.17   *

יֶקֶב = n.m   WINE-VAT, TROUGH   s Is 5.2   *

יָקַד = vb   TO BE KINDLED   Ho.imp.3f.s Je 15.14   *

יָקָר = adj   PRECIOUS   m.s Je 15.19   f.s 2Sm 12.30   *

יָקֹשׁ = vb   TO LAY SNARES   Qal.ptc.m.pl = FOWLERS Ps 124.7   *

יָרֵא = vb   TO FEAR @29c   Qal.pf.3m.s Gn 19.30; Ne 7.2   3f.s Gn 18.15

Qal.imp.2f.s 1Sm 4.20; Zp 3.7,15   1.s Gn 3.10; Ps 23.4

Qal.imp.3m.pl 1Sm 4.7; 2Sm 12.18; Jo 1.5; Ec 12.5

Qal.juss.2f.s Zp 3.16   2m.pl Ex 20.20; Ne 4.8

Qal.inf.cs Dt 8.6; Ne 1.11   ptc.m.s Jo 1.9   m.pl.cs Ps 22.24

Qal.ptc.m.pl+sfx Ps 22.26; 103.11

Ni.imp.2m.s Ps 130.4   ptc.m.s Dt 8.15; Zp 2.11; Ps 96.4; Ne 1.5

Pi.inf.cs+sfx Ne 6.19   ptc.m.pl Ne 6.9,14

יִרְאָה = n.f   FEAR   s Jo 1.10,16; Ps 2.11   +sfx Ex 20.20

s.cs Ps 19.10; Pr 8.13; Ne 5.9,15   *

יָרָבְעָם = n.pr.m   JEROBOAM   Hs 1.1   *

יְרֻבֶּשֶׁת =n.pr.m   JERUBESHETH (= JERUBAAL/GIDEON)   2Sm 11.21   *

יָרַד = vb   TO DESCEND @28b   Qal.pf.3m.s 2Sm 11.9; Jo 1.5; Ct 6.2

Qal.pf.2m.s 2Sm 11.10   1.s Jo 2.7; Ne 6.3   imp.3m.s Jo 1.3
Qal.coh.s Gn 18.21   imv.m.s @28c 2Sm 11.8   m.pl 1Sm 6.21
Qal.inf.cs @28c Ne 6.3   ptc.m.pl.cs Ps 22.30
Hi.pf.3m.pl 1Sm 6.15   imp.3m.s+sfx Ob 3   1.s+sfx Ob 4

יַרְדֵּן = n.pr   R. JORDAN   Je 12.5   *

יָרָה = vb   1. TO SHOOT   Hi.imp.3m.pl 2Sm 11.20,24
Hi.ptc.m.pl 2Sm 11.24   *
            2. TO TEACH   Hi.imp.3m.s+sfx Is 2.3   *

יְרוּשָׁלַ͏ִם = n.loc   JERUSALEM   2Sm 11.1; Is 5.3; Ob 11; Zp 1.4; Ct 1.5

יָרֵחַ = n.m   MOON   s Ps 8.4;121.6; Ec 12.2   *

יָרִיב = n.m   OPPONENT   pl+sfx Je 18.19   *

יְרִיעָה = n.f   CURTAIN   pl.cs Ct 1.5   *

יָרֵךְ = n.f   THIGH   s.cs Gn 24.9   s+sfx Gn 24.2; Ct 3.8
dual+sfx Ct 7.2

(?) יְרֵכָה = n.f   SIDE   dual.cs Jo 1.5 F.S p125; Ps 48.3 Rl p32   *

יִרְמְיָהוּ = n.pr.m   JEREMIAH   Je 18.18   *

יֶרֶק = n.m   GREEN PLANT   s.cs Gn 1.30   *

יָרֵשׁ = vb   TO TAKE POSSESSION   Qal.pf.3m.pl Ob 17,19
Qal.pf.2m.pl Dt 8.1   imp.3m.pl @29c Ob 20   *

יִשְׂרָאֵל = n.pr.m   ISRAEL   Ex 20.22; 1Sm 9.9; 2Sm 15.2; Je 31.31; Ps 121.4

יֵשׁ = n.m   SUBSTANCE, EXISTENCE, IT IS
s Gn 18.24; 1Sm 9.12; Jo 4.11; Ne 5.2,3,4,5   = WEALTH Pr 8.21
in question 1Sm 9.11; Ec 1.10   *

יָשַׁב = vb   TO DWELL, SIT @28b   Qal.pf.3m.s Gn 19.29; Ps 1.1
Qal.pf.2m.s Dt 8.12   1.s Je 15.17; Ne 1.4   3m.pl Ne 13.16
Qal.imp.3m.s Jo 3.6; Ps 29.10   3f.s Hs 3.3   3m.pl Zp 1.13; Ru 1.4
Qal.juss.3m.s 1Sm 5.7   imv.m.s @28c 2Sm 11.12; Ps 110.1
Qal.ptc.m.s Is 6.1; Es 2.21   f.s Na 3.8; Zp 2.15; Ct 8.13; Ne 2.6
Qal.ptc.m.pl 2Sm 11.11; Ne 4.6   f.pl Ct 5.12   m.pl.cs Zp 1.4; Ne 7.3
Hi.pf.1.s+sfx Hs 11.11
Hi = MARRY   pf.3m.pl Ne 13.23   inf.cs Ne 13.27

יְשׁוּעָה = n.f   SALVATION   s+הָ Jo 2.10   s+sfx Ps 22.2;96.2   *

יִשְׁמָעֵאל = n.pr.m   ISHMAEL   Gn 17.18,20,23,25,26   *

יָשֵׁן‎ = vb   TO SLEEP   Qal.imp.3m.s Gn 2.21; Ps 121.4   *

יָשֵׁן‎ = adj   SLEEPING   f.s Ct 5.2   m.pl Ct 7.10   *

יָשָׁן‎ = adj   OLD   m.pl Ct 7.14   *

יָשַׁע‎ = vb   TO SAVE, DELIVER   Ni.coh.s Je 17.14

   Hi.pf.1.s Zp 3.19   +sfx Hs 1.7   imp.3m.s Zp 3.17   +sfx 1Sm 4.3

   Hi.imp.1.s+sfx Hs 1.7   imv.m.s+sfx Je 17.14; Ps 6.5;22.22

   Hi.inf.cs+sfx Je 15.20   ptc.m.pl Ob 21   *

יֶשַׁע‎ = n.m   DELIVERANCE, RESCUE   s+sfx Ps 24.5   *

יְשַׁעְיָהוּ‎ = n.pr.m   ISAIAH   Is 1.1;2.1   *

יָשַׁר‎ = vb   TO BE/GO STRAIGHT   Qal.imp.3f.pl 1Sm 6.12 R1 p7, G/K 47k   *

יָשָׁר‎ = adj   STRAIGHT, UPRIGHT   m.pl Ps 19.9; Pr 8.9   *

יִשְׁרָה‎ = n.f   UPRIGHTNESS   s.cs 1Kg 3.6   H.L.

יָתוֹם‎ = n.m   ORPHAN   s Is 1.17,23; Ps 82.3   *

יָתַר‎ = vb   TO REMAIN OVER   Ni.pf.3m.s Ne 6.1   3f.s Is 1.8

   Hi.pf.3m.s Is 1.9   *

יֶתֶר‎ = n.m   REMAINDER   s Ne 2.16

   s.cs 2Sm 12.28; Zp 2.9; Ne 4.8,13;6.1,14   *

יִתְרוֹן‎ = n.m   ADVANTAGE, PROFIT (only Ec)   s Ec 1.3   *

כ

כְּ‎ = particle of comparison   LIKE   Zp 1.17; Ec 12.7

   +sfx @7c   1Kg 3.12; Je 15.18; Ps 29.6; Ne 6.11;13.26

      כ veritatis Ne 7.2 G/K 118x   = quantity ABOUT   1Sm 4.2

כְּאֵב‎ = n.m   PAIN   s+sfx Je 15.18   *

כָּבֵד‎ = vb   TO BE HEAVY, HONOURED   Qal.pf.3f.s Gn 18.20; 1Sm 5.11;
                                                      Ne 5.18

   Qal.imp.3f.s 1Sm 5.6   ptc.m.s 1Kg 3.9 F.S p121 or adj B.D.B. p458

   Ni.ptc.m.s 1Sm 9.6   m.pl.cs Pr 8.24   m.pl+sfx Na 3.10

   Pi = TO MAKE HEAVY, INSENSITIVE   pf.3m.pl 1Sm 6.6   imp.2m.pl 1Sm 6.6

   Pi = HONOUR, GLORIFY   imv.m.s Ex 20.12   m.pl+sfx Ps 22.24

   Hi.pf.3m.pl Ne 5.15   Hith.imv.f.s Na 3.15

   Hith.imv.m.s B.D.B. p458, Holl p150, or inf.abs as imv R2 p87
                                                      Na 3.15   *

כָּבֵד = adj   HEAVY   m.s 1Sm 4.18   m.s.cs Is 1.4   *

כֹּבֶד = n.m   MASS, ABUNDANCE   s.cs Na 3.3   *

כבה = vb   TO EXTINGUISH   Pi.inf.cs Ct 8.7   ptc.m.s Is 1.31   *

כָּבוֹד = n.m   HONOUR, GLORY   s 1Sm 4.21; 1Kg 3.13; Na 2.10; Ps 8.6

   s.cs Ps 19.2   s+sfx Is 6.3; Ps 96.3

כְּבָר = adv   ALREADY (late Hebrew, only in Ec)   Ec 1.10   *

כֶּבֶשׂ = n.m   LAMB   s Je 11.19   pl Is 1.11   *

כִּבְשָׂה = n.f   EWE-LAMB   s 2Sm 12.3,6   s.cs 2Sm 12.4   *

כָּבַשׁ = vb   TO SUBDUE, BRING INTO BONDAGE   Qal.imv.m.pl+sfx Gn 1.28

   Qal.ptc.m.pl Ne 5.5   Ni.ptc.f.pl Ne 5.5   *

כִּבְשָׁן = n.m   FURNACE   s Gn 19.28   *

כַּד = n.f   JAR   s Ec 12.6   *

כֹּה = adv   THUS   Ex 20.22; 1Sm 9.9; Je 11.21; Ez 37.5; Ob 1; Ne 13.18

כֵּהָה = n.f   DULLING, RELIEF   s Na 3.19   *

כֹּהֵן = n.m   PRIEST   s Je 18.18; Ps 110.4; Ne 13.4,13

   pl 1Sm 6.2; Zp 1.4; Ne 2.16   +sfx Zp 3.4   pl.cs 1Sm 5.5

כְּהֻנָּה = n.f   PRIESTHOOD   s Ne 13.29   *

כּוֹכָב = n.m   STAR   pl Gn 1.16; Ob 4; Ps 8.4; Ec 12.2; Ne 4.15

   pl.cs Na 3.16   *

כּוּל = vb   TO CONTAIN   Pil.inf.cs Je 20.9 @30g   *

כּוּן = vb   TO BE FIRM, SECURE   Ni.imp.3m.s Ps 101.7   2m.s Ps 93.1

   Ni.ptc.m.s or pf.3m.s Is 2.2; Ps 93.2

   Po.pf.2m.s Ps 8.4   imp.3m.s+sfx Ps 24.2;48.9

   Hi.pf.3m.s Zp 1.7; Ps 103.19   inf.cs+sfx Na 2.4; Pr 8.27

   Ho.pf.3m.s.wc Na 2.6   *

כּוֹס = n.f   CUP   s+sfx 2Sm 12.3; Ps 23.5   *

כּוּשׁ = n.loc   CUSH, ETHIOPIA   Gn 2.13; Na 3.9; Zp 3.10   *

כּוּשִׁי = 1. adj.gent   ETHIOPIAN   m.pl Zp 2.12   *

   2. n.pr.m   CUSHI   Zp 1.1   *

כָּזָב = n.m   LIE, FALSEHOOD   s Zp 3.13   *

כֹּחַ = n.m   STRENGTH   s Dt 8.18; Na 1.3;2.2; Ps 29.4;103.20

   s.cs Ne 4.4   s+sfx Dt 8.17; Ps 22.16; Ne 1.10   *

כָחֵשׁ = vb   TO DENY, SHRINK BACK

       Pi.imp.3f.s Gn 18.15   3m.pl Ps 81.16 R1 p39   *

כַּחַשׁ = n.m   LYING, DECEIT   s Na 3.1   *

    כִּי = conj   THAT, BECAUSE, FOR   Gn 1.4; Je 31.33; Ru 1.6; Ec 1.18

     emphatic = YEA   Hs 11.10; Zp 2.9;3.20   = THOUGH   Je 12.6; Ps 23.4

     temporal = WHEN   Je 12.1;18.22; Hs 11.1; Ps 8.4

     = BUT   Gn 24.4; Dt 8.3   כִּי אִם = EXCEPT, RATHER   2Sm 12.3; Ps 1.2

כָּכָה = adv   THUS (more emphatic than כֹּה)   Ct 5.9; Ne 5.13   *

כִּכָּר = n.f   ROUND THING   1.   AREA OF JORDAN VALLEY   Gn 19.17ff R1 p26

                                   2.   TALENT WEIGHT   s.cs 2Sm 12.30   *

    כֹּל = n.m   ALL, WHOLE   s Gn 24.1; Dt 8.1; 2Sm 15.2; 1Kg 3.13; Ps 2.12

     s+sfx Is 1.23; Je 31.34; Zp 3.9; Ps 29.9;82.6; Ec 11.8

     + adverbial ending 1Sm 6.4 R1 p6

כָּלָא = vb   TO SHUT UP, RESTRAIN   Qal.pf.3m.pl 1Sm 6.10   G/K 75nn   *

כֶּלֶב = n.m   DOG   s Ps 22.21   pl Ps 22.17   *

כָּלָה = vb   TO BE COMPLETE, AT AN END   Qal.pf.3f.s Ps 84.3

     Qal.pf.3m.pl Jb 19.27   imp.3m.pl Is 1.28; Je 20.18

     Pi.pf.3m.s Gn 18.33   3f.s Hs 11.6   imp.3m.s.apoc Gn 2.2;17.22

     Pi.imp.3m.pl Ne 3.34   inf.cs+sfx 2Sm 11.19   Pu.imp.3m.pl Gn 2.1   *

    כָּלָה = n.f   DESTRUCTION   s Na 1.8,9; Zp 1.18

     used adverbially = COMPLETELY   Gn 18.21   R2 p23   *

   כַּלָּה = n.f   1.   DAUGHTER-IN-LAW   s+sfx 1Sm 4.19   pl+sfx Ru 1.6   *

                  2.   BRIDE   s Ct 4.8ff;5.1

    כְּלִי = n.m   VESSEL, UTENSIL   s Ps 2.9   s.cs as abs Na 2.10

     pl Jo 1.5; Ne 13.5   +sfx 1Sm 9.7   pl.cs 1Sm 6.8,15; Ne 13.8,9   *

כִּלְיוֹן = n.pr.m   CHILION   Ru 1.2,5   *

כָּלִיל = adj   ENTIRE   as adv ENTIRELY Is 2.18   *

כְּלָיֹת = n.f.pl   KIDNEYS (inmost, sensitive part of mankind)

     pl Je 11.20;20.12   +sfx Je 12.2; Jb 19.27   *

כְּלִמָּה = n.f   DISGRACE, REPROACH   s.cs Je 20.11   *

   כְּמוֹ = 1. adv   AS, LIKE   Ct 6.10;7.2   *

           2. conj   WHEN   Gn 19.15   *

כָּמַר = vb   TO BECOME HOT   Ni.pf.3m.pl Hs 11.8   *

כֹּמֶר = n.m   IDOLATROUS PRIEST   pl Zp 1.4   *

כֵּן = adv   SO, THEREFORE   Gn 1.7; 1Sm 9.13; 2Sm 15.1; Jo 4.2; Na 1.12
  + לְ Is 1.24; Je 18.21; Ez 37.12; Hs 2.8; Zp 3.8

כִּנּוֹר = n.m   LYRE   s Ps 81.3;150.3   *

כָּנַס = vb   TO COLLECT, GATHER   Qal.inf.cs Ec 3.5   *

כָּנַע = vb   TO BE HUMBLE   Hi.imp.1.s = SUBDUE   Ps 81.15   *

כְּנַעַן = 1. n.loc   CANAAN   Gn 17.8; Zp 2.5   *
        2. n.m   MERCHANT   s Zp 1.11   *

כְּנַעֲנִי = adj.gent   CANAANITE   m.s Gn 24.3   m.pl Ob 20   *

כָּנָף = n.m   WING   s Gn 1.21   dual Is 6.2   *

כִּסֵּא = n.m   THRONE, SEAT   s 1Sm 4.13,18; Is 6.1
  s+sfx 1Kg 3.6; Jo 3.6; Ps 93.2;103.19

כָּסָה = vb   TO COVER   Pi.imp.3m.s Is 6.2   apoc Jo 3.6
  Pi.imp.3f.s+sfx Ob 10   juss.2m.s.apoc Ne 3.37   inf.cs Hs 2.11
  Pi.ptc.m.s Gn 18.17   Hith.juss.3m.pl Jo 3.8   *

כֵּסֶה = n.m   FULL MOON   s Ps 81.4   *

כְּסִיל = n.m   FOOL   pl Pr 8.5   *

כִּסְלֵו = n.pr   KISLEV (9th month, Nov/Dec)   Ne 1.1   *

כָּסַף = vb   TO LONG FOR   Ni.pf.3f.s Ps 84.3
  Ni.ptc.m.s Zp 2.1 = ?BE PALE B.D.B. p494, ?BE BROKEN   K/B and G
  Meaning of verse is disputed. For full discussion see R1 pp88-89   *

כֶּסֶף = n.m   SILVER, MONEY   s Gn 17.12; Ex 20.23; 1Sm 9.8; Hs 2.10
  s+sfx Gn 17.13,23; Is 1.22;2.20

כָּעַס = vb   TO BE ANGRY, VEXED   Qal.imp.3m.s Ne 3.33
  Hi.pf.3m.pl Ne 3.37   *

כַּעַס = n.m   ANGER, VEXATION   s Ps 6.8; Ec 1.18;11.10   *

כַּף = n.f   HOLLOW   1. of hand = PALM   2. of foot = SOLE
  s Na 3.19   s.cs 1Sm 4.3; Is 1.6; Je 15.21   dual Ps 24.4
  dual+sfx Is 1.15; Jo 3.8; Ps 81.7   pl.cs 1Sm 5.4; Ct 5.5   *

כְּפִיר = n.m   YOUNG LION   pl Na 2.12   +sfx Na 2.14   *

כְּפִירִים = n.loc   KEPHIRIM (site unknown)   Ne 6.2   H.L.
  This preferable (as in N.E.B. and J.B.) to pl of כָּפָר (R.S.V.)

כָּפַר = vb   TO COVER, BLOT OUT   Pi.juss.2m.s Je 18.23   *

כָּפָר = n.m   VILLAGE   pl Ct 7.12   *

כֹּפֶר = n.m   1. VILLAGE   s.cs 1Sm 6.18   H.L.

                2. HENNA PLANT   s Ct 1.14   pl Ct 4.13   *

כַּפְתֹּר = n.m   CAPITAL (of column)   pl+sfx Zp 2.14   *

כַּר = n.m   PASTURE   ?f.pl.cs Zp 2.6   R1 p90   *

Better than derivation given in B.D.B. p500 from כָּרָה CISTERN

כָּרָה = vb   1.   TO DIG   Qal.pf.3m.pl Je 18.20,22   *

              2.   TO BUY   Qal.imp.1.s+sfx Hs 3.2   R1 p67   *

כְּרוּב = n.m   CHERUB   pl Gn 3.24; 1Sm 4.4   *

כַּרְכֹּם = n.m   SAFFRON   s Ct 4.14   H.L.

כֶּרֶם = n.m   VINEYARD   s Is 1.8;5.1; Ct 8.11   s.cs Is 5.7

s+sfx Is 5.1ff; Ct 1.6;8.12   pl Zp 1.13; Ct 1.6;2.15;7.13

pl.cs Ct 1.14   pl+sfx Hs 2.17; Ct 2.15 (but see R2 p126); Ne 5.3

כַּרְמֶל = n.loc   MOUNT CARMEL   Na 1.4; Ct 7.6   *

כָּרַע = vb   TO BOW DOWN   Qal.imp.3f.s 1Sm 4.19   3m.pl Ps 22.30   *

כָּרַת = vb   TO CUT   (used in covenant formula)

Qal.pf.1.s Je 31.31,32; Hs 2.20   imp.1.s Je 31.33

Qal.coh.pl+sfx Je 11.19   ptc.pass.f.pl 1Sm 5.4

Ni.pf.3m.s Na 2.1   3f.s Gn 17.14   2m.s Ob 10   3m.pl Zp 1.11

Ni.imp.3m.s Ob 9; Zp 3.7   Hi.pf.1.s Na 2.14; Zp 1.3,4;3.6

Hi.imp.3f.s+sfx Na 3.15   1.s Na 1.14   inf.cs Ob 14; Ps 101.8   *

כְּרֵתִי = adj.gent   CERETHITE = CRETAN   m.pl Zp 2.5   *

כָּשַׁל = vb   TO STUMBLE, TOTTER   Qal.pf.3m.s Ne 4.4

Qal.imp.3m.pl Na 3.3 K but Q has pf

Ni.imp.3m.pl Je 20.11; Na 2.6   Ho.ptc.m.pl Je 18.23   *

כֶּשֶׁף = n.m   SORCERY   pl Na 3.4   +sfx Na 3.4   *

כָּתַב = vb   TO WRITE   Qal.imp.3m.s 2Sm 11.14,15

Qal.imp.1.s+sfx Je 31.33 @21e   ptc.pass.m.s Ne 6.6;13.1

Ni.imp.3m.s Es 2.23   imp.3m.pl Jb 19.23   *

כֹּתֶל = n.m   WALL (of house) Aramaic word   s+sfx Ct 2.9   H.L.

כֶּתֶם = n.m   GOLD   s Ct 5.11   *

כֻּתֹּנֶת/כְּתֹנֶת = n.f   TUNIC   s+sfx Ct 5.3   pl.cs Gn 3.21   *

כָּתַר = vb   TO SURROUND   Pi.pf.3m.pl+sfx Ps 22.13   *

כָּתַת = vb   TO BEAT   Pi.pf.3m.pl Is 2.4   *

ל

לְ = prep   TO, FOR, TOWARDS   Gn 24.2; 2Sm 15.1; 1Kg 3.5; Jo 1.6

לְמוֹ = לָהֶם Holl p177   Ps 2.4   of time Gn 3.8; Ne 13.6

= ON   Ps 29.10   = BELONGING TO   1Sm 9.3

לֹא = adv of negation   NO, NOT   Gn 24.3; 1Sm 9.4; 1Kg 3.7; Je 31.32

הֲלֹא 1Sm 6.6; 2Sm 11.3   expect a negative reply

As question expecting affirmative answer   Hs 11.5

לֹא עַמִּי = name of Hosea's 3rd child   Hs 1.9;2.25

לֹא רֻחָמָה = name of Hosea's 2nd child   Hs 1.6,8;2.25

לָאָה = vb   TO BE TIRED, WEARY   Qal.imp.3m.pl Gn 19.11

Ni.pf.1.s Is 1.14; Je 20.9   Hi.imp.3m.pl+sfx Je 12.5   *

לְאֹם = n.m   PEOPLE   pl Ps 2.1   *

לבב = vb.denom   ?TO AROUSE   Pi.pf.2f.s+sfx Ct 4.9   *

לֵבָב/לֵב = n.m   HEART, INNER MAN   s 1Kg 3.6; Je 11.20; Na 2.11; Ps 24.4

s.cs Jo 2.4   s+sfx 1Sm 4.20; Je 31.33; Ob 3; Zp 1.12; Ec 1.13

s = DISCERNMENT   Pr 8.5;9.4   pl+sfx Na 2.8

לְבֹנָה = n.f   FRANKINCENSE   s Ct 3.6;4.6,14; Ne 13.5,9   *

לְבוּשׁ = n.m   RAIMENT, CLOTHING   s+sfx Ps 22.19   *

לְבִיא = n.f   LIONESS   pl+sfx Na 2.13   *

לבן = vb   TO BE WHITE   Hi.imp.3m.pl Is 1.18   *

לְבָנָה = n.f   MOON   s Ct 6.10   *

לְבָנוֹן = n.loc   LEBANON   Is 2.13; Na 1.4; Ps 29.5,6; Ct 3.9;4.8;5.15

לָבַשׁ/לָבֵשׁ = vb   TO PUT ON   Qal.pf.3m.s Ps 93.1

Qal.imp.1.s+sfx Ct 5.3   3m.pl Jo 3.5   ptc.m.pl Zp 1.8

Hi.imp.3m.s+sfx Gn 3.21   *

לַהַב = n.m   FLAME   s.cs Na 3.3   *

לֶהָבָה = n.f   FLAME   s Ob 18   pl.cs Ps 29.7   *

לַהַט = n.m   FLAME   s.cs Gn 3.24   H.L.

לוּ = conj   IF ONLY, OH THAT   Gn 17.8   *

לוּבִים = adj.gent.m.pl   LYBIANS   Na 3.9   *

לָוָה = vb   TO BORROW   Qal.pf.1.pl Ne 5.4   *

לוּחַ = n.m   BOARD, PLANK   s.cs Ct 8.9   *

לוֹט = n.pr.m   LOT   Gn 19.1ff

לֵוִי = adj.gent   LEVITE   m.pl 1Sm 6.15; Ne 7.1;13.5ff

לוּלֵי = conj   IF NOT, UNLESS   Is 1.9; Ps 124.1,2   *

לוּן/לִין = vb   TO LODGE, SPEND NIGHT   Qal.pf.3m.s 2Sm 12.16
      Qal.imp.3m.s Is 1.21; Ct 1.13   3m.pl Zp 2.14; Ne 13.20
      Qal.imp.1.pl Gn 19.2   juss.3m.pl Ne 4.16   coh.pl Ct 7.12
      Qal.imv.m.pl Gn 19.2   ptc.m.pl Ne 13.21   *

לוּשׁ = vb   TO KNEAD   Qal.imv.f.s Gn 18.6   *

לְחוּם = n.m   ?FLESH   s+sfx Zp 1.17   R1 p88   *

לְחִי = n.m   JAW, CHEEK   dual+sfx Hs 11.4; Ct 1.10;5.13   *

לָחַם = vb   1. TO FIGHT   Ni.pf.1.s 2Sm 12.27   3m.pl Je 15.20
      Ni.pf.2m.pl 1Sm 4.9   imp.3m.s 2Sm 12.26,29; Ne 4.14
      Ni.imp.3m.pl 1Sm 4.10; 2Sm 11.17   imv.m.pl Ne 4.8
      Ni.inf.cs 2Sm 11.20; Ne 4.2   *
            2. TO EAT   Qal.imv.m.pl Pr 9.5   *

לֶחֶם = n.m   BREAD   s Gn 3.19; Dt 8.3; 1Sm 9.7; Ru 1.6; Ne 5.15
      s+sfx Je 11.19 R2 p91; Hs 2.7; Ob 7   R2 p102   s.cs Ne 5.14,18

לָחַשׁ = vb   TO WHISPER   Hith.ptc.m.pl 2Sm 12.19   *

לַיְלָה = n.m   NIGHT   s Gn 1.5; 1Kg 3.5; Ob 5; Jo 4.10; Ps 121.6
      pl Jo 2.1; Ps 134.1; Ct 3.1,8

לִיץ = vb   TO MOCK, SCORN   Qal.ptc.m.pl Ps 1.1   *

לָכַד = vb   TO CAPTURE   Qal.pf.1.s 2Sm 12.27
      Qal.imp.3m.s 2Sm 12.26   +sfx 2Sm 12.29   1.s 2Sm 12.28
      Qal.imv.m.s+sfx 2Sm 12.28   inf.cs+sfx Je 18.22   *

לָמַד = vb   TO LEARN   Qal.imp.3m.pl Is 2.4   imv.m.pl Is 1.17
      Pi.imp.2m.s+sfx Ct 8.2   3m.pl Je 31.34   Pu.ptc.m.pl.cs Ct 3.8   *

לָעַג = vb   TO MOCK, DERIDE   Qal.imp.3m.s Ps 2.4   ptc.m.s Je 20.7
      Hi.imp.3m.s Ne 3.33   3m.pl Ps 22.8; Ne 2.19   *

לָעַע = vb   ?TO LICK UP, SIP   Qal.pf.3m.pl Ob 16   *

לַפִּיד = n.m   FLASH, TORCH   pl of lightning Ex 20.18;
      pl of torches Na 2.5   *

לָקַח = vb   TO TAKE @22f

    Qal.pf   Qal.imp

    3m.s Gn 2.22   +sfx Gn 24.7   3m.s Ps 6.10   +sfx 2Sm 11.4

    3f.s Zp 3.2   3f.s Gn 3.6

    2m.s Gn 24.4; 2Sm 12.9   2m.s Gn 24.3; 2Sm 12.10

    1.s 2Sm 12.11; Hs 2.11   2f.s Zp 3.7

    3m.pl 1Sm 5.1   3m.pl 1Sm 5.2; Ne 5.15

    2m.pl 1Sm 6.8   juss.2m.s+sfx Je 15.15

    Qal.coh.m.s Gn 18.5   m.pl 1Sm 4.3; Je 20.10; Ne 5.2,3

    Qal.imv.m.s 1Sm 9.3; Hs 1.2; Jo 4.3   +sfx Hs 11.3   R1 p70

    Qal.imv.m.pl 1Sm 6.7; Pr 8.10   inf.cs 2Sm 12.4

    Qal.ptc.m.pl.cs Gn 19.14

    Ni.pf.3m.s 1Sm 4.11,22   3f.s 1Sm 4.17   inf.cs 1Sm 4.19,21

    Pu.pf.3m.s Gn 3.23; Is 53.8   3f.s Gn 2.23   2m.s Gn 3.19

    Ho.imp.3m.s Gn 18.4   R2 p21

לָקַט = vb   TO PICK, GATHER   Qal.inf.cs Ct 6.2   *

לָשׁוֹן = n.m/f   TONGUE   s Je 18.18   +sfx Ps 22.16; Ct 4.11

    s.cs Zp 3.13; Ne 13.24   *

לִשְׁכָּה = n.f   CHAMBER, HALL   s Ne 13.5,8   s.cs Ne 13.4   pl Ne 13.9 *

לָשַׁן = vb.denom   TO SLANDER   Po'el.ptc.m.s.cs Ps 101.5   R1 p45   *

לֶתֶךְ = n.m   LETHECH (grain measure)   s Hs 3.2   H.L.

מ

מְאֹד = adv   VERY   Gn 1.31; 1Sm 4.10; Is 52.13; Na 2.2; Ps 93.5; Ne 2.2

מֵאָה = number   HUNDRED   s Gn 17.17; Ne 5.17

    s.cs Ne 5.11 = ?HUNDREDTH   R2 p53   dual Ct 8.12 = 200   *

מְאוּמָה = pro   ANYTHING   Jo 3.7   *

מָאוֹר = n.m   LIGHT, LUMINARY   s Gn 1.16   pl Gn 1.14,15,16   *

מַאֲכָל = n.m   FOOD   s Gn 2.9;3.6   *

מָאַן = vb   TO REFUSE   Pi.pf.3f.s Je 15.18   3m.pl Hs 11.5

    Pi.imp.2m.pl Is 1.20   *

מָבוֹא = n.m   ENTRANCE   s.cs Pr 8.3   *

מַבּוּל = n.m   FLOOD   s Ps 29.10   *

מַבּוּעַ = n.m   SPRING OF WATER   s Ec 12.6   *

מְבוּקָה = n.f   DESOLATION   s Na 2.11   H.L.

מִבְצָר = n.m   FORTIFICATION   s 1Sm 6.18   pl+sfx Na 3.12,14   *

מֶגֶד = n.m   PRECIOUS THING   pl Ct 4.13;7.14   +sfx Ct 4.16   *

מִגְדָּל = n.m   TOWER   s Is 2.15;5.2   s.cs Ct 4.4;7.5   pl+sfx Ps 48.3
      pl   @9e Ct 8.10   pl.cs Ct 5.13   R2 pl30   *

מָגוּר = n.m   1. SOJOURNING PLACE   pl+sfx Gn 17.8   *
      2. TERROR   s Je 20.10   *

מְגֵרָה = n.f   AXE, CUTTING INSTRUMENT   pl.cs 2Sm 12.31   H.L.

מגן = vb.denom   TO HAND OVER   Pi.imp.1.s+sfx Hs 11.8   *

מָגֵן = n.m   SHIELD   s Ps 84.12; Ct 4.4   +sfx Ps 84.10
      s.cs Na 2.4   pl Ne 4.10   *

מַגֵּפָה = n.f   SLAUGHTER, PLAGUE   s 1Sm 4.17;6.4   *

מְגֵרָה = n.f   SAW   coll 2Sm 12.31   *

מַד = n.m   GARMENT   pl+sfx 1Sm 4.12   *

מִדְבָּר = n.m   1. WILDERNESS   s Dt 8.2; 1Sm 4.8; Hs 2.5; Zp 2.13; Ct 3.6
      2. MOUTH   s+sfx Ct 4.3 Q, not pl as K   *

מָדַד = vb   TO MEASURE   Ni.imp.3m.s Hs 2.1   *

מִדָּה = n.f   MEASURE   s.cs Ne 5.4   pl+sfx Ps 133.2 = GARMENT   *

מָדוֹן = n.m   STRIFE, DISPUTE   s Je 15.10   *

מַדּוּעַ = adv   WHY ?   2Sm 11.10;12.9; Is 5.4; Je 12.1; Ne 2.2;13.11

מְדִינָה = n.f   PROVINCE   s Ne 1.3   *

מַדְרֵגָה = n.f   ROCKY TERRACE, MOUNTAIN PATH   s Ct 2.14   *

מָה = pro.inter   HOW ?, WHAT ?   exclam   HOW !
      Gn 2.19; 1Sm 9.7; 1Kg 3.5; Jo 1.6; Ps 8.2; Jb 19.28; Ec 1.3

      = NOT   Ct 5.8;7.1;8.4

מַה־שֶׁ = THAT WHICH (late Hebrew)   Ec 1.9 G/K 137c

מהה = vb   TO LINGER   Hithpalpel imp.3m.s.wc Gn 19.16   *

מְהוּמָה = n.f   PANIC, CONFUSION   s 1Sm 5.9   s.cs 1Sm 5.11   *

מְהֵיטַבְאֵל = n.pr.m   MEHETABEL   Ne 6.10   *

מָהַל = vb ?TO DILUTE   Qal.ptc.pass.m.s Is 1.22   Rl p79   H.L.

מַהֲלָך = n.m   JOURNEY   s.cs Jo 3.3,4   s+sfx Ne 2.6   *

מַהְפֵּכָה = n.f   OVERTHROW   s.cs Is 1.17   *

מהר = vb   TO HASTEN   Pi.pf.3m.s 1Sm 4.14   imp.3m.s Gn 18.6,7

        Pi.imp.3m.pl Na 2.6   imv.m.s Gn 19.22; 1Sm 9.12   f.s Gn 18.6

        מַהֵר Zp 1.14 either inf.abs @25c, or ptc G/K 52s, Holl p185
        treated as adj B.D.B. p555, see Rl pp87-88   *

מוֹאָב = n.loc   MOAB   Gn 19.37; Zp 2.8,9; Ru 1.1,2,6   *

מוֹאָבִי = adj.gent   MOABITE   m.s Ne 13.1   f.pl Ru 1.4; Ne 13.23   *

מוג = vb   TO MELT   Ni.pf. 3m.s Na 2.7   Hithpolel.pf.3m.pl Na 1.5   *

מוט = vb   TO TOTTER   Ni.imp.3f.s Ps 93.1   3m.pl Ps 82.5   *

מוֹט = n.m   1. BAR   s+sfx Na 1.13   G/K 91d   *

          2. TOTTERING   s Ps 121.3   or vb Qal.inf.cs F.S. p123   *

מול = vb   TO CIRCUMCISE   Qal.imp.3m.s Gn 17.23

        Ni.pf.3m.s Gn 17.26   3m.pl Gn 17.27   imp.3m.s Gn 17.12,13,14

        Ni.inf.abs Gn 17.10,13   inf.cs+sfx Gn 17.24,25   *

מול = prep   IN FRONT OF   2Sm 11.15   *

מוֹלֶדֶת = n.f   KINDRED, RELATIONS   s+sfx Gn 24.4,7   *

מוּם = n.m   BLEMISH, DEFECT   s Ct 4.7   *

מוֹסָד = n.m   FOUNDATION   pl.cs Ps 82.5; Pr 8.29   *

מוֹסֵר = n.m   FETTER   pl+sfx @9e Na 1.13; Ps 2.3   Rl p41   *

מוּסָר = n.m   DISCIPLINE, CORRECTION   s Zp 3.2,7; Pr 8.33

        s+sfx Pr 8.10   s.cs Is 53.5   *

מוֹעֵד = n.m   APPOINTED TIME, SACRED SEASON   s Gn 17.21;18.14; Zp 3.18

        s+sfx Hs 2.11,13   pl Gn 1.14   +sfx Is 1.14   *

מוֹעֵצָה = n.f   COUNSEL, ADVICE   pl+sfx Hs 11.6; Ps 81.13   *

מוֹצָא = n.m   SOMETHING WHICH GOES OUT

        from mouth = UTTERANCE   s.cs Dt 8.3; Je 17.16

        of sun = RISING   s+sfx Ps 19.7   *

מוֹרֶה = n.m   EARLY RAIN   s Ps 84.7   *

מוֹרָשׁ = n.m   POSSESSION   pl+sfx Ob 17   *

מוש/מיש = vb   TO ESCAPE   Hi.imp.3m.s Na 3.1   *

מִשְׁוָב = n.m   COMPANY   s.cs Ps 1.1   *

מוּת = vb   TO DIE   @30d   Qal.pf.3m.s 1Sm 4.19: 2Sm 11.15
     Qal.pf.1.s Gn 19.19   3m.pl 1Sm 4.11;5.12   imp.3m.s 1Sm4.18; Ru 1.3
     Qal.imp.2m.s Gn 2.17; Je 11.21   3m.pl Je 11.22; Ru 1.5
     Qal.imp.2m.pl Gn 3.3; Ps 82.7   1.pl Ex 20.19
     Qal.inf.cs Jo 4.8; Ps 48.15   R1 p34 for emendation   +sfx 1Sm 4.20
     Qal.inf.abs Gn 2.17; 2Sm 12.14   Po.pf.3m.s+sfx Je 20.17
     Hi.pf.1.s+sfx Hs 2.5   imp.3m.s 1Sm 5.11   inf.cs Gn 18.25
     Hi.inf.cs+sfx 1Sm 5.10

מָוֶת = n.m   DEATH   s 1Sm 5.11; Is 53.12; Je 18.23; Jo 4.9; Ps 6.6
     s.cs Is 6.1   s+sfx Jo 4.3,8   s = PLAGUE   Je 18.21
     pl+sfx Is 53.9   (intensive pl?) but see R2 p110 for emendation

מִזְבֵּחַ = n.m   ALTAR   s.cs Ex 20.24,25   s+sfx Ex 20.26
     pl+sfx @9e Ps 84.4   *

מֶזֶג = n.m   MIXED WINE   s Ct 7.3   H.L.

מְזוּזָה = n.f   DOOR POST   pl.cs Pr 8.34   *

מָזוֹר = n.m   ?MAN-TRAP, ?SNARE   s Ob 7   H.L.

מְזִמָּה = n.f   DISCRETION   pl Pr 8.12   *

מִזְמוֹר = n.m   PSALM (song for musical accompaniment)
     in headings of Ps 6;8;19;22;23;24;29;48;84;100;101;110   *

מַזְמֵרָה = n.f   PRUNING-KNIFE   pl Is 2.4   *

מִזְרָח = n.m   EAST   s Ps 103.12   *

מָחָה = vb   TO WIPE OUT   Ni.juss.3f.s Ne 3.37
     Hi.juss.2m.s Ne 13.14   2f.s Je 18.23 R2 p98, G/K 75ii   *

מָחוֹל = n.m   DANCE   s Ps 150.4   *

מְחוֹלָה = n.f   DANCE   s.cs Ct 7.1   *

מְחִיר = n.m   PRICE   s.Je 15.13   *

מְחִלָּה = n.f   HOLE   pl.cs Is 2.19   H.L.

מַחְלוֹן = n.pr.m   MAHLON   Ru 1.2,5   *

מַחְמָד = n.m   DESIRABLE THING   pl Ct 5.16   *

מַחֲנֶה = n.f   CAMP   s 1Sm 4.3,5,6,7   *

מַחֲנַיִם = n.loc   MAHANAIM   Ct 7.1   R2 p131   *

מַחֲסֶה = n.m   REFUGE   s+sfx Je 17.17   *

מָחַץ = vb   TO SMITE   Qal.pf.3m.s Ps 110.5,6   *

מָחָר = n.m   TOMORROW   s 2Sm 11.12   *

מָחֳרָת = n.f   THE NEXT DAY   s Gn 19.34; 1Sm 5.3,4; 2Sm 11.12; Jo 4.7   *

מַחֲשָׁבָה = n.f   SCHEME, PLOT   pl Je 11.19;18.18   *

מְחִתָּה = n.f   TERROR   s Je 17.17   *

מַטֶּה = n.m   STAFF, SCEPTRE   s.cs Ps 110.2   *

מִטָּה = n.f   BED, COUCH   s+sfx Ps 6.7; Ct 3.7   *

מָטַר = vb.denom   TO RAIN   Hi.pf.3m.s Gn 2.5;19.24   inf.cs Is 5.6   *

מָטָר = n.m   RAIN   s Is 5.6   *

מִי = inter.pro   WHO ?   Gn 3.11; 1Sm 4.8; 1Kg 3.9; Is 1.12; Jo 1.8
        expression of desire   OH THAT !   2Sm 15.4; Jb 19.23; Ct 8.1

מַיִם = n.m.pl   WATER   Ex 20.4; Dt 8.7; 1Sm 9.11; Is 1.22; Jo 2.6
        +sfx Hs 2.7   cs Na 3.14; Ps 23.2;81.8
        cs duplicated form מֵימֵי @33e   Na 2.9

מִין = n.m   KIND, SPECIES   s+sfx Gn 1.11ff

מֵישָׁרִים = n.m.pl   UPRIGHTNESS   Pr 8.6; Ct 7.10   as adv Ct 1.4 R2 p124   *

מַכְאוֹב = n.m   PAIN   s Ec 1.18   pl+sfx Is 53.4   pl @9e Is 53.3   *

מַכָּה = n.f   WOUND   s 1Sm 4.8,10;6.19; Is 1.6   +sfx Je 15.18; Na 3.19 *

מָכַר = vb   TO SELL   Qal.pf.2m.pl Ne 5.18   inf.cs+sfx Ne 13.15
        Qal.ptc.f.s.cs Na 3.4   m.pl Ne 13.16   m.pl.cs Ne 13.20
        Ni.pf.3m.pl Ne 5.8   ptc.m.pl Ne 5.8   *

מֶכֶר = n.m   MERCHANDISE   s Ne 13.16   *

מִכְרֶה = n.m   PIT   s.cs Zp 2.9   H.L.

מַכְשֵׁלָה = n.f   CAUSE OF STUMBLING   pl Zp 1.3 R1 p85   *

מַכְתֵּשׁ = n.loc   MAKTESH (= hollow) (place near Jerusalem)   Zp 1.11   *

מָלֵא = vb   TO BE FULL   Qal.pf.3m.s Ps 110.6; Ec 1.7   3f.s Ps 48.11
        Qal.pf.3m.pl Is 1.15;2.6   imv.m.pl Gn 1.22,28   ptc.m.pl Is 6.1
        Ni.pf.3m.s Ct 5.2   Pi.pf.2m.s+sfx Je 15.17   imp.3m.s Na 2.13
        Pi.imp.3f.s Is 2.7,8; Ec 1.8   1.s Pr 8.21   +sfx Ps 81.11
        Pi.ptc.m.pl Zp 1.9   Pu.ptc.m.pl Ct 5.14   *

מָלֵא = adj   FULL   f.s Ez 37.1; Na 3.1   f.s.cs+archaic ending Is 1.21
        as adv = FULLY   Je 12.6; Na 1.10   *

מְלֹא = n.m   FULNESS   s.cs Is 6.3   s+sfx Ps 24.1   *

מַלְאָךְ = n.m   MESSENGER   s 2Sm 11.19ff   +sfx Gn 24.7
        pl Gn 19.1; 1Sm 6.21; 2Sm 11.4;12.27; Ne 6.3
        pl+sfx Na 2.14 R2 p84, G/K 91 l; Ps 103.20

מְלָאכָה = n.f   WORK, OCCUPATION   s Ex 20.10; Ne 2.16;4.5;6.3;13.10
        s.cs Ne 5.16   s+sfx Gn 2.2; Ex 20.9; Jo 1.8; Ne 4.9;13.30

מִלֵּאת = n.f   ?BRIMMING POOL   s Ct 5.12   H.L.

מַלְבּוּשׁ = n.m   GARMENT   s Zp 1.8   *

מַלְבֵּן = n.m   BRICK-KILN   s 2Sm 12.31Q; Na 3.14   *

מִלָּה = n.f   WORD, UTTERANCE   pl+sfx Ps 19.5; Jb 19.23   *

מְלוּכָה = n.f   KINGSHIP, ROYALTY   s 2Sm 12.26; Ob 21; Ps 22.29   *

מְלוּנָה = n.f   SHELTER, WATCHMAN'S HUT   s Is 1.8   *

מֶלַח = n.m   SALT   s Gn 19.26; Zp 2.9   *

מַלָּח = n.m   SEAMAN   pl Jo 1.5   *

מִלְחָמָה = n.f   BATTLE, WAR   s 1Sm 4.1; Is 2.4; Hs 1.7; Ob 1; Ps 24.8
        s+sfx @14e 2Sm 11.25

מלט = vb   TO ESCAPE   Ni.pf.3f.s Ps 124.7   3m.pl Ps 22.6
        Ni.pf.1.pl Ps 124.7   coh.s Gn 19.20   imv.m.s Gn 19.17,22
        Ni.inf.cs Gn 19.19   *

מָלַךְ = vb   1. TO TAKE COUNSEL   Ni.imp.3m.s Ne 5.7   H.L.
              2. TO BE/BECOME KING   Qal.pf.3m.s Ps 93.1
        Qal.imp.3m.pl Pr 8.15   Hi.pf.2m.s 1Kg 3.7   *

מֶלֶךְ = n.m   KING   s 2Sm 15.3; Is 6.1; Jo 3.7; Ps 29.10; Es 2.23
        s.cs Jo 3.6; Ps 24.7; Ne 13.26   s+sfx 2Sm 12.30; Hs 3.5; Ps 2.6
        pl 2Sm 11.1 R2 p29; 1Kg 3.13; Ps 48.5   pl.cs Gn 17.16; Is 1.1

מַלְכָּה = n.f   QUEEN   s Es 2.22   pl Ct 6.8,9   *

מַלְכוּת = n.f   KINGSHIP, ROYAL POWER   s+sfx Ps 103.19   *

מַלְכִּי־צֶדֶק = n.pr.m   MELCHIZEDEK   Ps 110.4   *

מִלְכֹּם = n.pr.m   MILCOM (god of the Ammonites)   Zp 1.5   *

מלכן = 2Sm 12.31K error for מַלְבֵּן as in Q

מָלַל = vb   TO CIRCUMCISE   Ni.pf.2m.pl Gn 17.11   *

מַלְקוֹחַ = n.m   JAW   dual+sfx Ps 22.16   H.L.

מִמְכָּר = n.m   SALEABLE THING, WARE   s Ne 13.20   *

מַמְלָכָה = n.f   KINGDOM, DOMINION   pl Na 3.5; Zp 3.8   *

מַמְלָכוּת = n.f   KINGDOM   s.cs Hs 1.4   *

מַמְרֵא = n.loc   MAMRE   Gn 18.1   *

מֶמְשָׁלָה = n.f   DOMINION, REALM   s.cs Gn 1.16   s+sfx Ps 103.22   *

מִמְשָׁק = n.m   ?GROUND, POSSESSION   s Zp 2.9   H.L.

מַמְתַקִּים = n.m.pl   SWEET THINGS   Ct 5.16   *

מָן = n.m   MANNA   s Dt 8.3,16   *

מֵן = n.m   STRING (of harp)   pl Ps 150.4   H.L.

מִן = prep   FROM, OUT OF   @9f   Gn 2.7; Ex 20.22; Jo 3.8; Zp 1.4;
   +sfx @9g Gn 2.17; 1Sm 6.3; Is 1.15; Zp 3.18; Ps 103.12
   in comparison = MORE THAN   Gn 19.9; Is 52.14; Na 3.16; Ps 93.4
   = SOME OF   Ne 13.25   = RATHER THAN Pr 8.10

מָנָה = vb   TO COUNT, APPOINT   Ni.pf.3m.s Ps 53.12   imp.3m.s 1Kg 3.8
   Ni.inf.cs Ec 1.15   Pi.imp.3m.s.apoc Jo 2.1;4.6,7,8   *

מִנְדָּר = n.m   GARRISON (Assyrian loan word)   pl+sfx Na 3.17   H.L.

מִנְחָה = n.f   GIFT   s Ne 13.5,9   s.cs Is 1.13   s+sfx Zp 3.10   *

מְנֻחָה = n.f   RESTING PLACE   pl Ps 23.2   *

מָנַע = vb   TO WITHHOLD   Qal.imp.3m.s Ps 84.12   *

מַנְעוּל = n.m   BOLT, LOCK   s Ct 5.5   *

מְנָת = n.f   PORTION   pl.cs Ne 13.10   *

מֵסַב = n.m   COUCH   s+sfx Ct 1.12   R2 pl25   *

מָסָה = vb   TO MELT, DISSOLVE   Hi.imp.1.s Ps 6.7   *

מָסַךְ = vb   TO MIX   Qal.pf.3f.s Pr 9.2   1.s Pr 9.5   *

מַסֵּכָה = n.f   CAST IMAGE   s Na 1.14   *

מִסְכֵּנָת = n.f   POVERTY   s Dt 8.9   H.L.

מְסִלָּה = n.f   HIGHWAY   s 1Sm 6.12   pl Ps 84.6   *

מָסַס = vb   TO DISSOLVE, MELT   Ni.ptc.m.s Na 2.11; Ps 22.15   *

מִסְפָּר = n.m   NUMBER   s Ct 6.8   s.cs 1Sm 6.4,18; Hs 2.1   *

מִסְתָּר = n.m   HIDING   s.cs Is 53.3   H.L.

      Perhaps repoint to vb Hi.ptc סתר R2 p108

מַעְגָּל = n.m   TRACK   pl.cs Ps 23.3   *

מֵעֶה = n.m   INWARD PART   pl.cs Jo 2.1,2   pl+sfx Ps 22.15; Ct 5.4,14   *

מָעוֹז = n.m   PLACE OF REFUGE   s Na 1.7;3.11   *

מָעוֹן = n.m   DWELLING, HABITATION   s.cs Na 2.12   s+sfx Zp 3.7   *

מָעַט = vb   TO BE SMALL, FEW IN NUMBER   Pi.pf.3m.pl Ec 12.3   *

מְעַט = n.m   A LITTLE   s 2Sm 12.8; Hs 1.4; Ps 8.6; Ne 2.12;7.4

      s.cs Gn 18.4   s+כִּ Is 1.9; Ps 2.12;81.15; Ct 3.4   *

מַעְיָן = n.m   SPRING   s Ps 84.7; Ct 4.12   s.cs Ct 4.15

      pl @9e Pr 8.24   *

מָעַל = vb   TO ACT UNFAITHFULLY   Qal.imp.2m.pl Ne 1.8

      Qal.inf.cs Ne 13.27   *

מַעַל = adv   ABOVE   Ex 20.4; Is 6.2; Pr 8.28

      + ה loc+prefix ל & מִן Ez 37.8   *

מַעֲלֶה = n.m   ASCENT   s.cs 1Sm 9.11   *

מַעֲלָה = n.f   STEP, STAIR   pl Ex 20.26

      pl in headings of Ps 121,124,130,131,133,134   *

מַעֲלָל = n.m   DEED   pl+sfx Is 1.16; Je 11.18   *

מַעֲמַקִּים = n.m.pl   DEPTHS   Ps 130.1   *

מַעַן = prep/conj   ON ACCOUNT OF, IN ORDER THAT

      only with ל Ex 20.12; Dt 8.1; Ob 9; Ps 8.3;48.12; Jb 19.29

מְעֹנָה = n.f   DEN, LAIR   pl.cs Ct 4.8   pl+sfx Na 2.13   *

מַעַר = n.m   BARE PLACE   s+sfx Na 3.5   *

מַעֲרָב = n.m   WEST   s Ps 103.12   *

מְעָרָה = n.f   CAVE   s Gn 19.30   pl.cs Is 2.19   *

מַעֲרָכָה = n.f   ROW, BATTLE LINE   s 1Sm 4.2,12,16   *

מַעֲשֶׂה = n.m   DEED, WORK   s.cs Is 2.8; Ps 8.4;19.2; Ct 7.2

      pl Ec 1.14   +sfx Jo 3.10; Ps 103.22; Ne 6.14   pl.cs Ps 8.7   *

מַעֲשֵׂר = n.m   TENTH PART, TITHE   s.cs Ne 13.5,12   *

מִפְעָל = n.m   WORK   pl+sfx Pr 8.22   H.L.

מַפְרֶקֶת = n.f   NECK   s+sfx @14e 1Sm 4.18   H.L.

מִפְתָּח = n.m   OPENING   s.cs Pr 8.6   H.L.

מִפְתָּן = n.m   ?THRESHOLD, PLATFORM   s 1Sm 5.4; Zp 1.9   s.cs 1Sm 5.5   *

מֹץ = n.m   CHAFF   s Zp 2.2; Ps 1.4   *

מָצָא = vb   TO FIND

Qal.pf   Qal.imp

3m.s Gn 2.20; Pr 8.35Q R2 pl19   3m.s Jo 1.3

3f.s Ps 84.4   3f.s Hs 2.8,9

1.s Gn 18.3   +sfx Ct 3.1   1.s Gn 18.26   +sfx Ct 8.1

3m.pl 1Sm 9.4   +sfx Ct 3.3   3m.pl+sfx Pr 8.17 G/K 60e

                                         2m.pl 1Sm 9.13; Ct 5.8

Qal.inf.cs Gn 19.11   1.pl Jb 19.28

Qal.ptc.m.s+sfx Pr 8.35   f.s Ct 8.10   m.pl.cs Pr 8.9

Ni.pf.3m.s 1Sm 9.8; Ne 13.1   3m.pl Je 15.16

Ni.imp.3m.s Zp 3.13; Es 2.23   3m.pl Gn 18.29ff   ptc.f.pl Gn 19.15

מַצֵּבָה = n.f   SACRED PILLAR, MASSEBAH   s Hs 3.4   *

מַצָּה = n.f   UNLEAVENED BREAD   s Gn 19.3   *

מִצְוָה = n.f   COMMANDMENT   s Dt 8.1   +sfx Dt 8.2K   s.cs Ps 19.9;
      pl Ne 1.7   +sfx Ex 20.6; Dt 8.2Q; 1Kg 3.14   pl.cs Dt 8.6

מְצוּלָה = n.f   DEEP, DEPTHS (of sea)   s Jo 2.4   *

מְצוּקָה = n.f   ANGUISH, AFFLICTION   s Zp 1.15   *

מָצוֹר = n.m   SIEGE   s Na 3.14   *

מְצוּרָה = n.f   RAMPART, SIEGE-WORK   s Na 2.2   *

מִצְעָר = n.m   SMALL, MODEST THING   s Gn 19.20   *

מַצְפֻּן = n.m   HIDDEN TREASURE   pl+sfx Ob 6   H.L.

מִצְרַיִם = n.loc   EGYPT   Ex 20.2; Dt 8.14; 1Sm 4.8; Je 31.32; Hs 2.17

מִקְוֶה = n.m   ACCUMULATION ·   s.cs Gn 1.10   *

מָקוֹם = n.m   PLACE (especially sanctuary)   s Gn 1.9; Ex 20.24; Zp 1.4
      s+sfx Gn 18.33; Na 1.8; Ec 1.5   s.cs Hs 2.1; Ps 24.3; Ne 4.14
      pl Ne 4.6   pl.cs Ps 103.22

מִקְנָה = n.f   PURCHASE, ACQUISITION   s.cs Gn 17.12,13,23,27   *

מִקְרָא = n.m   ASSEMBLY   s Is 1.13   *

מִקְרֶה = n.m   ACCIDENT, CHANCE   s 1Sm 6.9   *

מִקְשָׁה = n.f   CUCUMBER FIELD   s Is 1.8   *

מַר = adj   BITTER   m.s Zp 1.14   *

מֹר/מוֹר = n.m   MYRRH   s Ct 1.13;3.6;4.6,14;5.5,13   +sfx Ct 5.1   *

מַרְאֶה = n.m   SIGHT, APPEARANCE   s Gn 2.9; 2Sm 11.2; Is 53.2
      s+sfx Is 52.14; Na 2.5 G/K 93ss; Ct 2.14 R2 p126;5.15
      pl.cs Ec 11.9 R1 p109   *

מַרְבֵּץ = n.m   PLACE FOR LYING DOWN   s Zp 2.15   *

מָרַד = vb   TO REBEL   Qal.inf.cs Ne 6.6   ptc.m.pl Ne 2.19   *

מָרְדְּכַי = n.pr.m   MORDECAI   Es 2.21,22   *

מָרָה/מָרָא = vb   TO REBEL G/K 75rr   Qal.pf.2m.pl Is 1.20   ptc.f.s Zp 3.1 *

מָרוֹם = n.m   HEIGHT   s+בְּ Ps 93.4   s.cs Ob 3
      pl Pr 8.2   pl.cs Pr 9.3   *

מָרַט = vb   TO PLUCK OUT (hair)   Qal.imp.1.s+sfx Ne 13.25   *

מְרִיא = n.m   FATTENED CATTLE, FATLING   pl Is 1.11   *

מְרִיבָה = n.loc   MERIBAH (=place of strife)   Ps 81.8   *

מֶרְכָּב = n.m   SEAT (of litter)   s+sfx Ct 3.10   *

מֶרְכָּבָה = n.f   CHARIOT   s 2Sm 15.1; Na 3.2   pl.cs Ct 6.12
      pl+sfx Is 2.7   *

מִרְמָה = n.f   TREACHERY   s Is 53.9; Zp 1.9; Ps 24.4   *

מִרְמָס = n.m   TRODDEN DOWN PLACE   s Is 5.5   *

מַרְעֶה = n.m   PASTURE, FOOD   s Na 2.12   *

מַרְעִית = n.f   PASTURING   s+sfx Ps 100.3   *

מֶרְקָח = n.m   PERFUME, SPICE   pl Ct 5.13   H.L.

מַשָּׂא = n.m   1. LOAD, BURDEN   s Ne 13.15,19   *
      2. ORACLE, UTTERANCE   s.cs Na 1.1   *

מַשְׂאֵת = n.f   1. BURDEN   s Zp 3.18   *   2. GIFT   s.cs 2Sm 11.8   *

מִשְׂגָּב = n.m   PLACE OF SAFETY   s Ps 48.4   *

מְשׂוּכָה = n.f   HEDGE   s+sfx Is 5.5   H.L.

מָשׂוֹשׂ = n.m   EXALTATION, JOY   s.cs Ps 48.3   s+sfx Hs 2.13   *

מִפְשָׂע = n.m   ?BLOODSHED   s Is 5.7   H.L.

מַשָּׁא = n.m   DEBT, USURY   s Ne 5.7,10   *

מִשְׁבָּר = n.m   BREAKER (of sea)   pl.cs Ps 93.4   pl+sfx Jo 2.4   *

מֹשֶׁה = n.pr.m   MOSES   Ex 20.19ff; Ps 103.7; Ne 1.7,8;13.1

מְשׁוֹאָה = n.f   DESOLATION   s Zp 1.15   *

מְשׁוּבָה = n.f   APOSTASY, TURNING BACK   s+sfx Hs 11.7   *

מָשַׁח = vb   TO ANOINT   Qal.pf.1.s+sfx 2Sm 12.7   *

מִשְׁחָר = n.m   DAWN   s Ps 110.3   H.L.
B.D.B. suggests מ due to dittography and should read normal form
שַׁחַר. In any case, the meaning is the same.

מִשְׁחָת = n.m   DISFIGUREMENT (B.D.B p1008, Holl p218)   s Is 52.14   H.L.
Perhaps should repoint to Ho.ptc of שחת R2 p106

מָשִׁיחַ = n.m.   ANOINTED ONE   s+sfx Ps 2.2;84.10   *

מָשַׁךְ = vb   TO DRAG, DRAW   Qal.imp.1.s+sfx Hs 11.4
Qal.imv.m.s+sfx Ct 1.4   *

מִשְׁכָּב = n.m   COUCH, BED   s+sfx 2Sm 11.2,13; Ct 3.1   *

מִשְׁכָּן = n.m   DWELLING PLACE   pl.cs @9e Ct 1.8   pl+sfx Ps 84.2   *

מָשַׁל = vb   TO RULE, REIGN   Qal.pf.3f.s Ps 103.19   imp.3m.s Gn 3.16
Qal.juss.3m.pl Ps 19.14   inf.cs Gn 1.18
Qal.ptc.m.s Gn 24.2; Ps 22.29   Hi.imp.2m.s+sfx Ps 8.7   *

מְשֻׁלָּם = n.pr.m   MESHULLAM   Ne 6.18   *

מִשְׁמָר = n.m   GUARD, WATCH   s Ne 4.3,16,17   +sfx Ne 7.3
pl+sfx Ne 13.14   *

מִשְׁמֶרֶת = n.f   GUARD, WATCH   pl Ne 13.30   pl.cs Ne 7.3   *

מִשְׁנֶה = n.m   SECOND, DOUBLE   s Je 17.18   as n.loc Zp 1.10   *

מְשִׁסָּה = n.f   BOOTY, PLUNDER   s Zp 1.13   *

מִשְׁעֶנֶת = n.f   STAFF   s+sfx @14e Ps 23.4   *

מִשְׁפָּחָה = n.f   CLAN, FAMILY   pl Na 3.4; Ne 4.7   pl.cs Ps 22.28   *

מִשְׁפָּט = n.m   JUDGEMENT   s 2Sm 15.2; 1Kg 3.11; Is 5.7; Hs 2.21; Ec 11.9
s+sfx Zp 2.3;3.5   pl Je 12.1; Ps 103.6; Ne 1.7
pl.cs Ps 19.10   pl+sfx Dt 8.11; Ps 48.12

מִשְׁקָל = n.m   WEIGHT   s+sfx 2Sm 12.30   *

מִשְׁתֶּה = n.m   DRINK   s Gn 19.3   *

מָתוֹק = adj   SWEET   m.s Ct 2.3; Ec 11.7   m.pl Ps 19.11   *

מָתַי = inter   WHEN ?   Ps 101.2

    with עַד = HOW LONG ?   Je 12.4; Ps 6.4;82.2; Ne 2.6   *

מְתֹם = n.m   SOUNDNESS, WHOLENESS   s Is 1.6   *

מַתַּנְיָה = n.pr.m   MATTANIAH   Ne 13.13   *

מָתְנַיִם = n.m.dual   LOINS   Na 2.2,11   +sfx Ne 4.12   *

נ

נָא = particle of entreaty   PLEASE

    Gn 24.2; Is 5.1; Je 17.15; Jo 1.8; Ps 124.1; Ct 3.2; Ne 1.6

נֹא־אָמוֹן = n.loc   NO-AMON, THEBES   Na 3.8   *

    Hebrew rendering of Egyptian 'City of Amon'   R2 p86

נָאָה = vb   TO BE COMELY, FITTING

    In B.D.B. p610, Lang p204, and G/K 73g a Pilel form of this verb is
    suggested for Ps 93.5 and Ct 1.10.   Holl p223 suggests Qal.
    However, for different parsing from root אוה   see R1 p31.

נָאוֶה = adj   BEAUTIFUL   m.s Ct 2.14;4.3   f.s Ct 1.5;6.4   *

נְאֻם = n.m   UTTERANCE, DECLARATION (used in prophetic formulae)

    s.cs Is 1.24; Je 31.31; Ez 37.14; Hs 2.15; Ob 4; Na 2.14; Zp 1.2

נָאַף = vb   TO COMMIT ADULTERY   Qal.juss.2m.s Ex 20.14

    Pi.ptc.f.s Hs 3.1   *

נַאֲפוּף = n.m   ADULTERY   pl+sfx Hs 2.4   H.L.

נָאַץ = vb   TO SPURN, DESPISE   Pi.pf.2m.s 2Sm 12.14   3m.pl Is 1.4

    Pi.inf.abs 2Sm 12.14 for meaning of vb in this verse see R2 p39   *

נבא = vb.denom   TO PROPHESY, ACT AS   נָבִיא   Ni.pf.1.s Ez 37.7

    Ni.juss.2m.s Je 11.21   imv.m.s Ez 37.4,9,12   inf.cs+sfx Ez 37.7

    Hith.pf.1.s Ez 37.10   *

נְבוּאָה = n.f   PROPHECY (late Hebrew)   s Ne 6.12   *

נבט = vb   TO LOOK   Hi.imp.3f.s Gn 19.26   3m.pl Ps 22.18

    Hi.juss.2m.s Gn 19.17   imv.m.s Ps 84.10   inf.cs Jo 2.5   *

נָבִיא = n.m   PROPHET   s 1Sm 9.9; 2Sm 12.25; Je 18.18

          pl Ne 6.7,14   +sfx Zp 3.4   *

נְבִיאָה = n.f   PROPHETESS   s Ne 6.14   *

נָבֵל = vb   1. TO WITHER   Qal.imp.3m.s Ps 1.3   ptc.f.s.cs Is 1.30 *

             2. TO BE FOOLISH   Pi.pf.1.s+sfx Na 3.6 = TO RIDICULE   *

נֵבֶל = n.m   HARP   s Ps 81.3;150.3   *

נַבְלוּת = n.f   SHAME R1 p62, PRIVATE PARTS Foh p169   s+sfx Hs 2.12   H.L.

נבע = vb   TO POUR FORTH   Hi.imp.3m.s Ps 19.3   *

נֶגֶב = n.loc   NEGEB   Ob 19,20   *

נגד = vb   TO DECLARE   Hi.pf.3m.s Gn 3.11; Jo 1.10   1.s Ne 2.12,16

      Hi.imp.3m.s 1Sm 9.6; Es 2.22   3f.s 2Sm 11.5   1.s Ne 2.18

      Hi.imp.3m.pl 2Sm 11.10; Ps 22.32   2m.pl Ct 5.8

      Hi.coh.m.pl+sfx Je 20.10   imv.m.s @13a Jo 1.8; Ct 1.7

      Hi.imv.m.pl Je 20.10   inf.cs 1Sm 4.13; 2Sm 12.18   ptc.m.s Ps 19.2

נֶגֶד = adv/prep   OPPOSITE, IN FRONT OF, OVER AGAINST

      2Sm 12.12; Is 1.16; Ps 22.26; Ne 3.37   +sfx Is 1.7; Ct 6.5

      +מִן Ob 11   +כְ &sfx = CORRESPONDING TO Gn 2.18,20

נָגִיד = n.m   RULER   pl.abst Pr 8.6 = NOBLE THINGS   *

נְגִינָה = n.f   MUSIC   pl Ps 6.1   *

נָגַע = vb   TO TOUCH, SMITE   Qal.pf.3f.s 1Sm 6.9   imp.3m.s Jo 3.6

      Qal.juss.2m.pl Gn 3.3   ptc.pass.m.s Is 53.4

      Hi = ARRIVE pf.3m.s Ct 2.12   3m.pl Ec 12.1   *

נֶגַע = n.m   PLAGUE, BLOW   s Is 53.8   *

נָגַף = vb   TO STRIKE   Qal.pf.3m.s+sfx 1Sm 4.3

      Qal.imp.3m.s 2Sm 12.15   Ni.imp.3m.s 1Sm 4.2,10   *

נגר = vb   TO POUR OUT, SPILL   Hi.imv.m.s+sfx Je 18.21   *

נָגַשׂ = vb   TO OPPRESS   Ni.pf.3m.s Is 53.7   *

נָגַשׁ = vb   TO APPROACH @22d   Qal.imp.3m.s Gn 18.23   3m.pl Gn 19.9

      Qal.imv.m.s Gn 19.9   Ni.pf.3m.s Ex 20.21   2m.pl 2Sm 11.20,21   *

נְדָבָה = n.f   FREEWILL-OFFERING, NOBILITY, ROYAL GRACE

      pl Ps 110.3

      See B.D.B. p621, R1 p43

נָדַד = vb   TO FLEE   Qal.imp.3m.s Na 3.7   Po'el.3m.s Na 3.17   *

נָדַח = vb   TO BANISH   Ni.ptc.m.s+sfx Ne 1.9   f.s Zp 3.19   *

נָדִיב = adj   NOBLE   m.s Ct 7.2   m.pl Pr 8.16   *

נָדַף = vb   TO DRIVE AWAY, SCATTER   Qal.imp.3f.s+sfx Ps 1.4   *

נָדַר = vb   TO MAKE A VOW   Qal.pf.1.s Jo 2.10   imp.3m.pl Jo 1.16   *

נֶדֶר = n.m   VOW   pl Jo 1.16   +sfx Na 2.1; Ps 22.26   *

נָהַג = vb   1. TO GUIDE   Qal.imp.1.s+sfx Ct 8.2

Pi.imp.3m.s+sfx Ps 48.15   *

2. TO LAMENT, SOB   Pi.ptc.f.pl Na 2.8   H.L.

נָהַל = vb   TO LEAD (animals to water)   Pi.imp.3m.s+sfx Ps 23.2   *

נָהַר = vb   TO FLOW, STREAM   Qal.pf.3m.pl Is 2.2   *

נָהָר = n.m   RIVER, STREAM   s Gn 2.10ff; Jo 2.4; Ne 2.7,9

pl.cs Zp 3.10   pl @9e Na 1.4;2.7; Ps 24.2;93.3; Ct 8.7

נוֹד = vb   TO MOURN   Qal.imp.3m.s Na 3.7   *

נָוֶה = n.f   PASTURE   pl.cs Zp 2.6; Ps 23.2   *

נוֹח = vb   TO REST   Qal.imp.3m.s Ex 20.11

2 forms of Hi   1. הֵנִיחַ   2. הִנִּיחַ   Rl p98

1. Hi.pf.3m.s+sfx Ez 37.1   2. Hi.pf.1.s Ez 37.14

Hi.pf.3m.pl 1Sm 6.18   imp.3m.s+sfx Gn 2.15   3m.pl+sfx Gn 19.16   *

נוּם = vb   TO SLEEP   Qal.pf.3m.pl Na 3.18   imp.3m.s Ps 121.3,4   *

נוּס = vb   TO FLEE   Qal.pf.3m.s 1Sm 4.17   1.s 1Sm 4.16

Qal.pf.3m.pl Ct 2.17;4.6   imp.3m.pl 1Sm 4.10   inf.cs Gn 19.20

Qal.ptc.m.pl Na 2.9   *

נוּעַ = vb   TO SHAKE, TREMBLE   Qal.imp.3m.pl Ex 20.18

Ni.imp.3m.pl Na 3.12   Hi.imp.3m.s Zp 2.15   3m.pl Ps 22.8   *

נוֹעַדְיָה = n.pr.m   NOADIAH   Ne 6.14   *

נוּף = vb   TO WIELD   Hi.pf.2m.s Ex 20.25   *

נוֹף = n.m   HEIGHT, ELEVATION   s Ps 48.3   H.L.

נָזָה = vb   TO SPRINKLE   Hi.imp.3m.s Is 52.15   R2 p106   *

נָזַל = vb   TO FLOW   Qal.juss.3m.pl Ct 4.16   ptc.m.pl Ct 4.15   *

נֶזֶם = n.m   RING (for ear or nose)   s+sfx Hs 2.15   *

נָחָה = vb   TO LEAD   Hi.imp.3m.s+sfx Ps 23.3   *

נַחוּם = n.pr.m   NAHUM   Na 1.1   H.L.

נִחוּמִים = n.m.pl   COMPASSION, COMFORT   +sfx Hs 11.8   *

נָחַל = vb denom   TO TAKE POSSESSION, INHERIT   Qal.imp.2m.s Ps 82.8
    Qal.imp.3m.pl+sfx Zp 2.9   Hi.inf.cs Pr 8.21   *

נַחַל = n.m   1. STREAM, WADI   s Ps 110.7; Ne 2.15   + ה loc Ps 124.4
    pl Ec 1.7   pl.cs Dt 8.7   *
            2. DATE-PALM   s Ct 6.11   *

נַחֲלָה = n.f   POSSESSION, HERITAGE   s+sfx Ps 2.8   *

נחם = vb   TO REPENT (Ni), COMFORT (Pi)   Ni.pf.3m.s Je 20.16; Jo 3.9
    Ni.imp.3m.s Jo 3.10; Ps 110.4   1.s Is 1.24   ptc.m.s Jo 4.2
    Pi.imp.3m.s 2Sm 12.24   3m.pl+sfx Ps 23.4   ptc.m.pl Na 3.7   *

נְחֶמְיָה = n.pr.m   NEHEMIAH   Ne 1.1   *

נָחָשׁ = n.m   SERPENT   s Gn 3.1ff; Dt 8.15

נְחֹשֶׁת = n.m   COPPER, BRONZE   s Dt 8.9; Je 15.12,20   *

נָטָה = vb   TO STRETCH OUT   Qal.pf.1.s Zp 1.4   imp.3m.s.apoc Zp 2.13
    Hi.imp.1.s.apoc Hs 11.4   R1 p71   *

נָטִיל = adj   LADEN   m.pl.cs Zp 1.11 perhaps in passive sense
    However, if in active sense then = WEIGHER OF   R1 p87   *

נָטַע = vb   TO PLANT   Qal.pf.2m.s+sfx Je 12.2   3m.pl Zp 1.13
    Qal.imp.3m.s Gn 2.8   +sfx Is 5.2   inf.cs Ec 3.2
    Qal.ptc.pass.m.s Ec 3.2   *

נֶטַע = n.m   PLANTATION   s.cs Is 5.7   *

נָטַף = vb   TO DRIP   Qal.pf.3m.pl Ct 5.5   imp.3f.pl Ct 4.11
    Qal.ptc.f.pl Ct 5.13   *

נָטַר = vb   1. TO KEEP WATCH   Qal.pf.1.s Ct 1.6   ptc.f.s Ct 1.6
    Qal.ptc.m.pl Ct 8.11,12   *
            2. ?TO BE ANGRY   Qal.imp.3m.s Ps 103.9   ptc.m.s Na 1.2 *
    Second meaning "open to conjecture" Holl p236, though accepted by
    Foh.   See discussion in R1 p24 & R2 p76.

נָטַשׁ = vb   TO LEAVE, FORSAKE   Qal.pf.2m.s Is 2.6   G/K 44g
    Qal.imp.3f.s 1Sm 4.2   R1 p2.   B.D.B. p644 suggests emendation.

נִינְוֵה = n.loc   NINEVEH   Jo 1.2;3.2;4.11; Na 1.1;2.9; Zp 2.13

נִיסָן = n.pr   NISAN (name of 1st month March/April)   Ne 2.1   *

נִיצוֹץ = n.m   SPARK   s Is 1.31   H.L.

נכה = vb   TO STRIKE   Ni.pf.3m.s 2Sm 11.15

    Hi.pf.3m.s 1Sm 6.19; 2Sm 11.21   2m.s 2Sm 12.9   3m.pl Gn 19.11

    Hi.pf.3m.pl+sfx Ct 5.7   imp.3m.s+sfx Ps 121.6

    Hi.imp.3m.s.apoc 1Sm 5.6,9;6.19   3f.s.apoc Jo 4.7,8   1.s Ne 13.25

    Hi.imp.3m.pl 1Sm 4.2   coh.pl+sfx Je 18.18   ptc.m.pl 1Sm 4.8

    Ho.pf.3m.pl 1Sm 5.12   imp.2m.pl Is 1.5   ptc.m.s.cs Is 53.4

    Ho.ptc.m.pl.cs Je 18.21   *

נָכֹחַ = adj   STRAIGHT, RIGHT   m.pl 2Sm 15.3; Pr 8.9   *

נֶכַח = prep   IN FRONT OF   Je 17.16   *

נכר = vb   TO RECOGNISE, UNDERSTAND   Hi.imp.3m.s+sfx Ps 103.16

    Hi.coh.s Ne 6.12   ptc.m.pl Ne 13.24   *

נֶכֶר = n.m   MISFORTUNE, CALAMITY   s+sfx Ob 12   *

נֵכָר = n.m   FOREIGNNESS   s Gn 17.12,27; Ps 81.10; Ne 13.30   *

נָכְרִי = adj   FOREIGN   m.s Zp 1.8   f.pl Ne 13.26,27

    as subs = FOREIGNER, ALIEN   m.pl Is 2.6; Ob 11   *

נָמֵר = n.m   LEOPARD   pl Ct 4.8   *

נסה = vb   TO TEST, TRY   Pi.inf.cs Ex 20.20   +sfx Dt 8.2,16   *

נָסַךְ = vb   TO INSTALL, APPOINT   Qal.pf.1.s Ps 2.6   Rl p42

    Ni.pf.1.s Pr 8.23   B.D.B. p651, or from root 2. נסך = TO WEAVE
    so Holl p239   *

נְעוּרִים = n.m.pl   YOUTH, EARLY LIFE   +sfx Hs 2.17; Ps 103.5   Rl p24   *

נָעִים = adj   SWEET, PLEASANT   m.s Ps 81.3;133.1; Ct 1.16   *

נָעַל = vb   TO LOCK, BOLT   Qal.ptc.pass.m.s Ct 4.12   *

נַעַל = n.m   SANDAL, SHOE   pl Ct 7.2   *

נָעֵם = vb   TO BE LOVELY   Qal.pf.2f.s Ct 7.7   *

נָעֳמִי = n.pr.f   NAOMI   Ru 1.2,3   *

נָעַר = vb   TO SHAKE OUT   Qal.pf.1.s Ne 5.13   ptc.pass.m.s Ne 5.13

    Pi.juss.3m.s Ne 5.13   *

נַעַר = n.m   BOY, YOUTH, SERVANT   s Gn 18.7; 1Sm 9.8; 2Sm 12.16; 1Kg 3.7

    s+sfx 1Sm 9.5; Ne 4.16   pl 1Sm 9.3   +sfx Ne 4.10;5.10ff; 13.19

נַעֲרָה = n.f   GIRL, MAID   pl 1Sm 9.11   +sfx Pr 9.3   *

נְעֹרֶת = n.f   TOW (shaken from flax, used for tinder)   s Is 1.31   *

נָפַח = vb   TO BLOW   Qal.imp.3m.s Gn 2.7   imv.f.s Ez 37.9   *

נָפַל = vb   TO FALL   Qal.pf.3m.pl Na 3.12
    Qal.imp.3m.s Gn 17.3,17; 1Sm 4.10,18; 2Sm 11.17; Jo 1.7
    Qal.imp.3m.pl Ne 6.16   ptc.m.s 1Sm 5.3,4
    Hi = THROW DOWN   imp.3m.s Gn 2.21   3m.pl Jo 1.7; Ps 22.19
    Hi.coh.s Jo 1.7   *

נָפַץ = vb   TO SMASH   Pi.imp.2m.s+sfx Ps 2.9   *

נֶפֶשׁ = n.f   SOUL, SELF, PERSON, LIFE
    s Gn 17.14; Ps 19.8   s.cs Gn 1.20; 1Kg 3.11; Je 20.13; Jo 1.14
    s = ?THROAT, NECK   Jo 1.7   F.S. p126
    s+sfx 2Sm 11.11; Is 53.10; Jo 2.8; Ps 121.7; Pr 8.36; Ct 1.7

נֹפֶת = n.m   HONEY FROM THE COMB   s Ct 4.11   s.cs Ps 19.11   *

נָצַב = vb   TO STAND   Ni.pf.3f.s Pr 8.2
    Ni.ptc.m.s Ps 82.1   m.pl Gn 18.2   f.pl 1Sm 4.20   *

נָצַח = vb   ?TO BE PRE-EMINENT, SUPERVISE
    Pi.ptc.m.s+ל as liturgical direction in headings of Psalms.
    · Ps 6, 8, 19, 22, 81, 84   Usually translated CHOIRMASTER B.D.B. p664
    for other possible interpretations see R1 p27   *

נֶצַח = n.m   PERPETUITY   s Je 15.18   +ל Ps 103.9   *

נְצִיב = n.m   PILLAR   s.cs Gn 19.26   *

נָצַל = vb   TO SAVE, DELIVER, SNATCH AWAY
    Hi.pf.3m.s Je 20.13 1.s Hs 2.11   +sfx 2Sm 12.7; Je 15.21
    Hi.imp.3m.s+sfx 1Sm 4.8; Hs 2.12   juss.3m.s+sfx Ps 22.9
    Hi.imv.m.s Ps 22.21   m.pl Ps 82.4
    Hi.inf.cs Jo 4.6   +sfx Je 15.20; Zp 1.18   *

נִצָּנִים = n.m.pl   BLOSSOMS   Ct 2.12   H.L.

נָצַץ = vb   TO BLOOM, BLOSSOM   Hi.pf.3m.pl Ct 6.11;7.13
    Hi.imp.3m.s Ec 12.5   *   Exact derivation disputed, Lang p205 has
    verbal form נאץ   B.D.B. p665 takes to be denom of נִצָּה = BLOSSOM

נָצַר = vb   TO GUARD, KEEP WATCH   Qal.inf.abs as imv @11d Na 2.2
    Qal.ptc.pass.f.s Is 1.8   R1 p77   *

נְקֵבָה = n.f   FEMALE   s Gn 1.27   *

נְקֻדָּה = n.f   DROP, POINT, BEAD   pl.cs Ct 1.11   H.L.

נָקָה = vb   TO BE INNOCENT   Ni.pf.2m.s Gn 24.8   1.s Ps 19.14

    Pi = ACQUIT, LEAVE UNPUNISHED   imp.3m.s Ex 20.7; Na 1.3

    Pi.imv.m.s+sfx Ps 19.3   inf.abs Na 1.3   *

נָקִי = adj   CLEAN   m.s.cs Ps 24.4   *

נָקִיא = adj   INNOCENT   m.s Jo 1.14   *

נָקַם = vb   TO TAKE REVENGE   Qal.ptc.m.s Na 1.2

    Ni.imp.1.s Is 1.24   imv.m.s Je 15.15   Hith.ptc.m.s Ps 8.3   *

נְקָמָה = n.f   VENGEANCE, REQUITAL   s+sfx Je 11.20;20.10,12   *

נָקַף = vb   1. TO CUT OFF, DESTROY   Pi.pf.3m.pl Jb 19.26   Rl p101   *

    2. TO SURROUND   Hi.pf.3m.pl+sfx Ps 22.17

    Hi.imv.m.pl+sfx Ps 48.13   *

נְקָרָה = n.f   CREVICE, CLEFT   pl.cs Is 2.21   *

נֵר = n.m   LAMP   pl @9e Zp 1.12   *

נֵרְדְ = n.m   NARD   s Ct 4.14   +sfx Ct 1.12   pl Ct 4.13   *

נָשָׂא = vb   TO LIFT, CARRY, TAKE, FORGIVE

    Qal.pf.3m.s Is 53.4; Ps 24.4   1.s Gn 18.26;19.21   3m.pl Ps 93.3

    Qal.imp.3m.s Ex 20.7b; Is 2.4   3f.s Na 1.5   2m.s Gn 18.24

    Qal.imp.1.s Hs 1.6; Ps 121.1   3m.pl Jo 1.15; Ru 1.4   2m.pl Ps 82.2

    Qal.juss.2m.s Ex 20.7a; Is 2.9   imv.m.pl Ps 24.7;81.3

    Qal.imv.m.pl+sfx Jo 1.12   inf.abs Hs 1.6   Rl p56

    Qal.inf.cs Is 1.14   +sfx Je 15.15   ptc.m.pl Ne 4.11

    Ni.pf.3m.s Is 52.13   imv.m.pl Ps 24.7

    Ni.ptc.m.s Is 2.2,12;6.1   m.pl Is 2.13   f.pl Is 2.14

נָשַׂג = vb   TO OVERTAKE   Hi.imp.3f.s Hs 2.9   *

נָשִׂיא = n.m   CHIEF, PRINCE   pl Gn 17.20   *

נָשָׁא = vb   1. TO PRACTISE USURY   Qal.ptc.m.pl Ne 5.7K

    Q = נשׁה as in Ne 5.10   *

    2. TO DECEIVE   Hi.pf.3m.s+sfx Gn 3.13; Ob 3

    Hi.pf.3m.pl+sfx Ob 7   *

נָשָׁה = vb   TO PRACTISE USURY, LEND   Qal.pf.1.s Je 15.10

    Qal.pf.3m.pl Je 15.10   ptc.m.pl Ne 5.7Q,10,11   *

נְשִׁיקָה = n.f   KISS   pl.cs Ct 1.2   *

נִשְׁכָּה = n.f   CHAMBER (rare form of לִשְׁכָּה) s Ne 13.7   *

נְשָׁמָה = n.f   BREATH, BREATHING THING   s Is 2.22; Ps 150.6
    s.cs Gn 2.7   *

נָשַׁק = vb   TO KISS   Qal.imp.3m.s+sfx Ct 1.2   1.s+sfx Ct 8.1
    Pi.imv.m.pl Ps 2.12   *

נֶשֶׁר = n.m   EAGLE   s Ob 4; Ps 103.5   *

נְתִיבָה = n.f   PATH   pl Pr 8.2   +sfx Hs 2.8   pl.cs Pr 8.20   *

נָתַךְ = vb   TO GUSH FORTH   Ni.pf.3f.s Na 1.6   *

נָתַן = vb   TO GIVE, PUT, SET   @22e

Qal.pf   Qal.imp
3m.s Dt 8.10   +sfx Ec 12.7   3m.s Zp 3.5   +sfx Ne 13.26
3f.s Gn 3.12   3f.s Gn 3.6; Pr 8.1
2m.s Gn 3.12; 1Kg 3.9   2m.s 1Kg 3.6
1.s 1Kg 3.12; Je 31.33   +sfx Ob 2   1.s Je 15.13; Ct 7.13; Ne 5.7
3m.pl Hs 2.14; Ct 2.13;7.14   2m.pl Ne 13.25
2m.pl 1Sm 6.5,8

Qal.juss.2m.s Jo 1.14   3m.pl Ne 2.7   coh.s Gn 17.2; 2Sm 12.8
Qal.imv.m.s Je 18.21   +sfx Ne 1.11;3.36 m.pl Ps 81.3
Qal.imv.m.s.emphatic Ps 8.2   text corrupt, see R1 p27
Qal.inf.cs Ru 1.6   ptc.m.s Ex 20.12; Dt 8.18; Ne 2.12
Qal.ptc.m.pl Ne 13.5 m.pl.cs Hs 2.7   ptc.pass.m.s Ne 13.4
Ni.pf.3f.s.i.p or rare form of 3f.pl Ne 13.10 R2 p57

נָתָן = n.pr.m   NATHAN   2Sm 12.1,5,7,13,15,25   *

נָתַץ = vb   TO TEAR DOWN, DEMOLISH   Ni.pf.3m.pl Na 1.6   *

נִתֵּק = vb   TO TEAR UP, SNAP   Pi.imp.1.s Na 1.13
    Pi.coh.pl Ps 2.3   Hi.imv.m.s+sfx Je 12.3   *

ס

סְאָה = n.f   SEAH (a measure of grain)   pl Gn 18.6   *

סָבָא = vb   TO DRINK HEAVILY   Qal.ptc.pass.m.pl Na 1.10   *

סֹבֶא = n.m   WHEAT-BEER   s+sfx Is 1.22; Na 1.10   *

סָבַב = vb   TO TURN, GO AROUND   @31e   Qal.pf.3m.pl Ec 12.5
    Qal.pf.3m.pl+sfx Ps 22.13,17   juss.3m.s 1Sm 5.8   imv.m.s Ct 2.17
    Qal.imv.m.pl Ps 48.13   ptc.m.s Gn 2.11,13; Ec 1.6

```
        Qal.ptc.m.pl Ct 3.3;5.7      Ni.pf.3m.pl Gn 19.4
        Po.imp.3m.s Jo 2.4,6      coh.s Ct 3.2
        Hi.pf.3m.pl 1Sm 5.9,10      imp.3m.pl 1Sm 5.8      *
```

סָבִיב = subs   CIRCUIT, often used as adv AROUND
        s Je 20.10; Ez 37.2; Na 3.8; Ct 3.7   pl+sfx Ne 5.17;6.16
        pl+sfx as subs Ec 1.6   R1 p105   *

סָבַךְ = vb   TO INTERWEAVE   Qal.ptc.pass.m.pl Na 1.10   *

סָבַל = vb   TO BEAR A HEAVY BURDEN   Qal.pf.3m.s+sfx Is 53.4
        Qal.imp.3m.s Is 53.11   Hith.imp.3m.s Ec 12.5   @18g, R1 p111   *

סֵבֶל = n.m   LOAD, BURDEN   s Ps 81.7; Ne 4.11   *

סַבָּל = n.m   BURDEN-BEARER, PORTER   coll Ne 4.4   *

סָגָן = n.m   MINOR OFFICIAL (from Akkadian)   pl Ne 2.16;4.8,13;5.7,17;
                                                              13.11   *

סָגַר = vb   TO SHUT, CLOSE   Qal.pf.3m.s Gn 19.6   3m.pl Gn 19.10
        Qal.imp.3m.s Gn 2.21   coh.pl Ne 6.10   Ni.imp.3m.pl Ne 13.19
        Pu.pf.3m.pl Ec 12.4   Hi.juss.2m.s Ob 14   *

סְדֹם = n.loc   SODOM   Gn 18.16ff;19.1ff; Is 1.9,10; Zp 2.9

סֹהַר = n.m   ROUNDNESS   s Ct 7.3   H.L.

סוּג = vb   1. TO FENCE   Qal.ptc.pass.f.s Ct 7.3   *
             2. TO BACKSLIDE, FALL AWAY   Ni.ptc.m.pl Zp 1.6   *

סוֹד = n.m   COMPANY   s.cs Je 15.17   *

סוּךְ = vb   TO ANOINT   Qal.imp.3m.s 2Sm 12.20   *

סוּס = n.m   HORSE   s Na 3.2   pl 2Sm 15.1; Is 2.7; Je 12.5; Hs 1.7   *

סוּסָה = n.f   MARE   s.cs.with hireq compaginis Ct 1.9   R2 p125   H.L.

סוּף = vb   TO COME TO AN END   Hi.imp.1.s (juss form) Zp 1.2,3   *
        Probably need to emend pointing from אֹסֵף to אָסֵף .
        Full discussion in R1 p84, B.D.B. pp692-693, Holl p254

סוּף = n.m   REEDS, RUSHES (coll)   s Jo 2.6   *

סוּפָה = n.f   STORM WIND   s Na 1.3   *

סוֹפֵר = n.m   SCRIBE   s Ne 13.13   *

סוּר = vb   TO TURN ASIDE, DEPART   Qal.pf.3m.pl 1Sm 6.12
        Qal.imp.3m.s Ps 101.4   3f.s 1Sm 6.3; 2Sm 12.20   3m.pl Gn 19.3
        Qal.juss.3m.s Pr 9.4   imv.m.pl Gn 19.2; Ps 6.9

Hi.pf.3m.s Zp 3.15   1.s Hs 2.19; Ps 81.7   imp.1.s Zp 3.11

Hi.juss.2f.s Hs 2.4   coh.s Is 1.25   imv.m.s Ec 11.10

Hi.imv.m.pl Is 1.16   inf.abs Is 5.5   *

סֶטַ = n.m   ?DEVIATION, SWERVING   pl Ps 101.3   *

סִיג = n.m   DROSS   pl Is 1.22   +sfx Is 1.25   *

סִיר = n.m   THORN   pl Hs 2.8; Na 1.10   *

סֻכָּה = n.f   BOOTH, HUT   s Is 1.8; Jo 4.5   pl 2Sm 11.11   *

סֹכֵךְ = n.m   PROTECTOR, SHIELD, BARRICADE   s Na 2.6   H.L.

Technical term for shield used in seige.

סֶלָה = n.m   SELAH   s Ps 24.6,10;48.9;81.8;82.2;84.5,9   *

A musical term appearing 70 times in Ps.   It is left untranslated
in R.S.V.   See B.D.B. pp699-700, R1 p33

סָלַח = vb   TO FORGIVE   Qal.imp.1.s Je 31.34   ptc.m.s Ps 103.3   *

סְלִיחָה = n.f   FORGIVENESS   s Ps 130.4   *

סֶלַע = n.m   ROCK, CRAG   s Ob 3; Ct 2.14   pl Is 2.21   *

סֹלֶת = n.f   FINE FLOUR   s Gn 18.6   *

סְמָדַר = n.m   ?BLOSSOM   s Ct 2.13,15;7.13   etymology unknown   *

סָמַךְ = vb   TO SUPPORT, SUSTAIN   Pi.imv.m.pl+sfx Ct 2.5   *

סַנְבַלַּט = n.pr.m   SANBALLAT   Ne 2.10,19;3.33;4.1;6.1ff;13.28

סַנְוֵרִים = n.pl.intensive   BLINDING LIGHT, BLINDNESS   Gn 19.11   *

סַנְסִנִּים = n.m.pl   CLUSTER (of dates)   +sfx Ct 7.9   *

סָעַד = vb   TO SUPPORT, SUSTAIN   Qal.imv.m.pl Gn 18.5   *

סָעִיף = n.m   CLEFT, CRACK   pl.cs Is 2.21   *

סָעַר = vb   TO STORM, RAGE   Qal.ptc.m.s Jo 1.11,13   *

סַעַר = n.m   STORM   s Jo 1.4,12   *

סַף = n.m   THRESHOLD, SILL   s Zp 2.14; Es 2.21   *

סָפַד = vb   TO WAIL, LAMENT   Qal.imp.3f.s 2Sm 11.26

Qal.inf.cs Ec 3.4   ptc.m.pl Ec 12.5   *

סָפָה = vb   TO SWEEP AWAY   Qal.pf.3f.s.intra Je 12.4

Qal.imp.2m.s Gn 18.23,24   Ni.imp.2m.s Gn 19.15,17   *

סְפִינָה = n.f   SHIP, VESSEL   s Jo 1.5   H.L.

סַפִּיר = n.m   LAPIS LAZULI   pl Ct 5.13   *

סָסַף = vb   TO GUARD THE THRESHOLD, BE A DOORKEEPER
        Hithpolel.inf.cs Ps 84.11   H.L.

סָפַר = vb   TO COUNT   Qal.imv.m.pl Ps 48.13
        Ni.imp.3m.s 1Kg 3.8; Hs 2.1
        Pi = REPORT, TELL   imp.1.s Ps 22.18   2m.pl Ps 48.14
        Pi.coh.s Ps 2.7;22.23   imv.m.pl Ps 96.3   ptc.m.pl Ps 19.2
        Pu.pf.3m.s Is 52.15   imp.3m.s Ps 22.31   *

סֵפֶר = n.m   BOOK, WRITTEN DOCUMENT   s 2Sm 11.14,15; Jb 19.23
        s.cs Na 1.1; Es 2.23; Ne 13.1   *

סְפָרַד = n.loc   SEPHARAD   Ob 20   H.L.

סִקֵּל = vb   TO STONE   Pi.pf.3m.s+sfx Is 5.2 = CLEAR STONES AWAY   *

סָרָה = n.f   DEFECTION, APOSTASY   s Is 1.5   *

סָרִיס = n.m   EUNUCH   pl.cs Es 2.21   *

סֶרֶן = n.m   TYRANT, LORD (Philistine loan word)   pl 1Sm 6.18
        pl+sfx 1Sm 6.4   pl.cs 1Sm 5.8,11;6.4,12,16   *

סָרַר = vb   TO BE STUBBORN, REBELLIOUS   Qal.ptc.m.pl Is 1.23   *

סְתָו = n.m   WINTER (Aramaic)   s Ct 2.11K pronounce as Q סְתָיו H.L.

סָתַם = vb   TO STOP UP, SHUT UP   Ni.inf.cs Ne 4.1   *

סָתַר = vb   TO HIDE, CONCEAL   Ni.imp.2m.pl Zp 2.3
        Ni.ptc.m.s Ps 19.7   f.pl Ps 19.3   Hi.pf.3m.s Ps 22.25   *

סֵתֶר = n.m   HIDING PLACE, SECRET   s 2Sm 12.12; Ps 81.8;101.5
        s.cs Ct 2.14   *

ע

עָב = n.m   CLOUD   pl Is 5.6; Ec 12.2   *

עָבַד = vb   TO SERVE, WORK   Qal.pf.2m.s+sfx Dt 8.19   3m.pl 1Sm 4.9
        Qal.imp.3m.s+sfx Ps 22.31   2m.s Ex 20.9   2m.pl 1Sm 4.9
        Qal.imv.m.pl Ps 2.11;100.2   inf.cs Gn 2.5;3.23   +sfx Gn 2.15;
                                                            Zp 3.9
        Ho.pf.2m.s+sfx Ex 20.5   *

עֶבֶד = n.m   SLAVE, SERVANT   s Gn 24.5,9; Ne 2.10,19
        s+sfx Gn 24.2; Ex 20.10; 2Sm 15.2; 1Kg 3.6; Is 52.13; Ps 19.12

pl Ex 20.2; Dt 8.14; Ne 5.5   +sfx 2Sm 11.1; Ne 1.6b

pl.cs 2Sm 11.9;12.18; Ps 134.1

עֲבֹדָה = n.f   LABOUR, SERVICE   s Ne 5.18   *

עֹבַדְיָה = n.pr.m   OBADIAH   Ob 1.1   *

עֲבוּר = prep/conj   IN ORDER TO, ON ACCOUNT OF, FOR SAKE OF

used only with בְּ   Gn 18.29,31,32; Ex 20.20; 2Sm 12.21,25

+sfx Gn 3.17;18.26   + לְ also Ex 20.20   *

עָבַר = vb   TO PASS THROUGH

Qal.pf	Qal.imp
3m.s Zp 2.2; Ps 124.4; Ct 2.11	3m.s 1Sm 9.4a,b; 2Sm 11.27
3f.s Na 3.19; Ps 103.16	1.s Ne 2.14
1.s Ct 3.4	3m.pl 1Sm 9.4c; Pr 8.29
3m.pl Jo 2.4; Ps 48.5	3f.pl Ps 81.7
2m.pl Gn 18.5b	2m.pl Gn 18.5a

Qal.juss.2m.s Gn 18.3   inf.cs Na 2.1; Ne 2.14

Qal.ptc.m.s Na 1.8; Zp 3.6; Ps 8.9; Ct 5.5,13   m.pl.cs Ps 84.7

Hi.pf.3m.s 2Sm 12.13,31   +sfx Ez 37.2   1.s Je 15.14

Hi.imp.3m.s Jo 3.6   3m.pl+sfx Ne 2.7   imv.m.s Ec 11.10

עֵבֶר = n.m   BEYOND   s Zp 3.10; Ne 2.7,9   *

עֶבְרָה = n.f   FURY, WRATH   s Zp 1.15   s.cs Zp 1.18   *

עִבְרִי = adj.gent   HEBREW   m.s Jo 1.9   m.pl 1Sm 4.6,9   *

עֲבֹת = n.f   CORD, ROPE   s+sfx Ps 2.3   pl.cs Hs 11.4   *

עֻגָה = n.f   ROUND CAKE, LOAF   s Gn 18.6   *

עֵגֶל = n.m   CALF   s Ps 29.6   *

עֲגָלָה = n.f   CART, WAGON   s 1Sm 6.7,8,10,11,14   *

עַד = n.m   1. PERPETUITY   s Ps 48.15   +לְ Ps 19.10;22.27; Jb 19.24   *

2.   ?BOOTY   s Zp 3.8   or read as 1, perhaps change pointing
to עַד   - so G and R.S.V.   R1 p94   *

עַד = conj/prep   UNTIL, AS FAR AS

Gn 3.19; 1Sm 9.9; Je 31.34; Ob 7; Na 1.10; Ps 100.5;121.8; Ec 12.1

in question Je 12.4; Ps 6.4;82.2; Ne 2.6

+לֹא = BEFORE Pr 8.26

עֵד = n.m   WITNESS   s.cs Ex 20.16   (see also עַד 2)   *

עָדָה = vb   TO ADORN ONESELF   Qal.imp.3f.s Hs 2.15   *

עֵדָה = n.f   1. CONGREGATION, ASSEMBLY   s.cs Ps 1.5;22.17;82.1   *

                 2. SOLEMN STATEMENT   pl+sfx Ps 93.5   Rl p31   *

עֵדוּת = n.f   TESTIMONY, REMINDER   s Ps 81.6   s.cs Ps 19.8   *

עֲדִי = n.m   ORNAMENT   s+sfx Ps 103.5   obscure, see Rl p24   *

עֵדֶן = n.loc   EDEN   Gn 2.8,10,15;3.23,24   *

עֶדְנָה = n.f   PLEASURE, DELIGHT (sexual)   s Gn 18.12   H.L.

עָדַר = vb   1. TO HOE, WEED   Ni.imp.3m.s Is 5.6   *

                 2. TO BE MISSING (Ni)   Ni.pf.3m.s Zp 3.5   *

עֵדֶר = n.m   FLOCK, HERD   s.cs Ct 4.1,2;6.5,6   pl Zp 2.14
   pl.cs Ct 1.7   *

עוּגָב = n.m   FLUTE, PIPE   s Ps 150.4   *

עוּד = vb.denom   TO TESTIFY, WARN   Hi.pf.1.s Dt 8.19
   Hi.imp.1.s Ne 13.15   coh.s Ps 81.9; Ne 13.21   *

עוֹד = adv   STILL, AGAIN   Gn 17.5; Is 1.5; Je 31.34; Jo 3.4; Ps 103.16
   s = CONTINUALLY Ps 84.5   s+sfx Gn 18.22

עוּל = vb   TO NURSE, SUCKLE   Qal.ptc.f.pl 1Sm 6.7,10   *

עַוִּל = n.m   EVIL-DOER   s Zp 3.5   *

עָוֶל = n.m   INJUSTICE, WRONG   used adverbially Ps 82.2   *

עַוְלָה = n.f   INJUSTICE, WRONG   s Zp 3.5,13   *

עוֹלֵל/עוֹלָל = n.m   CHILD   pl Ps 8.3   +sfx Na 3.10   *

עוֹלָם = n.m   ETERNITY   s Gn 17.7; 2Sm 12.10; Zp 2.9
   + לְ Hs 2.21; Ob 10; Jo 2.7; Ps 117.2; Ec 1.4   + מִן Ps 93.2
   s+sfx Ec 12.5   pl+ לְ Ec 1.10

עָוֹן = n.m   INIQUITY, PUNISHMENT   s Is 1.4
   s.cs Gn 19.15; Ex 20.5; Is 53.6
   s+sfx Je 18.23;31.34; Ps 103.3; Ne 3.37   pl Ps 130.3
   pl.cs Jb 19.29 Rl p103   pl+sfx Is 53.5,11; Ps 103.10;130.8   *

עוּף = vb   TO FLY   Qal.imp.3m.s Na 3.16
   Po.imp.3m.s Gn 1.20; Is 6.2   *

עוֹף = n.m.coll   BIRDS   s Gn 1.20,22; Je 12.4
   s.cs Gn 1.21ff;2.19,20; Hs 2.20; Zp 1.3

עוּר = vb   TO AWAKE   Qal.imv.f.s Ct 4.16   ptc.m.s Ct 5.2
       Po.pf.1.s+sfx Ct 8.5   imp.2m.pl Ct 2.7;3.5;8.4
       Hi.imp.2m.pl Ct 2.7;3.5;8.4   *

עוֹר = n.m   SKIN   s Gn 3.21; Ez 37.6,8   +sfx Jb 19.26   *

עִוֵּר = adj   BLIND   m.pl Zp 1.17   *

עָוַת = vb   TO BE BENT, CROOKED   Pu.ptc.m.s Ec 1.15
       Hith.pf.3m.pl Ec 12.3   *

עַז = adj   STRONG   f.s Ct 8.6   *

עֵז = n.f   SHE-GOAT   pl @9e Ct 4.1;6.5   *

עוֹז / עֹז = n.m   STRENGTH, POWER   s Ps 8.3;29.1,11;84.6;93.1
       s+sfx Ps 81.2;110.2;150.1   *

עָזַב = vb   TO LEAVE, FORSAKE   Qal.pf.2m.s+sfx Ps 22.2   3m.pl Is 1.4
       Qal.imp.3m.s Gn 2.24   3m.pl Jo 2.9   coh.pl Ne 5.10
       Qal.imv.m.pl Pr 9.6   ptc.m.pl.cs Is 1.28   ptc.pass.f.s Zp 2.4
       Ni.pf.3m.s Ne 13.11   *
                ?2. TO REPAIR   Qal.imp.3m.pl Ne 3.34   R2 p50, K/B p694   *

עַזָּה = n.loc   GAZA   1Sm 6.17; Zp 2.4   *

עִזּוּז = adj   MIGHTY, POWERFUL   m.s Ps 24.8   *

עָזַז = vb   TO BE STRONG, FIRM   Qal.inf.cs Pr 8.28   *

[וֹ]עֻזִּיָּה = n.pr.m   UZZIAH   Is 1.1;6.1; Hs 1.1   *

עָזַק = vb   TO DIG, HOE   Pi.imp.3m.s+sfx Is 5.2   H.L.

עָזַר = vb   TO HELP   Qal.ptc.m.s Ps 22.12   *

עֵזֶר = n.m   HELP, HELPER   s Gn 2.18,20; 1Sm 4.1;5.1
       s+sfx Ps 121.1,2;124.8   *

עֶזְרָה = n.f   HELP, ASSISTANCE   s+sfx Na 3.9; Ps 22.20   *

עֵט = n.m   STYLUS, WRITING TOOL   s.cs Jb 19.24   *

עָטָה = vb   TO WRAP ONESELF   Qal.ptc.f.s Ct 1.7   R2 p125
       Hi.imp.3m.s Ps 84.7   *

עֲטַלֵּף = n.m   BAT   pl Is 2.20   *

עָטַף = vb   TO BE FEEBLE, FAINT   Hith.inf.cs Jo 2.8   *

עָטַר = vb.denom   TO CROWN   Pi.pf.3f.s Ct 3.11
       Pi.imp.2m.s+sfx Ps 8.6   ptc.m.s+sfx Ps 103.4   *

עֲטָרָה = n.f   CROWN   s Ct 3.11   s.cs 2Sm 12.30   *

עַיִן = n.f   1. EYE   s Ec 1.8   +sfx Ps 6.8

dual Gn 3.6; Ps 101.5; Ec 11.7   +sfx 1Sm 4.15; Jo 2.5; Jb 19.27

dual.cs Gn 3.7; 2Sm 11.27; 1Kg 3.10; Is 2.11; Hs 2.12

2. SPRING, WELL   s.cs Ne 2.13,14   pl Dt 8.7

pl.cs Pr 8.28   *

עֵין גֶּדִי = n.loc   EN-GEDI   Ct 1.14   *

עִיר = 1. n.m   RAGE   s Hs 11.9   *

2. n.f   CITY   s Gn 18.24; 1Sm 9.6; 2Sm 15.2; Is 1.8; Jo 1.2

s.cs 2Sm 12.26; Is 1.26; Na 3.1   pl @33e Gn 19.25; Je 20.16;

pl+sfx Is 1.7; Hs 11.6; Zp 3.6   pl.cs Gn 19.29a; 1Sm 6.18; Ob 20

עֵירֹם = adj   NAKED   m.s Gn 3.10,11   m.pl Gn 3.7   *

עַכְבָּר = n.m   MOUSE   pl+sfx 1Sm 6.5   pl.cs 1Sm 6.4,11,18   *

עָכוֹר = n.m   TROUBLE or n.pr.m   ACHOR   Hs 2.17   R1 p64   *

Name of valley W. or S.W. of Jericho. See Joshua 7.24-26

עַל = n.m   HEIGHT   s Hs 11.7   R1 p72   *

Text difficult

? name of god, - N.E.B. HIGH GOD; R.S.V. as עֹל = YOKE,

J.B. as בַּעַל = BAAL

עַל = prep   UPON, OVER, AGAINST etc

= UPON   Ex 20.5; 1Sm 4.12; Je 31.33; Ps 121.5; Jb 19.25; Ec 1.6

= OVER   Gn 1.7; 2Sm 12.7; Ez 37.2; Zp 1.9; Ps 103.11; Ec 1.12

= AGAINST   Ex 20.25; Is 2.12; Zp 1.4; Ps 29.3;124.2; Ne 2.19

= BY   Gn 18.2; Dt 8.3; 1Sm 4.1; 2Sm 15.2; Ps 1.3

= ON ACCOUNT OF   Gn 2.24; Dt 8.10; Jo 4.2   = AFTER   Ps 110.4

= AS FAR AS   Ps 48.11   = CONCERNING   Is 1.1;2.1; Jo 4.2

עַל-כֵּן = THEREFORE   1Sm 5.5; Ps 1.5; Ct 1.3

עַל-מָה = WHEREFORE   Is 1.5   R1 p76

for various possibilities of עַל-פְּנֵי Ex 20.3 see R1 p10

עַל +sfx @12e Dt 8.4; Ez 37.1; Hs 2.15; Jo 1.2; Ps 117.2

עֹל = n.m   YOKE   s 1Sm 6.7; Hs 11.4   *

עָלָה = vb   TO GO UP, ASCEND   Qal.pf.3m.s Gn 19.15; 1Sm 6.7; Ez 37.8

Qal.pf.3f.s Jo 1.2; Ne 4.1   3m.pl Hs 2.2; Ob 21; Ct 4.2

Qal.imp.3m.s Gn 2.6; 1Sm 9.13   apoc Is 53.2; Jo 4.6

Qal.imp.3f.s 2Sm 11.20   apoc 1Sm 5.12   1.s Ct 7.9   1.pl Is 2.3

Qal.juss.2m.s Ex 20.26   imv.m.pl 1Sm 9.13   ptc.m.s Ne 2.15

Qal.ptc.f.s Ct 3.6;8.5   Hi.pf.1.s Ez 37.6,12   3m.pl 1Sm 6.14,15

Hi.imp.2m.s.apoc Jo 2.7   3m.pl 1Sm 7.1   imv.m.pl 1Sm 6.21

Hi.inf.cs+sfx Ez 37.13   ptc.m.s Na 3.3   +sfx Ps 81.11

Ho.pf.3f.s Na 2.8

עָלֶה = n.m   LEAF   s.cs Gn 3.7   s+sfx Is 1.30; Ps 1.3   *

עֹלָה = n.f   WHOLE BURNT OFFERING   s 1Sm 6.14   pl 1Sm 6.15

pl.cs Is 1.11   pl+sfx Ex 20.24   *

עָלַז = vb   TO EXULT   Qal.imp.1.s Je 15.17   imv.f.s. Zp 3.14   *

עֲלֵי = prep   BESIDE (old form of עַל , usually in poetry)   Pr 8.2   *

עֵלִי = n.pr.m   ELI   1 Sm 4.4ff

עֶלְיוֹן = adj   HIGHEST, SUPREME   m.s Ps 82.6   *

Used like n.m as epithet of God. Here in phrase בְּנֵי עֶלְיוֹן

עַלִּיז = adj   ARROGANT, EXULTANT   f.s Zp 2.15   m.pl.cs Zp 3.11   *

עֲלִילָה = n.f   DEED, ACTION   pl+sfx Zp 3.7,11; Ps 103.7   *

עָלַל = vb   TO MOCK, MAKE A FOOL OF   Hith.pf.3m.s 1Sm 6.6   *

עֹלֵלוֹת = n.f.pl   GLEANINGS   Ob 5   *

עָלַם = vb   TO HIDE, CONCEAL   Ni.ptc.f.s Na 3.11 = SWOON

Hi.imp.1.s Is 1.15   *

עַלְמָה = n.f   YOUNG WOMAN   pl Ct 1.3;6.8   *

עָלַף = vb   TO COVER   Pu.ptc.f.s. Ct 5.14

Hith.imp.3m.s Jo 4.8 = FAINT   *

עַם/עָם = n.m   1. PEOPLE   s Ex 20.18; 1Sm 9.12; 1Kg 3.8; Je 31.33; Jo 1.8

s.cs Is 1.10; Zp 2.10   s+sfx 1Kg 3.8; Is 1.3; Ez 37.13; Ru 1.6

pl Gn 17.16; Zp 3.9; Ps 96.3; Ne 1.8   pl.cs Zp 3.20

          2. KINSMAN   s+sfx in phrase בֶּן עַמִּי Gn 19.38

pl+sfx Gn 17.14   *

עִם = prep   WITH, BESIDE   Gn 18.23; 1Kg 3.6a; Hs 2.20; Na 3.12

+sfx @31f Gn 3.6; Ex 20.19; 1Sm 9.5; 1Kg 3.6b; Jo 1.3; Ps 130.4

Ideomatic of a thought or purpose Dt 8.5 B.D.B. p768 No.4a

עִמָּד = prep   WITH (Alternative to above)

only occurs with suffix @31f   Gn 3.12;19.19; Ps 23.4;101.6

עָמַד = vb   TO STAND   Qal.pf.3m.s Gn 19.27; 2Sm 15.2; Ps 1.1

Qal.imp.3m.s Ex 20.21; Jo 1.15   3f.s 1Sm 6.14   2m.s Je 15.19

Qal.imp.3m.pl Ex 20.18; Ez 37.10   juss.2m.s Gn 19.17; Ob 14

Qal.imv.m.pl Na 2.9   inf.cs 1Sm 6.20   +sfx Je 18.20; Ob 11

Qal.ptc.m.s Gn 18.8; Ct 2.9   f.s Ps 19.10; Ec 1.4

Qal.ptc.m.pl Is 6.2; Ps 134.1   Hi.pf.2m.s Ne 6.7   1.s Ne 6.1

Hi.imp.1.s Ne 4.7   +sfx Ne 13.11   1.pl Ne 4.3   imv.m.s Ne 7.3

עֹמֶד = n.m   STATION, PLACE   s+sfx Ne 13.11   *

עַמּוּד = n.m   PILLAR, COLUMN   pl.cs Ct 5.15   pl+sfx Pr 9.1; Ct 3.10   *

עַמּוֹן = n.pr.gent   AMMON   Gn 19.38; 2Sm 11.1;12.9,26,31; Zp 2.8,9   *

עַמּוֹנִי = adj.gent   AMMONITE   m.s Ne 2.10,19;3.35;13.1

m.pl Ne 4.1   f.pl Ne 13.23   *

עַמִּינָדָב = ?n.pr.m   AMMINADIB   Ct 6.12   very uncertain   R2 p131   H.L.

עָמַל = vb   TO TOIL   Qal.pf.2m.s Jo 4.10   imp.3m.s Ec 1.3   *

עָמָל = n.m   TOIL, LABOUR   s Je 20.18   +sfx Ec 1.3   s.cs Is 53.11   *

עָמַס/עָמַשׂ = vb   TO CARRY A LOAD   Qal.ptc.m.pl Ne 4.11;13.15   *

עֵמֶק = n.m   VALLEY   s 1Sm 6.13   s.cs Hs 1.5;2.17; Ps 84.7

pl Ct 2.1   *

עֲמֹרָה = n.loc   GOMORRAH   Gn 18.20;19.24,28; Is 1.9,10; Zp 2.9   *

עֵנָב = n.m   GRAPE   pl Is 5.2,4; Hs 3.1; Ne 13.15   *

עָנָה = vb   1. TO ANSWER   Qal.pf.3m.s Ct 2.10   +sfx Ct 5.6

Qal.pf.3f.s 1Sm 4.20; Hs 2.17   2m.s+sfx Ps 22.22 R1 p48

Qal.imp.3m.s.apoc Gn 18.27; 1Sm 4.17   +sfx Jo 2.3   3f.s Hs 2.24

Qal.imp.2m.s Ps 22.3   1.s Hs 2.23   +sfx Ps 81.8   3m.pl Hs 2.23,24

Qal.imp.3f.pl 1Sm 9.12   juss.2m.s Ex 20.16   inf.cs 1Sm 9.8   *

2. TO BE WRETCHED, AFFLICTED   Ni.ptc.m.s Is 53.7

Pi.pf.1.s+sfx Na 1.12   imp.3m.s+sfx Dt 8.3   1.s+sfx Na 1.12

Pi.inf.cs+sfx Dt 8.2,16   ptc.m.pl+sfx Zp 3.19

Pu.ptc.m.s Is 53.4   *

3. TO BE OCCUPIED WITH   Qal.inf.cs Ec 1.13 R1 p105   *

עָנִו = n.m   HUMBLE, AFFLICTED ONE   pl Ps 22.27   pl.cs Zp 2.3   *

עֲנָוָה = n.f   HUMILITY   s Zp 2.3   *

עֱנוּת = n.f   AFFLICTION   s.cs Ps 22.25   H.L.

עָנִי = adj   WRETCHED   m.s Zp 3.12; Ps 22.25;82.3   *

82

עִנְיָן = n.m   OCCUPATION, TASK (only Ec)   s Ec 1.13   *

עָנַן = vb   TO MAKE APPEAR, CONJURE UP
     Po'el.ptc.m.pl (minus מְ , G/K 52s) = SORCERERS   Is 2.6   *

עָנָן = n.m   CLOUD-MASS   s Na 1.3; Zp 1.15   *

עֲנָק = n.m   NECKLACE, PENDANT   s Ct 4.9   *

עֲנָתוֹת = n.loc   ANATOTH   Je 11.21,23   *

עָסִיס = n.m   JUICE   s.cs Ct 8.2   *

עֹפֶל = n.m   TUMOUR, BOIL   pl 1Sm 5.6,9,12
     pl.cs 1Sm 6.4   pl+sfx 1Sm 6.5   *
     In each case Q replaces with טְחוֹר

עָפָר = n.m   DUST, MUD   s Gn 2.7; Is 2.10; Zp 1.17; Jb 19.25; Ec 12.7
     s.cs Ps 22.16   pl.cs Pr 8.26   s = RUBBLE Ne 3.34;4.4

עֹפֶר = n.m   FAWN, HART   s.cs Ct 2.9,17;8.14   pl Ct 4.5;7.4   *

עֹפֶרֶת = n.m   LEAD   s Jb 19.24   *

עֵץ = n.m   TREE, WOOD   s Gn 1.12; Je 11.19; Ps 1.3; Es 2.23
     s.cs Gn 1.11ff   pl Ne 2.8;13.31   pl.cs 1Sm 6.14; Ct 2.3;3.9;4.14

עֶצֶב = n.m   PAIN   s Gn 3.16   *

עִצָּבוֹן = n.m   PAIN, TOIL   s Gn 3.17   +sfx Gn 3.16   *

עֵצָה = n.f   PLAN, COUNSEL   s Je 18.18; Pr 8.14
     s.cs Ps 1.1   s+sfx Je 18.23; Ne 4.9   *

עָצוּם = adj   MIGHTY, NUMEROUS   m.s Gn 18.18   m.pl Is 53.12   *

עֶצֶם = n.f   BONE   s Gn 2.23;17.23; Ez 37.7   +sfx Ez 37.7
     pl Ez 37.1ff   +sfx Je 20.9; Ez 37.11; Ps 22.15,18
     pl+sfx @9e Gn 2.23; Ps 6.3

עֹצֶם = n.m   MIGHT   s+sfx Na 3.9   s.cs Dt 8.17   *

עָצַר = vb   TO RESTRAIN, SHUT UP   Qal.ptc.pass.m.s Je 20.9; Ne 6.10   *

עֹצֶר = n.m   (POWER OF) RESTRAINT   s Is 53.8   R2 p109   *

עֲצָרָה = n.f   FESTIVE ASSEMBLY   s Is 1.13   *

עָקֵב = n.m   HEEL   s Gn 3.15   pl.cs Ct 1.8   *

עֵקֶב = conj   AS A CONSEQUENCE, BECAUSE OF   Dt 8.20; 2Sm 12.6,10
     as n.m = REWARD Ps 19.12   *

עָקַר = vb   TO UPROOT   Qal.inf.cs Ec 3.2   Ni.imp.3f.s Zp 2.4   *

עַקְרָב = n.m   SCORPION   s Dt 8.15   *

עֶקְרוֹן = n.loc   EKRON   1Sm 5.10;6.16,17; Zp 2.4   *

עֶקְרוֹנִי = adj.gent   EKRONITE   m.pl 1Sm 5.10   *

עִקֵּשׁ = adj   TWISTED, PERVERTED   m.s Ps 101.4; Pr 8.8   *

עָרַב = vb   TO GIVE IN PLEDGE, MORTGAGE   Qal.ptc.m.pl Ne 5.3   *

עָרֵב = adj   SWEET, PLEASANT   m.s Ct 2.14   *

עֶרֶב = n.m   EVENING   s Gn 1.5ff;19.1; 2Sm 11.2,13; Zp 2.7;3.3

עֵרֶב = n.m   MIXED RACE, PEOPLE OF FOREIGN DESCENT   s Ne 13.3   *

עֹרֵב = n.m   RAVEN   s Ct 5.11   *

עַרְבִי = adj.gent   ARAB   m.s Ne 2.19;6.1   m.pl Ne 4.1   *

עָרָה = vb   TO LAY BARE, EXPOSE   Pi.pf.3m.s Zp 2.14

Hi.pf.3m.s Is 53.12   *

עֲרוּגָה = n.f   GARDEN-BED   s.cs Ct 5.13   pl.cs Ct 6.2   *

עֶרְוָה = n.f   NAKEDNESS, GENITALS   s+sfx Ex 20.26; Hs 2.11   *

עָרוֹם = adj   NAKED   f.s Hs 2.5   m.pl Gn 2.25   *

עָרוּם = adj   CRAFTY, SUBTLE   m.s Gn 3.1   *

עָרִיץ = adj   AWE INSPIRING   m.s Je 20.11

m.pl.subs in bad sense = THE RUTHLESS (R.S.V.) Je 15.21   *

עָרַךְ = vb   TO ARRANGE IN ORDER   Qal.pf.3f.s Pr 9.2

Qal.imp.2m.s Ps 23.5   3m.pl 1Sm 4.2   *

עָרֵל = adj   HAVING FORESKIN i.e. UNCIRCUMCISED   m.s Gn 17.14   *

עָרְלָה = n.f   FORESKIN   s+sfx Gn 17.11,14,23,24,25   *

עָרְמָה = n.f   SHREWDNESS   s Pr 8.5,12   *

עֲרֵמָה = n.f   HEAP   s.cs Ct 7.3   pl Ne 13.15   pl.cs Ne 3.34   *

עֲרָפֶל = n.m   DARKNESS, STORM-CLOUD   s Ex 20.21; Zp 1.15   *

עָרַץ = vb   TO TERRIFY, CAUSE TO TREMBLE   Qal.inf.cs Is 2.19,21   *

עֶרֶשׂ = n.f   COUCH   s+sfx Ps 6.7; Ct 1.16   *

עֵשֶׂב = n.m.coll   HERBAGE   s Gn 1.11,12,29,30

s.cs Gn 2.5;3.18; Je 12.4   *

עָשָׂה = vb   TO DO, MAKE, USE

      Qal.pf   Qal.imp

      3m.s Ex 20.11   +sfx Ps 100.3   3m.s Zp 1.18   apoc Gn 1.7

      2m.s 1Kg 3.6; Jo 1.10   2m.s Gn 18.5; Je 12.5

      2f.s Gn 3.13   1.s 2Sm 12.12; Ne 6.13

      1.s 1Kg 3.12; Ez 37.14   3m.pl Gn 3.7; 1Sm 6.10

      3m.pl Gn 18.21; Is 2.8   1.pl Jo 1.11; Ne 5.12

      2m.pl 1Sm 6.5; Ne 1.9   juss.2m.s Ex 20.4,10

                                          juss.2m.pl Gn 19.8; Ex 20.23

      Qal.imv.m.s Je 18.23   f.s Gn 18.6 m.pl 1Sm 6.7

      Qal.inf.cs Dt 8.1; Jo 3.10; Ne 2.12 +sfx Ps 103.18

      Qal.ptc.m.s Ex 20.6; Zp 3.19 m.s.cs Ps 121.2;134.3

      Qal.ptc.m.pl Ne 2.19;3.34 m.pl.cs Ps 103.20; Ne 13.10

      Ni.pf.3m.s Ec 1.9,13   3f.s Ne 6.16   3m.pl Ec 1.14; Ne 5.18

      Ni.imp.3m.s Ob 15; Ec 1.9   3f.s Ne 6.9   ptc.m.s Ne 5.18

עֵשָׂו = n.pr.m   ESAU   Ob 6,8,9,18,19,21   *

עֶשֶׂר/עֲשָׂרָה = number   TEN @25d   m Ru 1.4; Ne 4.6

      f Gn 18.32   f.cs Ne 5.18   *

עָשָׂר/עֶשְׂרֵה = number   TEN (In compound numbers)   @26c

      m Gn 17.20; Hs 3.2   f Gn 17.25; Jo 4.11   *

עֶשְׂרִים = number   TWENTY   Gn 18.31; Ne 1.1;2.1;5.14;6.15   *

עָשִׂיר = adj   RICH   m.s 2Sm 12.1,2,4; Is 53.9   R2 p110   *

עָשָׁן = n.m   SMOKE   s Na 2.14; Ct 3.6   *

עָשֵׁן = adj   SMOKING   m.s Ex 20.18   *

עָשַׁק = vb   TO OPPRESS   Qal.ptc.pass.m.pl Ps 103.6   *

עֹשֶׁר = n.m   WEALTH   s 1Kg 3.11,13; Pr 8.18   *

עָשַׁשׁ = vb   TO DISINTEGRATE   Qal.pf.3f.s Ps 6.8   *

עֶשֶׁת = n.m   ?TABLET   s.cs Ct 5.14   R2 p130   H.L.

עָשַׁת = vb   TO SPARE A THOUGHT   Hith.imp.3m.s Jo 1.6   H.L.

עֵת = n.f   TIME   s Pr 8.30; Ec 3.1ff; Ne 6.1;13.21

      s.cs Ct 2.12; Ec 3.8   s+sfx Hs 2.11; Ps 1.3;81.16

      s+בְּ Zp 1.12; Ne 4.16   +כְּ Gn 18.10; 1Sm 4.20   +לְ 2Sm 11.1,2

      pl (late Hebrew) Ne 13.31

עַתָּה = adv   NOW   Gn 3.22; 1Sm 9.6; 1Kg 3.7; Is 1.21; Jo 4.3; Ps 121.8

עַתּוּד = n.m   RAM, HE-GOAT   pl Is 1.11   *

עָתֵק = 1. vb   TO GROW OLD   Qal.pf.3f.s Ps 6.8   *
          2. adj   ?OUTSTANDING   m.s Pr 8.18   H.L.

Meaning not clear, though linked to root meaning 'ancient', thus
OUTSTANDING B.D.B. p801, Lang p264 or INHERITED Holl p287, Foh p217

עָתָר = n.m   WORSHIPPER, SUPPLIANT   pl+sfx Zp 3.10   H.L.

פ

פָּארוּר = n.m   REDNESS, FLUSH   s Na 2.11   *

Meaning dubious, probably linked to root פָּרַר, so R2 p83.   See
also Holl p288, Lang p264 and B.D.B. pp802-803 under פָּאַר

פַּג/פַּגָּה = n.m. or n.f   UNRIPE FIG   pl+sfx Ct 2.13   H.L.

פָּגַע = vb   TO LET FALL UPON, TO INTERCEDE   Hi.pf.3m.s Is 53.6
Hi.pf.1.s Je 15.11   imp.3m.s Is 53.12   *

פֶּגֶר = n.m   CORPSE   s.i.p Na 3.3   *

פָּדָה = vb   TO RANSOM   Qal.pf.2m.s Ne 1.10   1.s+sfx Je 15.21
Qal.imp.3m.s Ps 130.8   Ni.imp.3f.s Is 1.27   *

פְּדוּת = n.f   RANSOM   s Ps 130.7   *

פְּדָיָה = n.pr.m   PEDAIAH   Ne 13.13   *

פֶּה = n.m   MOUTH   s+sfx @33e Hs 2.19; Ob 12; Ps 81.11; Pr 8.8; Ct 1.2
s.cs @33e Dt 8.3; Is 1.20; Na 3.12; Ps 8.3; Pr 8.13
s.cs = ENTRANCE Pr 8.3   = EXTREMITY Ps 133.2

פֹּה = adv   HERE   Gn 19.12   *

פּוּחַ = vb   TO BREATHE   Qal.imp.3m.s Ct 2.17;4.6
Hi.imv.f.s Ct 4.16   *

פּוּט = n.loc   PUT = ?SOMALIA   Na 3.9   *

פּוּץ = vb   TO SCATTER   Qal.ptc.pass.m.pl+sfx Zp 3.10
Hi.imp.1.s Ne 1.8   ptc.m.s Na 2.2 (noun in B.D.B. p807)   *

פּוּק = vb   TO OBTAIN   Hi.imp.3m.s Pr 8.35   *

פּוּשׁ = vb   ?TO BE DISPERSED   Ni.pf.3m.pl Na 3.18 R2 pp88-89   H.L.

פָּז = n.m   PURE GOLD   s Ps 19.11; Pr 8.19; Ct 5.11,15   *

פַּח = n.m   BIRD-TRAP   s Ps 124.7   s.cs Ps 124.7   pl Je 18.22   *

פָּחַד = vb   TO BE IN AWE/DREAD   Qal.pf.3m.pl Hs 3.5   *

פַּחַד = n.m   TERROR, DREAD   s Ct 3.8   s.cs Is 2.10,19,21   *

פֶּחָה = n.m   GOVERNOR (Assyrian loan word)   s Ne 5.14,18   +sfx Ne 5.14
      pl Ne 5.15   pl.cs Ne 2.7,9   *

פָּחַז = vb   TO BRAG, BE INSOLENT   Qal.ptc.m.pl Zp 3.4   *

פָּטַר = vb   TO SEPARATE (lips), GRIMACE   Hi.imp.3m.pl Ps 22.8   *

פִּילֶגֶשׁ = n.f   CONCUBINE   pl @9e Ct 6.8,9   *

פִּינְחָס = n.pr.m   PHINEAS   1Sm 4.4,11,17,19   *

פִּישׁוֹן = n.pr   R. PISHON   Gn 2.11   H.L.

פָּלָא = vb   TO BE EXTRAORDINARY, WONDERFUL   Ni.imp.3m.s Gn 18.14
      Ni.ptc.f.pl Ps 131.1   +sfx Ps 96.3   *

פֶּלֶג = n.m   WATER CHANNEL   pl.cs Ps 1.3   *

פְּלָדָה = n.f   ?BUNTING, FITTINGS ON CHARIOTS   pl Na 2.4   H.L.
      Meaning unclear, see R2 p81

פֶּלַח = n.f   1. HALF, CLEAVAGE   s.cs Ct 4.3;6.7   *
                2. MILLSTONE   s.cs 2Sm 11.21   *

פָּלַט = vb   TO RESCUE, DELIVER   Pi.imp.2m.s+sfx Ps 22.5
      Pi.juss.3m.s+sfx Ps 22.9   imv.m.pl Ps 82.4   *

פָּלִיט = n.m   SURVIVOR   pl+sfx Ob 14   *

פְּלֵטָה = n.f   ESCAPED REMNANT   s Ob 17; Ne 1.2   *

פָּלַל = vb   TO INTERCEDE   Hith.imp.3m.s Jo 2.2;4.2   1.s Ne 2.4
      Hith.imp.1.pl Ne 4.3   ptc.m.s Ne 1.4,6   *

פְּלִשְׁתִּי = adj.gent   PHILISTINE   m.pl 1Sm 4.1ff; Is 2.6; Ob 19; Zp 2.5

פֶּן = conj   LEST, ELSE   Gn 24.6; Ex 20.19; Dt 8.11; 1Sm 9.5; Hs 2.5

פָּנָה = vb   TO TURN   Qal.pf.3m.s Ct 6.1   1.pl Is 53.6
      Qal.imp.3m.pl Gn 18.22   ptc.m.pl Hs 3.1
      Pi = TO REMOVE pf.3m.s Zp 3.15   Hi.ptc.m.s Na 2.9   *

פִּנָּה = n.f   PINNACLE, TOWER   pl Zp 1.16   +sfx Zp 3.6   *

פָּנִים = n.m.pl   FACE, PRESENCE   cs Gn 1.2; Is 2.10; Ez 37.2; Jb 19.29
      +sfx Gn 24.7; 1Sm 9.12; 2Sm 15.1; Jo 1.2; Na 1.5; Ps 100.2
      ?pl = FACES Is 53.3   + לְ = FORMERLY 1Sm 9.9; 1Kg 3.12; Ec 1.10

פְּנִינִים = n.m.pl   CORALS   Pr 8.11   *

פַסְּגוּ = vb   ?TO PASS THROUGH   Pi.imv.m.pl Ps 48.14   H.L.

פְּסִיל = n.m   IDOL   pl Hs 11.2   *

פֶּסֶל = n.m   IDOL, IMAGE   s Ex 20.4; Na 1.14   *

פָּעַל = vb   TO DO, MAKE   Qal.pf.3m.pl Zp 2.3
     Qal.ptc.m.pl.cs Ps 6.9;101.8   *

פֹּעַל = n.m   DEED, WORK   s+sfx Is 1.31   *

פַּעַם = n.f   1. OCCURRENCE   s Ne 6.5;13.20   pl Ne 4.6;6.4
     s+הַ = THIS TIME Gn 2.23;18.32   dual = TWICE Na 1.9   *
            2. FOOT   dual+sfx Ct 7.2   *

פָּצָה = vb   TO OPEN WIDE   Qal.pf.3m.pl Ps 22.14   *

פָּצַע = vb   TO BRUISE, WOUND   Qal.pf.3m.pl+sfx Ct 5.7   *

פֶּצַע = n.m   BRUISE, WOUND   s Is 1.6   *

פָּצַר = vb   TO URGE   Qal.imp.3m.s Gn 19.3   3m.pl Gn 19.9   *

פִּק = n.m   SHAKING, TOTTERING   s.cs Na 2.11   H.L.

פָּקַד = vb   TO VISIT, ATTEND TO (either in good or bad sense)
     Qal.pf.3m.s Ru 1.6   1.s Hs 1.4;2.15; Zp 1.8,9,12;3.7
     Qal.imp.3m.s+sfx Zp 2.7   2m.s+sfx Ps 8.5   imv.m.s+sfx Je 15.15
     Qal.ptc.m.s Ex 20.5; Je 11.22   Ni.imp.3m.pl Ne 7.1   *

פְּקֻדָּה = n.f   VISITATION, PUNISHMENT   s+sfx Je 11.23   *

פִּקּוּדִים = n.m.pl   DIRECTIONS, PRECEPTS   +sfx Ps 103.18   cs Ps 19.9   *

פָּקַח = vb   TO OPEN (eyes)   Ni.pf.3m.pl Gn 3.5   imp.3f.pl Gn 3.7   *

פַּר = n.m   BULL   pl Is 1.11; Ps 22.13   *

פָּרַד = vb   TO DIVIDE   Ni.imp.3m.s Gn 2.10   ptc.m.pl Ne 4.13
     Hith.pf.3m.pl Ps 22.15   *

פַּרְדֵּס = n.m   PARK (Persian loan word)   s Ne 2.8   s.cs Ct 4.13   *

פָּרָה = 1. vb   TO BE FRUITFUL   Qal.imv.m.pl Gn 1.22,28
     Hi.pf.1.s Gn 17.6,20   *
        2. n.f   COW, HEIFER   pl 1Sm 6.7,10,12,14   *

פְּרָזִי = n.m   HAMLET DWELLER   s 1Sm 6.18   *

פָּרַח = vb   TO BUD, SPROUT   Qal.pf.3f.s Ct 6.11;7.13   *

פֶּרַח = n.m   BUD, BLOOM   s.cs Na 1.4   *

פְּרִי = n.m   FRUIT   s Gn 1.11,12; Je 12.2
s.cs Gn 1.29;3.2,3; Ct 4.13,16   s+sfx Gn 3.6; Ps 1.3; Pr 8.19

פָּרַע = vb   TO NEGLECT, IGNORE   Qal.juss.2m.pl Pr 8.33   *

פַּרְעֹה = n.m   PHARAOH   1Sm 6.6; Ct 1.9   *

פָּרַץ = vb   TO BREAK DOWN   Qal.pf.3m.s Ne 3.35   inf.abs Is 5.5
Qal.inf.cs Ec 3.3   ptc.pass.m.pl Ne 2.13;4.1
Pu.ptc.f.s Ne 1.3   *

פֶּרֶץ = n.m   BREACH   s Ne 6.1   *

פֶּרֶק = n.m   1. PLUNDER   s Na 3.1   H.L.
2. PARTING OF THE WAYS   s Ob 14   H.L.

פָּרַר = vb   TO BREAK, FRUSTRATE   Hi.pf.3m.s Gn 17.14   3m.pl Je 31.32
Hi.imp.3m.s Ne 4.9   3f.s Ec 12.5 usually emended to Ho   *

פָּרַשׂ = vb   TO SPREAD OUT   Pi.inf.cs+sfx Is 1.15   *

פָּרָשׁ = n.m   HORSEMAN   s Na 3.3   pl Hs 1.7; Ne 2.9   *

פְּרָת = n.pr   R. EUPHRATES   Gn 2.14   *

פָּשַׁט = vb   TO STRIP OFF   Qal.pf.3m.s Na 3.16   1.s Ct 5.3
Qal.ptc.m.pl Ne 4.17   Hi.imp.1.s+sfx Hs 2.5   *

פָּשַׁע = vb   TO REBEL, SIN   Qal.pf.2f.s Zp 3.11   3m.pl Is 1.2
Qal.ptc.m.pl Is 1.28;53.12   *

פֶּשַׁע = n.m   SIN, TRANSGRESSION   s Ps 19.14   s.cs Is 53.8
pl+sfx Is 53.5; Ps 103.12   *

פֵּשֶׁת = n.m   FLAX, LINEN   s+sfx Hs 2.7,11   *

פַּת = n.f   FRAGMENT, MORSEL   s.cs Gn 18.5   s+sfx 2Sm 12.3   *

פִּתְאֹם = adv   SUDDENLY   Je 18.22   *

פָּתָה = vb   TO BE SIMPLE, NAÏVE   Ni.imp.1.s.apoc Je 20.7
Pi = PERSUADE, SEDUCE pf.2m.s+sfx Je 20.7   ptc.m.s+sfx Hs 2.16
Pu.imp.3m.s Je 20.10   *

פָּתַח = vb   TO OPEN   Qal.pf.1.s Ct 5.6   imp.3m.s Is 53.7
Qal.imp.3m.pl+sfx Ne 13.19   imv.f.s Ct 5.2   inf.abs Na 3.13
Qal.inf.cs Ct 5.5   +sfx Ez 37.13   ptc.m.s Ez 37.12
Qal.ptc.pass.f.s Ne 6.5   f.pl Ne 1.6   Ni.pf.3m.pl Na 2.7;3.13
Ni.juss.3m.pl Ne 7.3   Pi.pf.3m.s Ct 7.13   *

פֶּתִי = adj   SIMPLE, NAÏVE   m.s Ps 19.8; Pr 9.4   m.pl Pr 8.5;9.6   *

פָּתַל = vb   TO TWIST   Ni.ptc.m.s Pr 8.8   *

צ

צֹאן = n.f.coll   FLOCK, SHEEP and GOATS

s 2Sm 12.2; Is 53.6; Je 12.3; Jo 3.7; Zp 2.6; Ps 100.3; Ct 1.8
Ne 5.18

s+sfx Ex 20.24; Dt 8.13; 2Sm 12.4

n.b. pll form צֹנֶה Ps 8.8   *

צָבָא = n.m   ARMY, HOST   s.cs Zp 1.5   s+sfx Gn 2.1

pl+sfx Ps 103.21   pl @9e Is 1.9; Na 2.14; Zp 2.9; Ps 48.9

צְבֹאיִם = n.loc   ZEBOIM (near Sodom)   Hs 11.8   *

צָבַב = vb   TO POUR OUT   Ho.pf.3m.s Na 2.8   H.L.

Conjectural, not translated in B.D.B. p246. See discussion on
possible renderings in R2 p82

צְבִי = n.m   GAZELLE   s Ct 2.9,17;8.14   pl @9e Ct 2.7;3.5   *

צְבִיָּה = n.f   FEMALE GAZELLE   s Ct 4.5;7.4   *

צַד = n.m   SIDE   s+sfx 1Sm 6.8   *

צָדָה = vb   TO BE DEVASTATED, LAID WASTE   Ni.pf.3m.pl Zp 3.6   H.L.

צָדוֹק = n.pr.m   ZADOK   Ne 13.13   *

צַדִּיק = adj   RIGHTEOUS   m.s Gn 18.23,25; Is 53.11; Je 12.1;20.12; Zp 3.5

m.pl Gn 18.24,26,28; Ps 1.5,6   *

צָדַק = vb   TO BE JUST, RIGHTEOUS   Qal.pf.3m.pl Ps 19.10

Hi.pf.1.s+sfx 2Sm 15.4   imp.3m.s Is 53.11   imv.m.pl Ps 82.3   *

צֶדֶק = n.m   RIGHTEOUSNESS, JUSTICE

s Is 1.21,26; Je 11.20; Hs 2.21; Zp 2.3; Ps 23.3;48.11; Pr 8.8,15,16 *

צְדָקָה = n.f   RIGHTEOUSNESS

s Gn 18.19; 1Kg 3.6; Is 1.27;5.7; Ps 24.5; Pr 8.18,20

s+sfx Ps 22.32;103.17   s = RIGHT, LEGAL CLAIM Ne 2.20

pl = RIGHTEOUS DEEDS Ps 103.6   *

צָהֳרַיִם = n.m.pl   NOON   Je 20.16; Zp 2.4; Ct 1.7   *

צַוָּאר = n.m   NECK, BACK OF NECK   s+sfx Ct 1.10;4.4;7.5   *

צָוָה = vb   TO APPOINT, ORDER, DIRECT

     Pi.pf.3m.s Na 1.14; Ps 133.3; Ne 5.14   +sfx Ez 37.10

     Pi.pf.2m.s Ne 1.7,8   1.s+sfx Gn 3.11,17   imp.3m.s Gn 18.19

     Pi.imp.3m.s.apoc Gn 2.16; 2Sm 11.19   1.s Is 5.6; Ne 7.2

     Pi.ptc.m.s+sfx Dt 8.1,11   Pu.pf.1.s Ez 37.7   *

צוּם = vb   TO FAST   Qal.pf.2m.s 2Sm 12.21   1.s 2Sm 12.22

     Qal.imp.3m.s 2Sm 12.16   ptc.m.s 2Sm 12.23; Ne 1.4   *

צוֹם = n.m   FAST   s 2Sm 12.16; Jo 3.5   *

צוֹעַר = n.loc   ZOAR   Gn 19.22,30   +ה loc Gn 19.23   *

צוּף = 1.n.m   HONEYCOMB   pl Ps 19.11   *

     2.n.loc   ZUPH   1Sm 9.5   *

צוּץ = vb   1. TO BLOSSOM   Qal.imp.3m.s Ps 103.15   *

     2. TO PEEP   Hi.ptc.m.s Ct 2.9   *

צוּר = vb   TO BESEIGE, ENCLOSE   Qal.imp.3m.pl 2Sm 11.1   1.pl Ct 8.9 *

צוּר = n.m   ROCK, CLIFF   s Dt 8.15; Is 2.10; Ps 81.17; Jb 19.24

     s+sfx Ps 19.15   pl Is 2.19,21; Na 1.6   *

צַוְּרוֹן = n.m   NECKLACE   pl +sfx Ct 4.9   H.L.

צַח = adj   RADIANT, DAZZLING   m.s Ct 5.10   *

צְחִיחַ = n.m   OPEN SPACE   pl Ne 4.7   *

צָחַק = vb   TO LAUGH   Qal.pf.3f.s Gn 18.13   2f.s Gn 18.15

     Qal.pf.1.s Gn 18.15   imp.3m.s Gn 17.17   3f.s Gn 18.12

     Pi.ptc.m.s Gn 19.14   *

צֵידָ = n.m   PROVISION, FOOD   s Ne 13.15   *

צִיָּה = n.f   ARIDITY   s Is 53.2; Hs 2.5; Zp 2.13   *

צִיּוֹן = n.loc   ZION   Is 1.8; Ob 17; Zp 3.14; Ps 2.6;134.3; Ct 3.11

צִיץ = n.m   BLOSSOM, FLOWER   s.cs Ps 103.15   *

צִיר = n.m   1. MESSENGER   s Ob 1   *

     2. PANG, CONVULSION   pl+sfx 1Sm 4.19   *

צֵל = n.m   SHADOW   s Jo 4.5,6   s.cs Gn 19.8

     s+sfx Ps 121.5; Ct 2.3   pl צְלָלִים Ct 2.17;4.6   *

צָלֵח = vb   TO PROSPER   Qal.pf.3f.s Je 12.1   imp.3m.s Is 53.10

     Hi.imp.3m.s Ps 1.3; Ne 2.20   imv.m.s Ne 1.11   *

צָלַל = vb   TO BECOME DARK   Qal.pf.3m.pl Ne 13.1   *

צֶלֶם = n.m   IMAGE   s.cs Gn 1.27   s+sfx Gn 1.26,27
        pl.cs 1Sm 6.5,11   *

צַלְמָוֶת = n.m   SHADOW OF DEATH   s Ps 23.4   Rl p51   *

צָלַע = vb   TO LIMP   Qal.ptc.f.s Zp 3.19   *

צֶלַע = n.m   STUMBLING   s+sfx Je 20.10   *

צֵלָע = n.f   RIB   s Gn 2.22   pl+sfx Gn 2.21   *

צֶלְצְלִים = n.m.pl   CYMBALS   cs Ps 150.5   *

צָמָא = n.m   THIRST   s Hs 2.5   *

צִמָּאוֹן = n.m   THIRSTY GROUND   s Dt 8.15   *

צַמָּה = n.f   WOMAN'S VEIL   s+sfx Ct 4.1,3;6.7   *

צָמַח = vb   TO SPRING, SPROUT UP   Qal.imp.3m.s Gn 2.5
        Hi.imp.3m.s Gn 2.9   3f.s Gn 3.18   *

צֶמַח = n.m   GROWTH   s.cs Gn 19.25   *

צֶמֶר = n.m   WOOL   s Is 1.18   +sfx Hs 2.7,11   *

צָמַת = vb   TO SILENCE, DESTROY   Hi.imp.1.s Ps 101.5,8   *

צֹאן = n.m.coll   SHEEP AND GOATS   s Ps 8.8   H.L.

צָעִיר = adj   LITTLE, YOUNG   f.s Gn 19.31,34,35,38   *

צְעָקָה = n.f   CRY OF DISTRESS, CALL FOR HELP
        s 1Sm 4.14; Is 5.7; Zp 1.10   +sfx Gn 18.21;19.13   s.cs Ne 5.1   *

צָפָה = vb   TO KEEP WATCH, LOOK OUT   Qal.ptc.m.s Ct 7.5
        Pi.imv.m.s Na 2.2   ptc.m.s 1Sm 4.13   *

צָפוֹן = n.f   NORTH   s Je 15.12; Zp 2.13; Ps 48.3; Ec 1.6
        = NORTH WIND s Ct 4.16   *

צִפּוֹר = n.f   BIRD   s Hs 11.11; Ps 84.4;124.7; Ec 12.4
        s.cs Ps 8.9   pl @9e Ne 5.18   *

צָפַן = vb   TO TREASURE, STORE UP   Qal.pf.1.s Ct 7.14   *

צְפַנְיָה = n.pr.m   ZEPHANIAH   Zp 1.1   *

צַר = n.m   ADVERSARY, OPPRESSOR   pl+sfx Is 1.24; Na 1.2; Ps 81.15
                                        Ne 4.5   *

צָרָה = n.f   DISTRESS, TROUBLE
        s Je 15.11; Ob 12,14; Jo 2.3; Na 1.7,9; Zp 1.15; Ps 22.12;81.8   *

צְרוֹר = n.m   BUNDLE, POUCH, BAG   s.cs Ct 1.13   *

צָרַח = vb   TO CRY, ROAR   Qal.ptc.m.s Zp 1.14   *

צֹרִי = adj.gent   TYRIAN   m.pl Ne 13.16   *

צָרַף = vb   TO SMELT   Qal.imp.1.s Is 1.25   *

צָרְפַת = n.loc   ZAREPHATH   Ob 20   *

צָרַר = vb   1. TO BE HOSTILE   Qal.ptc.m.pl+sfx Ps 6.8;8.3;23.5   *

2. intra   TO BE NARROW

Hi.pf.1.s Zp 1.17 = PRESS IN ON, CAUSE DISTRESS   *

ק

קָאַת = n.f   ?OWL (Holl p310, Foh p241), ?HERON (B.D.B. p866, Lang p293)

s Zp 2.14   unclean bird inhabiting ruins   *

קָבַץ = vb   TO GATHER   Qal.imp.1.s+sfx Ne 13.11

Qal.inf.cs Zp 3.8 Rl p94   ptc.pass.m.pl Ne 5.16

Ni.pf.3m.pl Hs 2.2   juss.2m.pl Ne 4.14   Pi.pf.3m.pl Na 2.11

Pi.imp.1.s Zp 3.19   +sfx Ne 1.9   inf.cs+sfx Zp 3.20

Pi.ptc.m.s Na 3.18   *

קֶבֶר = n.m   GRAVE   s+sfx Is 53.9; Je 20.17; Na 1.14

pl+sfx Ez 37.12,13   pl.cs @9e Ne 2.3,5   *

קָדוֹשׁ = adj   SACRED, HOLY   m.s 1Sm 6.20; Is 6.3; Hs 11.9; Ps 22.4

m.s.cs Is 1.4   *

קָדַח = vb   TO BE KINDLED   Qal.pf.3f.s Je 15.14   *

קָדִים = n.m   EAST   s רוּחַ קָדִים = SIROCCO Jo 4.8; Ps 48.8   *

קֶדֶם = n.m   EAST, FRONT   s Gn 2.8;3.24; Is 2.6; Jo 4.5

temporal sense s.cs Pr 8.22   pl.cs Pr 8.23   *

קָדַם = vb.denom   TO ANTICIPATE   Pi.pf.1.s Jo 4.2   3m.pl Ne 13.2   *

קִדְמָה = n.f   FRONT   , EAST   s.cs Gn 2.14   *

קֵדָר = n.pr   KEDAR (bedouin tribe)   Ct 1.5   *

קָדַשׁ = vb   TO SET APART, CONSECRATE   Pi.imp.3m.s Gn 2.3

Pi.imp.3m.s+sfx Ex 20.11   inf.cs Ne 13.22   +sfx Ex 20.8

Hi.pf.3m.s Zp 1.7   imv.m.s+sfx Je 12.3   Hith.ptc.f.s 2Sm 11.4   *

קָדֵשׁ = n.loc   KADESH   Ps 29.8

קֹדֶשׁ = n.m   HOLINESS, SANCTUARY   s Ob 17; Zp 3.4; Ps 29.2;134.2
s+sfx Ob 16; Jo 2.5; Ps 2.6;24.3;48.2;103.1;150.1

קָהָל = n.m   ASSEMBLY   s Ps 22.23,26; Ne 5.13   s.cs Ne 13.1   *

קְהִלָּה = n.f   ASSEMBLY, CONGREGATION   s Ne 5.7   *

קֹהֶלֶת = n.m   PREACHER   s Ec 1.1,2,12;12.8 G/K 122r   *

קָו = n.m   SOUND (so Vss) s+sfx Ps 19.5   * From sense STRING?
but may derive from root קוה = TO CALL   R2 p62

קָוָה = vb   1. TO WAIT FOR   Pi.pf.3f.s Ps 130.5
Pi.pf.1.s Is 5.4; Ps 130.5   imp.3m.s.apoc Is 5.2,7   *
          2. TO COLLECT   Ni.juss.3m.pl Gn 1.9   *

קוֹל = n.m   SOUND, VOICE   s Ez 37.7; Zp 2.14;3.2
s.cs Gn 3.8; Dt 8.20; Je 18.19; Jo 2.10; Ps 103.20; Ec 12.4
s+sfx 2Sm 12.18; Jo 2.3; Ps 93.3   pl @9e Ex 20.18
  pl.cs Ps 93.4

קוּם = vb   TO ARISE, STAND   @30b   Qal.pf.3f.s 1Sm 4.15 R1 p3
Qal.pf.2m.s 2Sm 12.21   1.s Ct 5.5   imp.3m.s 1Kg 3.12; Jo 1.3
Qal.imp.3f.s Gn 19.35; Na 1.9; Ru 1.6   1.s Ne 2.12;4.8
Qal.imp.3m.pl Gn 18.16; 2Sm 12.17   1.pl Ne 2.18,20
Qal.coh.s Ct 3.2   pl Ob 1   imv.m.s Jo 1.2; Ps 82.8   @13a
Qal.imv.f.s Ct 2.10,13   m.pl Gn 19.14; Ob 1
Qal.inf.cs Ps 124.2   +sfx Gn 19.33; Is 2.19,21; Zp 3.8
Hi.pf.1.s Gn 17.7,19   imp.3m.s Ne 5.13   1.s Gn 17.21
Hi.ptc.m.s 2Sm 12.11

קוֹמָה = n.f   HEIGHT, STATURE   s+sfx Ct 7.8   *

קוֹץ = n.m   THORN BUSH   coll.s Gn 3.18   *

קְוֻצּוֹת = n.f.pl   LOCKS OF HAIR   +sfx Ct 5.2,11   *

קוֹרָה = n.f   RAFTER, BEAM   s+sfx Gn 19.8   pl.cs Ct 1.17   *

קֶטֶל = n.m   SLAUGHTER, MURDER   s Ob 9   H.L.

קָטֹן = adj   SMALL   m.s+sfx Jo 3.5   + לְ + מִן Je 31.34
f.s. 2Sm 12.3; Ct 8.8   m.pl Ct 2.15   *

קָטָן = adj   SMALL, YOUNG   m.s Gn 1.16;19.11; 1Sm 5.9; 1Kg 3.7; Ob 2   *

קָטַר = vb.denom   TO SEND UP SMOKE (of sacrifice or incense)
Pi.imp.3m.pl Hs 11.2   Pu.ptc.f.s.cs Ct 3.6 = PERFUMED
Hi.imp.3f.s Hs 2.15   *

קְטֹרֶת = n.f SMOKE, INCENSE s Is 1.13 *

קִיא = vb TO VOMIT Qal/Hi.imp.3m.s Jo 2.11 F.S. p126 *

קִיטֹר = n.m THICK SMOKE s.cs Gn 19.28 *

קִיקָיוֹן = n.m CASTOR-OIL PLANT, CLIMBING GOURD s Jo 4.6,7,9,10 *

קִישׁ = n.pr.m KISH 1Sm 9.3 *

קָלוֹן = n.m SHAME, PRIVATE PARTS s+sfx Na 3.5 *

קָלַל = vb TO BE SLIGHT @31 Qal.pf.2m.s Na 1.14
Pi = TO CURSE imp.1.s+sfx Ne 13.25 inf.cs+sfx Ne 13.2
Pi.ptc.m.s+sfx Je 15.10 is erroneous, modify to pf.3m.pl+sfx
i.e. read כלה כיקללוני as כְּלֵהֶם קִלְלוּנִי R2 p94, G/K 61h
Hi.imp.3m.s 1Sm 6.5 inf.cs Jo 1.5 *

קְלָלָה = n.f CURSE s Ne 13.2 *

קֶלֶס = n.m DERISION, RIDICULE s Je 20.8 *

קֶמַח = n.m FLOUR, MEAL s Gn 18.6 *

קֵן = n.m NEST s Ps 84.4 +sfx Ob 4 *

קַנָּא = adj JEALOUS m.s Ex 20.5 *

קִנְאָה = n.f ZEAL, ARDOUR s Ct 8.6 +sfx Zp 1.18;3.8 *

קָנָה = vb TO GET, BEGET Qal.pf.3m.s 2Sm 12.3 +sfx Pr 8.22
Qal.pf.1.pl Ne 5.8,16 ptc.m.s+sfx Is 1.3 *

קָנֶה = n.m CALAMUS (type of aromatic reed) s Ct 4.14 *

קַנּוֹא = adj JEALOUS m.s Na 1.2 *

קִנָּמוֹן = n.m CINNAMON s Ct 4.14 *

קָסַם = vb.denom TO PRACTISE DIVINATION Qal.ptc.m.pl 1Sm 6.2 *

קָפָא = vb TO THICKEN, CONGEAL Qal.ptc.m.pl Zp 1.12 *

קִפֹּד = n.m TYPE OF OWL s Zp 2.14 Rl p92, Holl p321, N.E.B. *
Rather than traditionally PORCUPINE B.D.B. p891, HEDGEHOG Lang p302

קָפַץ = vb TO DRAW TOGETHER, SHUT Qal.imp.3m.pl Is 52.15
Pi.ptc.m.s = LEAPING, BOUNDING Ct 2.8 *

קֵץ = n.m END s.cs Ne 13.6 *

קָצַב = vb TO SHEAR, CUT OFF Qal.ptc.pass.f.pl Ct 4.2 *

קֵצֶב = n.m   EXTREMITY   pl.cs Jo 2.7   *

קָצָה = n.f   END   pl+sfx Ps 19.7   *

קָצֶה = n.m   END   s Gn 19.4   s.cs Ps 19.5,7; Ne 1.9   *

קָצֶה = n.m   END (always with אֵין)   s Is 2.7; Ne 2.20;3.3,9   *

קְצָו = n.m   END (only in pl.cs)   Ps 48.11   *

קָצִין = n.m   CHIEF, RULER   pl.cs Is 1.10   *

קָצִיר = n.m   GRAIN HARVEST   s.cs 1Sm 6.13   *

קָצַף = vb   TO BE ANGRY   Qal.pf.3m.s Es 2.21   *

קָצַר = vb   TO REAP, HARVEST   Qal.ptc.m.pl 1Sm 6.13   *

קָרָא = vb   1. TO CALL, PROCLAIM

Qal.pf   Qal.imp

3m.s Gn 1.5;19.22; Is 6.3   3m.s Gn 1.5; 2Sm 12.24K;15.2

2m.s Gn 17.19; Ps 81.8   3f.s 2Sm 12.24Q; Pr 8.1;9.3

1.s Jo 2.3 +sfx Ps 130.1   2f.s Hs 2.18

3m.pl Je 12.6; Hs 11.2   1.s Je 20.8; Ps 22.3; Ne 5.12

                                   3m.pl Jo 1.14 +sfx Hs 11.7

Qal.imv.m.s Hs 1.4; Jo 1.2   juss.3m.pl Jo 3.8

Qal.inf.cs Is 1.13; Zp 3.9; Ne 6.7

Qal.ptc.pass.m.pl 1Sm 9.13   +sfx Zp 1.7

Ni.pf.3m.s 2Sm 12.28; Je 15.16; Ne 13.1

Ni.imp.3m.s Gn 2.23;17.5; 1Sm 9.9; Is 1.26

           2. TO ENCOUNTER   Qal.inf.cs 1Sm 4.1,2 +sfx Gn 18.2;19.1 *

קָרֵב = vb   TO COME, DRAW NEAR   Qal.pf.3f.s Zp 3.2

Qal.imp.3m.s Jo 1.6   2m.pl (for 3f.pl R1 p99) Ez 37.7   *

קֶרֶב = n.m   INWARD PART, MIDST   s.cs Ps 48.10;82.1;110.2

s+sfx Gn 24.3; 1Sm 4.3; Hs 11.9; Zp 3.3   pl+sfx Ps 103.1

קָרְבָּן = n.m   OFFERING   s.cs Ne 13.31   *

קָרָה = vb.denom   TO BUILD WITH BEAMS

Pi.pf.3m.pl+sfx Ne 3.3,6   inf.cs Ne 2.8   *

קָרָה = n.f   COLD   s Na 3.17   *

קָרוֹב = adj   NEAR, IMMINENT   m.s Je 12.2; Ob 15; Zp 1.7,14

m.s = RELATED TO Ne 13.4   f.s Gn 19.20; Ps 22.12   *

קֹרַח = n.pr.m   KORAH   Ps 48.1;84.1   *

Refers to some musical guild of compilers or singers

קְרִיאָה = n.f   PROCLAMATION   s Jo 3.2   H.L.

קִרְיָה = n.f   TOWN, CITY   s Is 1.21,26   s.cs Ps 48.3   *

קִרְיַת יְעָרִים = n.loc   KIRIATH-JEARIM   1Sm 6.21;7.1   *

קָרַם = vb   TO SPREAD OVER   Qal.pf.1.s Ez 37.6   imp.3m.s Ez 37.8   *

קֶרֶן = n.f   HORN   s Is 5.1   dual.cs Ps 22.22   *

קָרַע = vb   TO TEAR   Qal.inf.cs Ec 3.7   ptc.pass.m.pl 1Sm 4.12   *

קֶרֶת = n.f   CITY, TOWN   s Pr 8.3;9.3   *

קַשׁ = n.m   STUBBLE   s Ob 18; Na 1.10   *

קָשַׁב = vb   TO ATTEND, LISTEN   Hi.coh.pl Je 18.18
Hi.imv.m.s Je 18.19   ptc.m.pl Ct 8.13   *

קַשֻּׁב = adj   ATTENTIVE   f.s Ne 1.6,11   *

קַשֻּׁב = adj   ATTENTIVE   f.pl Ps 130.2   *

קָשְׁתָה = vb   TO BE HARD, SEVERE   Qal.pf.3f.s 1Sm 5.7   *

קָשָׁה = adj   HARD, SEVERE   f.s Ct 8.6   *

קָשַׁר = vb   TO BIND TOGETHER, CONSPIRE   Qal.imp.3m.pl Ne 4.2
Ni.imp.3f.s Ne 3.38   *

קָשַׁשׁ = vb   TO GATHER, ASSEMBLE   Qal.imv.m.s Zp 2.1
Hith.imv.m.s Zp 2.1   elsewhere vb always Po'el meaning TO GATHER
STUBBLE see Rl pp88-89   *

קֶשֶׁת = n.f   BOW   s Hs 1.7;2.20   s.cs Hs 1.5   pl Ne 4.10
pl+sfx Ne 4.7   *

ר

רָאָה = vb   TO SEE

Qal.pf	Qal.imp
3m.s Ec 1.16	3m.s Jo 4.5 apoc Jo 3.10
1.s Ez 37.8; Ne 13.15,23	3f.s.apoc Gn 3.6
3m.pl Jb 19.27 +sfx Ct 6.9	2m.s+sfx Je 12.3
2m.pl Ex 20.22; 1Sm 6.9	1.s Is 6.1 apoc Ne 4.8
1.pl Ps 48.9	3m.pl 1Sm 6.13; Ps 22.18
	1.pl+sfx Is 53.2

Qal.juss.2m.s Ob 12,13   2m.pl+sfx Ct 1.6   1.pl Ct 7.13

Qal.coh.s. Je 11.20   imv.m.s 2Sm 15.3; Ec 1.10   f.pl Ct 3.11

Qal.inf.cs Gn 2.19; 1Sm 4.15; Ec 1.8   ptc.m.s Je 20.12

Qal.ptc.m.s+sfx Na 3.7   m.pl Ex 20.18   f.pl Ec 12.3

Ni.pf.3m.s 1Kg 3.5   3m.pl Ct 2.12   imp.3m.s Ps 84.8

Ni.imp.3m.s.apoc Gn 17.1   juss.3f.s Gn 1.9   inf.cs Is 1.12

Hi.pf.2m.s+sfx Je 11.18   1.s Na 3.5   imv.f.s+sfx Ct 2.14

רֹאֶה = n.m   SEER   s 1Sm 9.9,11   *

רְאִי = n.m   SPECTACLE   s Na 3.6   *

רְאֵם = n.m   WILD OX   pl Ps 22.22;29.6   *

רֹאשׁ = n.m   HEAD   s Gn 3.15; Is 1.5; Hs 2.2; Ps 110.6; Pr 8.23

s.cs 2Sm 12.30; Jo 4.8; Ct 4.8   s+sfx Jo 2.6; Ps 23.5; Ne 3.36

pl @33e Gn 2.10   +sfx Ps 24.7   pl.cs Ct 4.14

רִאשׁוֹן = adj   FORMER, FIRST   m.s Hs 2.9   m.pl Ec 1.11; Ne 5.15

f.s with prep & used adverbially = FORMERLY Is 1.26   *

רֵאשִׁית = n.f   BEGINNING   s or s.cs Gn 1.1   F.S p120   s.cs Pr 8.22   *

רַב = 1. adj   GREAT, MANY ,MUCH

m.s 1Kg 3.8; Jo 4.2   i.p Ps 19.11;48.3   f.s Jo 4.11; Ps 110.6

m.pl 1Kg 3.11; Hs 3.3; Na 1.12; Ps 29.3   f.pl Ez 37.2

2. n.m   CHIEF, CAPTAIN   s.cs Jo 1.6   *

רֹב = n.m   ABUNDANCE   s 1Kg 3.8

s.cs Is 1.11; Na 3.3,4; Ps 150.2; Ec 1.18; Ne 13.22   *

רָבַב = vb   TO BE GREAT   Qal.pf.3f.s Gn 18.20   *

רְבָבָה = number   TEN THOUSAND   s Ct 5.10   *

רָבָה = vb   TO INCREASE, BECOME NUMEROUS   Qal.pf.2m.pl Dt 8.1

Qal.imp.3m.s Dt 8.13   3m.pl Dt 8.13   juss.3m.s Gn 1.22

Qal.imv.m.pl Gn 1.22,28   Hi.pf.2m.s Na 3.16   R2 pp87-88

Hi.pf.1.s Gn 17.20; Hs 2.10   imp.1.s Gn 3.16   2m.pl Is 1.15

Hi.coh.s @13e Gn 17.2   inf.abs before מִן = MORE THAN   Jo 4.11

Hi.inf.abs used adverbially = ABUNDANTLY Gn 3.16; 2Sm 12.2; Ec 1.16

Hi.ptc.m.pl Ne 6.17

רַבָּה = n.loc   RABBAH   2Sm 11.1;12.27   + ה loc 2Sm 12.29

cs רַבַּת בְּנֵי עַמּוֹן 2Sm 12.26   *

רִבּוֹ = number   TEN THOUSAND   s Jo 4.11   *

רְבִיעִי = ordinal number   FOURTH   Gn 1.19;2.14   *

רֹבַע = n.m   FOURTH PART   s.cs 1Sm 9.8   *

רִבֵּעַ = n.m   DESCENDANT OF FOURTH GENERATION   pl Ex 20.5   *

רָבֵץ = vb   TO LIE DOWN   Qal.pf.3m.pl Zp 2.14;3.13   imp.3m.pl Zp 2.7

Hi.imp.3m.s+sfx Ps 23.2   2m.s Ct 1.7   *

רָגַל = vb.denom   TO GO ON FOOT   Tiph'el.pf.1.s Hs 11.3   *

Meaning is causative TEACH TO WALK   R1 p70, G/K 55h

רֶגֶל = n.f   FOOT   s Is 1.6   +sfx Dt 8.4; Ps 121.3

dual.cs Na 2.1   dual+sfx Gn 18.4; 2Sm 11.8; Is 6.2; Ez 37.10

רַגְלִי = n.m   FOOT-SOLDIER   s 1Sm 4.10   pl Je 12.5   *

רֶגַע = n.m   MOMENT   s Ps 6.11   *

רָגַשׁ = vb   TO BE IN TUMULT, RESTLESS   Qal.pf.3m.pl Ps 2.1   H.L.

רָדָה = vb   TO RULE, GOVERN   Qal.juss.3m.pl Gn 1.26

Qal.imv.m.s Ps 110.2   m.pl Gn 1.28   *

רְדִיד = n.m   MANTLE, WRAPPER   s+sfx Ct 5.7   *

רָדַם = vb   TO BE IN A DEEP SLEEP   Ni.imp.3m.s Jo 1.5

Ni.ptc.m.s Jo 1.6   *

רָדַף = vb   TO PURSUE   Qal.imp.3m.pl+sfx Ps 23.6   1.pl Jb 19.28

Qal.ptc.m.s Is 1.23   m.pl+sfx Je 15.15;17.18;20.11

Pi.pf.3f.s Hs 2.9   imp.3m.s Na 1.8   *

רַהַט = n.m   ?LOOM BEAMS   pl Ct 7.6   H.L.

So R2 pp131-132   rather than LOCKS B.D.B. p923, Lang p314, or

WATERING TROUGH Holl p334, Foh p256

רָהִיט = n.m.coll   RAFTER   s+sfx Ct 1.17   H.L.

So read Q for K רחיט

רוּחַ = n.f   WIND, BREATH, SPIRIT

s Ez 37.5; Jo 1.4; Ps 103.16; Ec 1.6   +sfx Ez 37.14

s.cs Gn 1.2;3.8; Ez 37.1; Jo 4.8   pl Ez 37.9

רְוָיָה = n.f   OVERFLOW, SATURATION   s Ps 23.5   *

רוּם = 1. vb   TO BE HIGH, EXALTED   Qal.pf.3m.pl Ps 131.1

Qal.imp.3m.s Is 52.13   ptc.m.s Dt 8.14; Is 2.12;6.1

Qal.ptc.m.pl Is 2.13,14   Po.pf.1.s Is 1.2   imp.3m.s Hs 11.7

Hi.imp.3m.s Ps 110.7   ptc.m.pl.cs Hs 11.4   *

2. n.m   HAUGHTINESS   s.cs Is 2.11,17   *

רוע = vb   TO RAISE A SHOUT   Hi.imp.3m.pl 1Sm 4.5
Hi.imv.m.pl Zp 3.14; Ps 81.2;100.1   *

רוץ = vb   TO RUN   Qal.pf.3m.s Gn 18.7   2m.s Je 12.5
Qal.imp.3m.s Gn 18.2; 1Sm 4.12   coh.pl Ct 1.4   inf.cs Ps 19.6
Qal.ptc.m.pl 2Sm 15.1   Po.imp.3m.pl Na 2.5   *

רוש = vb   TO BE POOR, NEEDY   Qal.ptc.m.s 2Sm 12.1,3,4; Ps 82.3   *

רות = n.pr.f   RUTH   Ru 1.4   *

רזה = vb   TO MAKE LEAN   Qal.pf.3m.s Zp 2.11   Rl p91   *

רזן = vb   TO BE WEIGHTY, JUDICIOUS B.D.B. p931
Only in form of Qal.ptc.m.pl as subs = RULER   Ps 2.2; Pr 8.15   *

רחב = vb   TO MAKE WIDE   Hi.pf.3m.pl+sfx Ct 6.5
Hi.imv.m.s Ps 81.11 = OPEN (mouth)   *

רחב = adj   WIDE, BROAD   m.s.cs Ps 101.5   f.s Ne 4.13
f.s.cs Ne 7.4   *

רחוב = n.f   OPEN SPACE, PLAZA   s Gn 19.2   pl Na 2.5; Ct 3.2   *

רחום = adj   COMPASSIONATE   m.s Jo 4.2; Ps 103.8   *

רחוק = adj   DISTANT, FAR OFF   m.s Je 12.2; Ps 22.2   m.pl Ne 4.13
m.s+מן = AT A DISTANCE   Ex 20.18,21   *

רחל = n.f   EWE   s Is 53.7   pl Ct 6.6   *

רחם = vb.denom   TO SHOW LOVE, HAVE COMPASSION   Pi.pf.3m.s Ps 103.13
Pi.pf.1.s Hs 2.25   imp.1.s Hs 1.6,7;2.6   inf.cs Ps 103.13
Pu.pf.3f.s Hs 1.6,8;2.3,25   *

רחם = n.m   WOMB   s+sfx Je 20.17   s.cs+מן Ps 110.3
s+מן Je 20.17,18   = FROM BIRTH   Ps 22.11   *

רחמים = n.m.pl.intensive   TENDER LOVE   Hs 2.21; Ps 103.4; Ne 1.11   *

רחף = vb   TO HOVER   Pi.ptc.f.s Gn 1.2   *

רחץ = vb   TO WASH   Qal.pf.1.s Ct 5.3   imp.3m.s 2Sm 12.20
Qal.imv.m.s 2Sm 11.8   m.pl Gn 18.4;19.2; Is 1.16
Qal.ptc.f.s 2Sm 11.2   f.pl Ct 5.12   *

רחצה = n.f   WASHING   s Ct 4.2;6.6   *

רחק = vb   TO BE/BECOME DISTANT   Qal.juss.2m.s Ps 22.12,20
Qal.inf.cs Ps 103.12; Ec 3.5   Ni.pf.3m.s Ec 12.6K   Rl p112

Hi.pf.3m.s Ps 103.12   *

רמשׂ = vb ^{Pi} TO DASH IN PIECES   Pu.imp.3m.pl Na 3.10   *

ריב = 1. vb   TO CONTEND, PLEAD   Qal.imp.3m.s Ps 103.9

     Qal.imp.l.s Je 12.1; Ne 13.25   coh.s Ne 5.7;13.11,17

     Qal.imv.m.pl Is 1.17;   Hs 2.4   *

      2. n.m   DISPUTE, LAWSUIT   s 2Sm 15.2,4; Je 15.10

     s.cs Is 1.23   s+sfx Je 11.20;20.12   *

ריח = n.m   SCENT, FRAGRANCE   s Ct 2.13;7.14   +sfx Ct 1.12

     s.cs Ct 1.3;4.10,11:7.9   *

ריק = n.m   VANITY, MISCHIEF   s Ps 2.1   *

ריקם = adv   EMPTY HANDED   1Sm 6.3   *

רך = adj   TENDER   m.s Gn 18.7   *

רכב = vb   TO RIDE   Qal.ptc.m.s Ne 2.12   *

רכב = n.m   1. CHARIOT   s Na 2.4,5   +sfx Na 2.14   pl.cs Ct 1.9   *

      2. in phrase פלח רכב = UPPER MILL-STONE   s 2Sm 11.21   *

רכך = vb   TO BE TENDER, SOFT   Pu.pf.3f.s Is 1.6   *

רכל = vb   TO GO ABOUT (for trade)   ptc as subs = MERCHANT

     Qal.ptc.m.s Ct 3.6   m.pl Ne 13.20   +sfx Na 3.16   *

רמון = n.m   POMEGRANATE   s Dt 8.8; Ct 4.3;6.7   +sfx Ct 8.2

     pl Ct 4.13;6.11;7.13   *

רמח = n.m   SPEAR, LANCE   pl Ne 4.10,15   +sfx Ne 4.7   *

רמיה = n.f   DECEIT, TREACHERY   s Ps 101.7   *

רמס = vb   TO TRAMPLE   Qal.imv.f.s Na 3.14   inf.cs Is 1.12   *

רמשׂ = vb   TO GLIDE ABOUT, CREEP   Qal.ptc.m.s Gn 1.26,30

     Qal.ptc.f.s Gn 1.21,28   *

רמשׂ = n.m.coll   ANIMALS, REPTILES   s Gn 1.24,26   s.cs Gn 1.25;

                                                        Hs 2.20   *

רנה = n.f   SHOUT OF JOY   s Zp 3.17   *

רנן = vb   TO SHOUT WITH JOY, CRY ALOUD

     Qal.imp.3f.s Pr 8.3 (for ending see R2 pl16)   imv.f.s Zp 3.14

     Pi.imp.3m.pl Ps 84.3   Hi.imv.m.pl Ps 81.2   *

רננה = n.f   SHOUT OF JOY   s Ps 100.2   *

רְסִיסֵי = n.m   DROP (of moisture)   pl.cs Ct 5.2   H.L.

רַע = 1. n.m   EVIL   s Gn 2.9;3.5; 1Kg 3.9; Zp 3.15; Ps 121.7

2. adj   EVIL   m.s   2Sm 12.9; Ec 1.13; Ne 6.13;13.17

m.pl Je 15.21; Ne 2.2   *

רֵעַ = n.m   FRIEND   s Hs 3.1   R1 p67

s+sfx Ex 20.16,17; Ct 5.16   pl Ct 5.1   *

רֹעַ = n.m   BADNESS, SADNESS   s.cs Is 1.16; Ne 2.2   *

רָעֵב = vb   TO BE HUNGRY   Hi.imp.3m.s+sfx Dt 8.3   *

רָעָב = n.m   FAMINE   s Je 11.22;18.21; Ru 1.1; Ne 5.3   *

רְעָדָה = n.f   TREMBLING   s Ps 2.11;48.7   *

רָעָה = 1. vb   TO FEED A FLOCK, PASTURE   Qal.imp.2m.s Ct 1.7

Qal.imp.3m.pl Zp 2.7;3.13   juss.3m.pl Jo 3.7   imv.f.s Ct 1.8

Qal.inf.cs Ct 6.2   ptc.m.s Je 17.16 R2 p96; Ct 2.16;6.3

Qal.ptc.m.s+sfx Ps 23.1   m.pl Zp 2.6; Ct 1.8;4.5   +sfx Na 3.18   *

2. n.f   EVIL   s 1Sm 6.9; 2Sm 12.11; Je 18.20; Ec 12.1; Ne 1.3

s.cs Je 12.4   s+sfx Ob 13; Jo 1.2;4.6; Na 3.19

רֵעֶה = n.m   FRIEND   s+sfx 2Sm 12.11 G/K 93ss; Je 31.34 F.S p123

Jo 1.7; Ps 101.5   *

רְעוּת = n.f   PASTURING   s.cs Ec 1.14   *

See R1 p105 where linked to root רעה = TO PASTURE, rather than
B.D.B. p946 where linked to another (supposed) root רעה = TO DESIRE

רַעְיָה = n.f   COMPANION, BELOVED   s+sfx Ct 1.9,15;2.2,10,13;4.1,7;5.2
6.4 *

רַעְיוֹן = n.m   PASTURING   s.cs Ec 1.17   see R1 p106 & רְעוּת   *

רָעַל = vb   TO SHAKE, QUIVER   Ho.pf.3m.pl Na 2.4   H.L.

רָעַם = vb.denom   TO THUNDER   Hi.pf.3m.s Ps 29.3   *

רַעַם = n.m   THUNDER   s Ps 81.8   *

רַעֲנָן = adj   LUXURIANT, FRESH, GREEN   f.s Ct 1.16   *

רָעַע = vb   1. TO BE EVIL, DISPLEASING

Qal.imp.3m.s 2Sm 11.27; Jo 4.1; Ne 2.10;13.8   3m.pl Ne 2.3

Qal.juss.3m.s 2Sm 11.25   Hi.imp.3m.s Zp 1.12   1.pl Gn 19.9

Hi.juss.2m.pl Gn 19.7   inf.abs Is 1.16 R1 p78, G/K 113d

Hi.ptc.m.pl Is 1.4; Je 20.13; Ps 22.17   *

2. TO BREAK   Qal.imp.3m.s Je 15.12   2m.s+sfx Ps 2.9   *

רָעַשׁ = vb   TO SHAKE, QUAKE   Qal.pf.3m.pl Na 1.5   *

רַעַשׁ = n.m   SHAKING, QUAKING   s Ez 37.7   s.cs Na 3.2   *

רָפָא = vb   TO HEAL   Qal.pf.1.s+sfx Hs 11.3
Qal.imv.m.s+sfx Je 17.14; Ps 6.3   inf.cs Ec 3.3   ptc.m.s Ps 103.3
Ni.pf.3m.s Is 53.5   imp.1.s Je 17.14   2m.pl 1Sm 6.3
Ni.inf.cs Je 15.18   *

רָפַד = vb   TO SUPPORT, REFRESH   Pi.imv.m.pl+sfx Ct 2.5   *

רָפָה = vb   TO BE LIMP, RELAX, SINK DOWN   Qal.imp.3m.pl Ne 6.9
Qal.juss.3m.pl Zp 3.16   Hi.imp.1.s+sfx Ct 3.4; Ne 6.3   *

רְפִידָה = n.f   ?BACK SUPPORT   s+sfx Ct 3.10 R2 pp127-128   H.L.

רָפַק = vb   TO LEAN, RECLINE   Hith.ptc.f.s Ct 8.5   H.L.

רָצוֹן = n.m   PLEASURE, FAVOUR, ACCEPTANCE   s Pr 8.35   +sfx Ps 103.21
s+לְ Ps 19.15   *

רָצַח = vb   TO MURDER   Qal.juss.2m.s Ex 20.13   Pi.ptc.m.pl Is 1.21   *

רָצַף = vb   TO INLAY   Qal.ptc.pass.m.s Ct 3.10   H.L.

רָצַץ = vb   TO CRUSH   Qal.imp.3f.s Ec 12.6a intra = GET CRUSHED
Ni.pf.3m.s Ec 12.6b   *

רַק = adv   ONLY   Gn 19.8;24.8; 1Sm 5.4   *

רֵק = adj   EMPTY   m.s Ne 5.13   *

רָקַד = vb   TO SKIP ABOUT   Qal.inf.cs Ec 3.4
Pi.ptc.f.s Na 3.2   Hi.imp.3m.s+sfx Ps 29.6   *

רַקָּה = n.f   TEMPLE (of head)   s+sfx Ct 4.3;6.7   *

רֶקַח = n.m   SPICE   s Ct 8.2   H.L.

רָקִיעַ = n.m   FIRMAMENT (of heaven) see R1 p23   s Gn 1.6,7,8; Ps 19.2
s.cs Gn 1.14,15,17,20; Ps 150.1   *

רָשָׁע = adj   SINFUL, GUILTY   m.s Gn 18.23,25
m.pl Is 53.9; Je 12.1; Zp 1.3; Ps 1.1;82.2   m.pl.cs Ps 101.8

רֶשַׁע = n.m   WICKEDNESS, WRONG   s Ps 84.11; Pr 8.7   *

רֶשֶׁף = n.m   FLAME   pl.cs Ct 8.6   pl+sfx Ct 8.6   *

רֻתַּק = vb(Pu)   TO BE BOUND   Pu.pf.3m.pl Na 3.10   *

שָׂבַ(ע) = vb   TO BE FULL, SATISFIED   Qal.pf.2m.s Dt 8.10,12   1.s Is 1.11

Qal.imp.3m.s Is 53.11   3f.s Ec 1.8   3m.pl Ps 22.27

Hi.imp.1.s+sfx Ps 81.17   ptc.m.s Ps 103.5   *

שָׂבַר = vb(Qal)   TO INSPECT   Qal.ptc.m.s Ne 2.13,15   *

Vb elsewhere always in Pi = TO HOPE.   Treated as two distinct verbs
in B.D.B. p960 but as one in K/B p914, Foh p268, Holl p349

שָׂגַב = vb   TO BE HIGH, EXALTED   Ni.pf.3m.s Is 2.11,17   *

שָׂדֶה = n.m   FIELD, OPEN COUNTRY   s Gn 2.5; 1Sm 4.2; Hs 2.14; Ps 103.15

s.cs 1Sm 6.1,14,18; Ob 19; Ru 1.6   s+sfx Ne 13.10

pl.cs Ru 1.1,2,6   pl+sfx @9e Ne 5.3,4,5,11

שָׂדַי = n.m   FIELD, OPEN COUNTRY   s Ps 8.8 (original form of שָׂדֶה)   *

שֶׂה = n.m   SHEEP or GOAT   s Is 53.7   *

שׂוּך = vb   TO HEDGE, SHUT IN   Qal.ptc.m.s Hs 2.8   *

שׂישׂ/שׂוּשׂ = vb   TO EXULT, REJOICE   Qal.imp.3m.s Zp 3.17; Ps 19.6   *

שָׂחָה = vb   TO SWIM   Hi.imp.1.s Ps 6.7   *

שְׂחוֹק = n.m   LAUGHING-STOCK   s Je 20.7   *

שָׂחַק = vb   TO LAUGH   Qal.imp.3m.s.i.p Ps 2.4   inf.cs Ec 3.4

Pi.ptc.f.s Pr 8.30,31   m.pl Je 15.17   *

שִׂיח = vb   TO CONSIDER   Po.imp.3m.s Is 53.8   *

שִׂיחַ = n.m   BUSH, SHRUB   s.cs Gn 2.5   *

שִׂים / שׂוּם = vb   TO PUT, PLACE, MAKE   @30b

Qal.pf		Qal.imp	
3m.s Ps 19.5	+sfx Ps 81.6	3m.s Gn 24.9	+sfx 2Sm 15.4
3f.s+sfx Ct 6.12		3f.s Is 53.10	
1.s+sfx Hs 2.5; Na 3.6; Zp 3.19		1.s Na 1.14	+sfx Hs 11.8
3m.pl Hs 2.2	+sfx Ct 1.6	3m.pl 1Sm 6.11; 2Sm 12.20; Ob 7	

Qal.juss.3m.s Zp 2.13 Rl p92   2m.pl 1Sm 6.8

Qal.imv.m.s Gn 24.2   +sfx Ct 8.6   inf.cs+sfx Pr 8.29

Qal.ptc.pass.m.s Ob 4

שְׂכִיָּה = n.f   ?SHIP   pl.cs Is 2.16   meaning dubious, Rl p82   H.L.

שָׂכַל = vb   TO BE PRUDENT, PROSPEROUS, ATTENTIVE   Hi.pf.3m.pl Je 20.11

Hi.imp.3m.s Is 52.13   coh.s Ps 101.2   imv.m.pl Ps 2.10
Hi.inf.cs Gn 3.6   *

שִׂכְלוּת = n.f   FOLLY   s Ec 1.17   root סכל. שׂ is error for ס.
Word only found in Ec. See Ec 2.3 for correct spelling   *

שָׂכַר = vb   TO HIRE   Qal.pf.3m.s+sfx Ne 6.12
Qal.imp.3m.s Ne 13.2   ptc.pass.m.s Ne 6.13   *

שָׂכָר = n.m   FARE   s+sfx Jo 1.3   *

שַׂלְמָה = n.f   MANTLE, CLOAK   pl+sfx Ct 4.11   *

שְׂמֹאול = n.m   LEFT, LEFT SIDE   s 1Sm 6.12   +sfx Jo 4.11; Ct 2.6;8.3   *

שָׂמַח = vb   TO REJOICE, BE GLAD   Qal.imp.3m.s Jo 4.6   3m.pl 1Sm 6.13
Qal.juss.3m.s Ps 48.12; Ec 11.8   2m.s Ob 12   coh.pl Ct 1.4
Qal.imv.m.s Ec 11.9   f.s Zp 3.14   Pi.pf.3m.s+sfx Je 20.15 G/K 59f
Pi.inf.abs Je 20.15   ptc.m.pl.cs Ps 19.9   *

שִׂמְחָה = n.f   JOY,GLADNESS   s Jo 4.6; Zp 3.17; Ps 100.2
s.cs Je 15.16; Ct 3.11   *

שִׂמְלָה = n.f   MANTLE, GARMENT   s+sfx Dt 8.4   pl+sfx 2Sm 12.20 Q   *

שָׂנֵא = vb   TO HATE   Qal.pf.3f.s Is 1.14   1.s Ps 101.3; Pr 8.13
Qal.inf.cs Pr 8.13; Ec 3.8   ptc.m.pl+sfx Ex 20.5
Pi.ptc.m.pl+sfx Pr 8.36   m.pl.cs Ps 81.16   *

שְׂנִיר = n.loc   SENIR (Amorite name of Hermon: Dt 3.9)   Ct 4.8   *

שֵׂעָר = n.m.coll   HAIR   s+sfx Ct 4.1;6.5   *

שְׂעָרָה = n.f   STORM, TEMPEST   s Na 1.3   *

שְׂעֹרָה = n.f   BARLEY   s Dt 8.8   pl Hs 3.2   *

שָׂפָה = n.f   LIP, LANGUAGE   s Zp 3.9; Ps 22.8   s.cs Ps 81.6
dual+sfx Je 17.16; Pr 8.6,7   dual.cs Ct 7.10   pl+sfx Ct 4.3,11
                                                  5.13   *

שָׂפַק = vb   either 1. TO SUFFICE (K/B, Foh)   or 2. TO CLAP HANDS (B.D.B)
Hi.imp.3m.pl Is 2.6 Rl p81   *

שַׂק = n.m   SACKCLOTH   s Jo 3.6   pl Jo 3.5,8   *

שַׂר = n.m   OFFICIAL, CHIEF   s.cs Ne 7.2   s.i.p Hs 3.4
pl Zp 1.8; Ps 82.7; Pr 8.16; Ne 4.10   +sfx Is 1.23; Zp 3.3
pl.cs Ne 2.9   *

שָׂרָה = n.pr.f   SARAH   Gn 17.15ff;18.6ff

שָׂרַי = n.pr.f   SARAI (before change of name to Sarah)   Gn 17.15   *

שָׂרִיד = n.m   SURVIVOR   s Is 1.9; Ob 18   pl+sfx Ob 14   *

שִׂרְיוֹן = n.loc   SIRION (Sidonian name of Hermon: Dt 3.9)   Ps 29.6   *

שָׂרַף = vb   TO BURN   Qal.ptc.pass.f.pl Ne 3.34   f.pl.cs Is 1.7   *

שָׂרָף = n.m   1. SERPENT   s Dt 8.15   *
           2. SERAPH   pl Is 6.2   *

שֹׂרֵק = n.m   CHOICE SPECIES OF VINE   s Is 5.2   *

שָׂרַר = vb.denom   TO RULE, DIRECT   Qal.imp.3m.pl Pr 8.16   *

שָׂשׂוֹן = n.m   JOY, EXULTATION   s Je 15.16   *

שָׂתַר = vb   TO BREAK OUT   Ni.imp.3m.pl 1Sm 5.9   H.L.

שׁ

·שׁ = relative particle   THAT, WHICH   @33d
(־) Jo 4.10; Ps 124.1; Ct 1.12; Ec 1.11   = BECAUSE   Ct 1.6;5.2
+בְ = ON ACCOUNT OF   Jo 1.7,12   + לְמָה = LEST   Ct 1.7

שָׁאַב = vb   TO DRAW (water)   Qal.imv.f.s Na 3.14   inf.cs 1Sm 9.11   *

שָׁאַג = vb   TO ROAR   Qal.imp.3m.s.i.p Hs 11.10
Qal.ptc.m.s Ps 22.14   m.pl Zp 3.3   *

שְׁאָגָה = n.f   ROARING   s+sfx Ps 22.2   *

שֹׁאָה = n.f   RUIN, DESTRUCTION   s Zp 1.15   *

שְׁאוֹל = n.pr   SHEOL, UNDERWORLD   Jo 2.3; Ps 6.6; Ct 8.6   *

שָׁאוּל = n.pr.m   SAUL   1Sm 9.3ff; 2Sm 12.7   *

שָׁאַל = vb   TO ASK, INQUIRE   Qal.pf.3m.s 1Kg 3.10   2m.s 1Kg 3.11,13
Qal.imp.3m.s 2Sm 11.7;12.20; Jo 4.8   1.s+sfx Ne 1.2
Qal.imv.m.s 1Kg 3.5; Ps 2.8   Ni.pf.1.s Ne 13.6 R2 p57   *

שָׁאַף = vb   TO PANT   Qal.ptc.m.s Ec 1.5   *

שָׁאַר = vb   TO BE LEFT, REMAIN   Ni.pf.3m.s 1Sm 5.4   3m.pl Ne 1.2,3
Ni.imp.3f.s Ru 1.3,5   ptc.m.pl Ne 1.3
Hi.pf.1.s Zp 3.12   imp.3m.pl Ob 5   *

שְׁאָר = n.m   REMNANT   s.cs Zp 1.4   *

שְׁאֵרִית = n.f   REMNANT, REMAINDER   s Je 11.23   s.cs Zp 2.7,9;3.13   *

שָׁבָה = vb   TO TAKE CAPTIVE   Qal.inf.cs Ob 11   *

שְׁבוּעָה/שְׁבֻעָה = n.f   OATH   s Ne 6.18   +sfx Gn 24.8   *

שְׁבוּת/שְׁבִית = n.f   RESTORATION   s+sfx Zp 2.7   pl+sfx Zp 3.20   *
          Full discussion of word in Rl pp90-91

שָׁבַח = vb   TO PRAISE   Pi.imv.m.pl Ps 117.1   *

שֵׁבֶט = n.m   1. ROD, SCEPTRE   s.cs Ps 2.9   s+sfx Ps 23.4   *
          2. TRIBE   pl.cs 2Sm 15.2   *

שְׁבִי = n.m   CAPTIVITY   s Na 3.10; Ne 1.2,3   *

שִׁבְיָה = n.f   CAPTIVITY   s Ne 3.36   *

שְׁבִיעִי = ordinal number   SEVENTH   Gn 2.2,3; Ex 20.10,11; 2Sm 12.18   *

שָׁבַע = vb   TO SWEAR, ADJURE (in Ct)
          Ni.pf.3m.s Gn 24.7; Dt 8.1,18; Ps 24.4;110.4   imp.3m.s Gn 24.9
          Ni.ptc.m.pl Zp 1.5   Hi.pf.2f.s+sfx Ct 5.9
          Hi.pf.1.s Ct 2.7;3.5;5.8;8.4   imp.1.s+sfx Gn 24.3; Ne 5.12;13.25   *

שִׁבְעָה = number   SEVEN   @25d   f 1Sm 6.1; Pr 9.1   *

שִׁבְעִים = number   SEVENTY   1Sm 6.19   *

שָׁבַר = vb   TO BREAK   Qal.pf.1.s Hs 1.5   imp.1.s Hs 2.20; Na 1.13
          Qal.imv.m.s+sfx Je 17.18   inf.cs Gn 19.9   ptc.m.s Ps 29.5
          Ni.imp.3f.s 1Sm 4.18; Ec 12.6   inf.cs Jo 1.4   ptc.m.s Ps 124.7
          Pi.imp.3m.s Ps 29.5   2m.s Ps 48.8   *

שֵׁבֶר = n.m   BREAKING   s Zp 1.10   +sfx Na 3.19   s.cs Is 1.28   *

שִׁבָּרוֹן = n.m   BREAKING   s Je 17.18   *

שָׁבַת = vb   TO CEASE, DESIST   Qal.pf.3m.s Gn 2.3   imp.3f.s Ne 6.3
          Hi.pf.1.s Hs 1.4;2.13   1.pl Ne 4.5   inf.cs Ps 8.3   *

שַׁבָּת = n.f   SABBATH   s Ex 20.8ff; Is 1.13; Ne 13.15   +sfx Hs 2.13

שָׁגַח = vb   TO GAZE   Hi.ptc.m.s Ct 2.9   *

שְׁגִיאָה = n.f   ERROR   pl Ps 19.13   H.L.

שֵׁגָל = n.f   QUEEN CONSORT, CHIEF CONCUBINE   s Ne 2.6   *

שַׁד = n.m   BREAST   dual Ct 8.8   dual.cs Ps 22.10; Ct 8.1
          dual+sfx Hs 2.4; Ct 1.13;4.5;7.4,8,9;8.10   *

שֹׁד = n.m   DESTRUCTION, HAVOC   s Je 20.8   *

שָׁדַד = vb   TO DEVASTATE, LAY WASTE   Qal.ptc.m.pl.cs Ob 5

107

Pu.pf.3f.s Na 3.7 *

שַׁדַּי = n.pr of deity ALMIGHTY Gn 17.1 *
Used in divine name אֵל שַׁדַּי and identified with יהוה

שֹׁהַם = n.m ONYX (name of precious gem) s Gn 2.12 *
Traditionally onyx, but may be carnelian or lapis lazuli Holl p361

שָׁוְא = n.m VANITY, FOLLY s Ex 20.7; Is 1.13; Jo 2.9; Ps 24.4 *

שׁוּב = vb TO RETURN, TURN BACK

Qal.pf	Qal.imp	Qal.juss,coh,imv
3m.s Zp 2.7	3m.s Hs 11.5	juss.3m.s 1Sm 5.11
1.s Ps 23.6	3f.s Ru 1.6	juss.3m.pl Jo 3.8
3m.pl Jo 3.10	2m.s Gn 3.19	coh.s Hs 2.9
2m.pl 2Sm 11.15	1.s Gn 18.10	coh.pl 1Sm 9.5
	3m.pl Je 15.19	imv.m.s @13a Ps 6.5
	2m.pl Ne 4.6	imv.f.s Ct 7.1
	1.pl Ne 4.9	

Qal.inf.abs Gn 18.10   inf.cs Hs 11.5   +sfx Zp 3.20
Qal.ptc.m.s Ec 1.6   m.pl Ec 1.7   +sfx Is 1.27
Po.imp.3m.s Ps 23.3

Hi.pf	Hi.imp	Hi.juss,coh,imv
3m.pl 1Sm 6.17,21	2m.s Gn 24.6	juss.2m.s Gn 24.8
2m.pl 1Sm 6.7,8	1.s Ps 81.15	coh.s Is 1.25,26
	3m.pl 1Sm 5.3	imv.m.s Ne 3.36
	2m.pl 1Sm 6.3	imv.f.s Ct 6.5
	1.pl Ne 5.12	imv.m.pl Ne 5.11

Hi.inf.abs Gn 24.5   inf.cs Jo 1.13   +sfx 2Sm 12.23
Hi.ptc.f.s.cs Ps 19.7

שָׁוָה = vb TO BE EQUAL TO, LEVEL   Qal.imp.3m.pl Pr 8.11
Pi = MAKE LEVEL i.e. RESTRAIN   pf.1.s Ps 131.2 *

שׁוּחָה = n.f PIT   s Je 18.20,22Q *

שׁוֹט = n.m WHIP   s Na 3.2 *

שׁוּל = n.m SKIRT   pl+sfx Is 6.1; Na 3.5 *

שׁוּלַמִּית = adj.gent.f WOMAN OF SHULEM   s Ct 7.1 R2 pl31 H.L.

שׁוע = vb TO CRY FOR HELP   Pi.pf.1.s Jo 2.3   inf.cs+sfx Ps 22.25 *

שַׁוְעָה = n.f   CRY FOR HELP   s.cs 1Sm 5.12   *

שׁוּעָל = n.m   FOX   s Ne 3.35   pl Ct 2.15   *

שׁוֹעֵר = n.m   GATEKEEPER   pl Ne 7.1;13.5   *

שׁוּף = vb   TO BRUISE   Qal.imp.3m.s+sfx Gn 3.15

   Qal.imp.2m.s+sfx @21e Gn 3.15   *

שׁוֹפָר/שֹׁפָר = n.m   RAM'S HORN   s Ex 20.18; Zp 1.16; Ps 81.4;150.3; Ne 4.12,
                                                    Ne 4.14   *

שׁוֹק = n.f   LEG   dual+sfx Ct 5.15   *

שׁוּק = n.m   STREET   s Ec 12.4,5   pl Ct 3.2   *

שׁוּר = vb   1. TO DEPART   2. TO LOOK   3. TO LEAP

   Qal.juss.2f.s Ct 4.8   *   Could be any of above, though 1. most
   likely, R2 p128, Holl p365.   2. is cited by B.D.B. p1003.   Existence
   of 3. is disputed.

שׁוֹר = n.m   OX, BULLOCK   s Is 1.3; Ne 5.18   +sfx Ex 20.17   *

שׁוּשַׁן = n.loc   SUSA   Ne 1.1   *

שׁוֹשַׁן / = n.m/f   LILY   m.pl Ct 2.16;4.5;5.13;6.2,3;7.3
שׁוֹשַׁנָּה f.s Ct 2.2   f.s.cs Ct 2.1   *

שָׁזַף = vb   TO CATCH SIGHT OF   Qal.pf.3f.s+sfx Ct 1.6 (of sun = TAN)*

שֹׁחַד = n.m   BRIBE   s Is 1.23   *

שָׁחָה = vb   TO BOW DOWN   Hithpalel forms given in lexicons
e.g B.D.B. p1005, Foh p280, now disputed in light of Ugaritic. For
alternative derivation as Hištap'el of vb חוה see p 32.

שָׁחַח = vb   TO STOOP, BOW DOWN   Qal.pf.3m.s Is 2.11,17

   Ni.imp.3m.s Is 2.9   3m.pl Ec 12.4   *

שַׁחַק = n.m   SKY, CLOUD   pl Pr 8.28   *

שָׁחַר = vb.denom   TO SEEK DILIGENTLY   Pi.ptc.m.pl+sfx Pr 8.17   *

שַׁחַר = n.m   DAWN   s Gn 19.15; Jo 4.7; Ps 22.1; Ct 6.10; Ne 4.15   *

שָׁחוֹר = adj   BLACK   f.s Ct 1.5   f.pl Ct 5.11   *

שַׁחֲרוּת = n.f   PRIME OF LIFE   s Ec 11.10 R1 p109   H.L.
   Either from root שָׁחַר = DAWN, or better שָׁחַר = BE BLACK

שְׁחַרְחֹרֶת = adj   SWARTHY   f.s Ct 1.6   H.L.

שָׁחַת = vb   TO SPOIL, DESTROY   Pi.pf.3m.pl Na 2.3
   Pi.inf.cs Gn 19.29; Hs 11.9   +sfx Gn 19.13   Hi.pf.3m.pl Zp 3.7

Hi.imp.2m.s Gn 18.28   l.s Gn 18.28,31,32   3m.pl 2Sm 11.1
Hi.coh.pl Je 11.19   ptc.m.s Gn 19.14   m.pl Gn 19.13; 1Sm 6.5
                                                        Is 1.4   *

שַׁחַת = n.f   PIT (= SHEOL)   s Jo 2.7; Ps 103.4   *

שָׁטַף = vb   TO OVERFLOW   Qal.pf.3m.pl+sfx Ps 124.4
Qal.imp.3m.pl+sfx Ct 8.7   *

שֶׁטֶף = n.m   FLOOD   s Na 1.8   *

שִׁיחָה = n.f   PIT   s Je 18.22K   *

שִׁיר = 1. vb   TO SING   Qal.coh.s Is 5.1; Ps 101.1
Qal.imv.m.pl Je 20.13; Ps 96.1,2   Po.imp.3m.s Zp 2.14
Po.ptc.m.pl Ne 7.1;13.5,10   *
    2. n.m   SONG   s Ec 12.4   s.cs Ct 1.1   pl Ct 1.1
s in titles of Psalms 48,96,121,124,130,131,133,134   *

שִׁירָה = n.f   SONG   s.cs Is 5.1   *

שִׁית = vb   TO PUT, SET   Qal.pf.3f.s 1Sm 4.20; Ps 84.4   2m.s Ps 8.7
Qal.pf.1.s+sfx Hs 2.5   imp.1.s Gn 3.15; Ps 101.3;110.1   +sfx Is 5.6
Qal.imp.3m.pl+sfx Ps 84.7   imv.m.pl Ps 48.14   *

שַׁיִת = n.m.coll   WEEDS, THORN BUSHES   s.i.p Is 5.6   *

שָׁכַב = vb   TO LIE DOWN   Qal.pf.3m.s 2Sm 12.11,16   l.s Gn 19.34
Qal.imp.3m.s 2Sm 11.4,9;12.24; Jo 1.5   3f.s Gn 19.33,35; 2Sm 12.3
Qal.imp.3m.pl Gn 19.4   coh.pl Gn 19.32   imv.f.s Gn 19.34
Qal.inf.cs 2Sm 11.11,13   +sfx Gn 19.33,35
Hi.pf.1.s+sfx Hs 2.20   *

שַׁכּוּל = adj   BEREAVED   f.s Ct 4.2;6.6   f.pl Je 18.21   *

שָׁכַח = vb   TO FORGET   Qal.pf.3f.s Hs 2.15   2m.s Dt 8.14
Qal.imp.2m.s Dt 8.11,19   juss.3f.s Ps 103.2   inf.abs Dt 8.19
Ni.imp.3f.s Je 20.11   *

שָׁכַם = vb.denom   TO MAKE AN EARLY START, BE EAGER
Hi.pf.3m.s 2Sm 15.2   3m.pl Zp 3.7   2m.pl Gn 19.2
Hi.imp.3m.s Gn 19.27   3m.pl 1Sm 5.3,4   coh.pl Ct 7.13   *

שְׁכֶם = n.m   SHOULDER   s Zp 3.9   +sfx Ps 81.7   *

שָׁכַן = vb   TO SETTLE, DWELL   Qal.pf.1.s Pr 8.12   imp.3m.pl Na 3.18
Qal.ptc.m.s+old ending Ob 3   Pi.inf.cs Ne 1.9
Hi = PUT imp.3m.s Gn 3.24   *

שְׁכַנְיָה = n.pr.m   SHECANIAH   Ne 6.18   *

שָׁכַר = vb   TO BE DRUNK   Qal.imp.2f.s Na 3.11   imv.m.pl Ct 5.1

   Pi = MAKE DRUNK imp.3m.s+sfx 2Sm 11.13   *

שֶׁלֶג = n.m   SNOW   s Is 1.18   *

שָׁלָה = vb   TO BE TRANQUIL, AT EASE   Qal.pf.3m.pl Je 12.1   *

שִׁלֹה = n.loc   SHILOH   1Sm 4.3,4,12   *

שַׁלְהֶבֶת = n.f   FLAME   שַׁלְהֶבֶתְיָה   Ct 8.6 could be intensive form.
   Perhaps should repoint either to שַׁלְהֶבַת יָה , Holl p370, Foh p284,
   or to pl+3f.sfx R2 p133.   *

שָׁלוֹם = n.m   PEACE, WELFARE   s Je 12.5; Na 2.1; Ps 29.11; Ct 8.10
   s+sfx Is 53.5; Je 20.10; Ob 7   s.cs 2Sm 11.7

שָׁלַח = vb   TO SEND, STRETCH OUT
   Qal.pf.3m.s Ct 5.4; Ne 6.19   +sfx 2Sm 11.22; Ne 6.12   3f.s Pr 9.3
   Qal.imp.3m.s Gn 24.7; Ps 110.2   +sfx Ne 2.6   3f.s 2Sm 11.5
   Qal.imp.2m.s+sfx Ne 2.5   1.s Ne 13.21   3m.pl Gn 19.10; 1Sm 5.8
   Qal.juss.2f.pl Ob 13   coh.s Ne 6.3,8   imv.m.s 2Sm 11.6
   Qal.inf.cs Es 2.21

   Pi.pf   Pi.imp   Pi
   3m.pl+sfx Ob 7   3m.s Gn 19.29   +sfx Gn 3.23 juss.2m.pl 1Sm 6.3
   2m.pl 1Sm 6.8   1.s+sfx 2Sm 11.12; Ps 81.13 imv.m.pl 1Sm 5.11
                     3m.pl 1Sm 5.10   inf.cs+sfx Gn 18.16
                     1.pl+sfx @21e 1Sm 6.2   ptc.m.pl 1Sm 6.3

   Pu.pf.3m.s Ob 1

שֶׁלַח = n.m   1. MISSILE, JAVELIN   s Ne 4.11   +sfx Ne 4.17   *
                2. SPROUT, SHOOT   dual+sfx Ct 4.13   *

שֻׁלְחָן = n.m   TABLE   s Ps 23.5   +sfx Pr 9.2; Ne 5.17   *

שָׁלַט = vb   TO DOMINEER, TYRANNIZE   Qal.pf.3m.pl Ne 5.15   *

שֶׁלֶט = n.m   SHIELD   pl.cs Ct 4.4   *

שְׁלִישִׁי = ordinal number   THIRD   Gn 1.13;2.14   *

שָׁלַךְ = vb   TO THROW   Hi.pf.3f.s 2Sm 11.21   1.s Na 3.6
   Hi.imp.3m.s Is 2.20   2m.s+sfx Jo 2.4   coh.s Ne 13.8
   Hi.coh.pl Ps 2.3   inf.cs Ec 3.5,6   Ho.imp.1.s Ps 22.11   *

שָׁלָל = n.m   BOOTY, PLUNDER   s Is 53.12   s.cs 2Sm 12.30   *

שָׁלֵם = vb   TO BE COMPLETE, SOUND   Qal.imp.3f.s Ne 6.15

Pi = REPAY, FULFIL   imp.3m.s 2Sm 12.6   l.s Ps 22.26   coh.s Jo 2.10

Pi.imv.f.s Na 2.1   Pu.imp.3m.s Je 18.20   *

שָׁלֵם = adj   COMPLETE   m.pl Ne 1.12 of army at full strength   *

שְׁלֶם = n.m   PEACE-OFFERING   pl+sfx Ex 20.24   *

שְׁלֹמֹה = n.pr.m   SOLOMON   2Sm 12.24; 1Kg 3.5; Ct 1.1; Ne 13.26

שֶׁלֶמְיָה = n.pr.m   SHELEMIAH   Ne 13.13   *

שִׁלְמֹנִין = n.m   BRIBE, REWARD   pl Is 1.23   H.L.

שָׁלֹשׁ / = number   THREE   m.cs Gn 17.25;18.6

שְׁלֹשָׁה } f Gn 18.2; Jo 2.1; Ne 2.11   f.cs Jo 3.3   *

שִׁלֵּשׁ = n.m   DESCENDANT OF THE THIRD GENERATION   pl Ex 20.5   *

שָׁלִשָׁה = n.loc   SHALISHAH   1Sm 9.4   *

שְׁלֹשִׁים = number   THIRTY   Gn 18.30; 1Sm 4.10; Ne 5.14;13.6   *

שִׁלְשֹׁם = n.m   DAY BEFORE YESTERDAY   1Sm 4.7   *

שָׁם = adv   THERE, THITHER   Gn 24.5; 1Sm 9.6; Jo 4.5; Ru 1.2; Ne 1.3

+הloc Gn 19.20,22;24.6,8; Ct 8.5; Ne 4.14

שֵׁם = n.m   NAME   s Zp 3.19,20; Ne 6.13   +sfx Hs 1.4; Ps 8.2

s.cs Gn 2.11; Ru 1.2; Es 2.22   pl @9e Gn 2.20   pl.cs Hs 2.19

שַׁמָּה = n.f   RUIN   s Zp 2.15   *

שְׁמוּעָה = n.f   REPORT   s 1Sm 4.19; Ob 1   +sfx Is 53.1   *

שָׁמַיִם = n.m.pl   HEAVENS, SKY   Gn 1.1; 1Sm 5.12; Jo 1.9; Ps 96.5; Ec 3.1

+sfx Ps 8.4

שְׁמִינִית = ordinal number   EIGHTH   Ps 6.1 Rl p45   *

שָׁמִיר = n.m.coll   THORN BUSHES   s Is 5.6   *

שָׁמֵם = vb   TO BE DESOLATE (of area), HORRIFIED (of people)

Qal.pf.3m.pl Is 52.14   Ni.pf.3m.pl Zp 3.6

Hi.pf.l.s Hs 2.14   imp.3m.s+sfx 1Sm 5.6   *

שְׁמָמָה = n.f   DESOLATION, RUIN   s Is 1.7; Zp 1.13;2.4,9,13   *

שֶׁמֶן = n.m   OIL   s Dt 8.8; Is 1.6; Ps 23.5;133.2; Ct 1.3

s.i.p Is 5.1   s+sfx Hs 2.7   pl+sfx Ct 1.3;4.10   *

שְׁמֹנֶה / }= number   EIGHT @25d   m 1Sm 4.15   f.cs Gn 17.12   *

שְׁמֹנָה }

שְׁמֹנִים = number   EIGHTY   Ct 6.8   *

שָׁמַע = vb   TO HEAR, LISTEN TO

Qal.pf		Qal.imp	
3m.s 2Sm 12.18; Ps 6.9;81.12		3m.s 1Sm 4.14; Ne 2.10,19	
3f.s Ru 1.6		3f.s 1Sm 4.19; 2Sm 11.26	
2m.s Gn 3.17; Jo 2.3		2m.s Ps 81.9	
1.s Gn 3.10 +sfx Gn 17.20		1.s Ps 81.6	
3m.pl Is 52.15; Ne 4.9;6.16		3m.pl Gn 3.8; 1Sm 4.6	
2m.pl Is 1.19		2m.pl Dt 8.20; Ne 4.14	
1.pl Ob 1; Ps 48.9		1.pl Ne 13.27	

Qal.coh.pl Ex 20.19   imv.m.s Je 18.19; Ps 81.9   m.pl Is 1.2
Qal.inf.cs 1Kg 3.11; Ps 103.20; Ec 1.8   +sfx Ne 1.4;13.3
Qal.ptc.m.s 2Sm 15.3; 1Kg 3.9   f.s Gn 18.10   m.pl.cs Na 3.19
Ni.pf.3m.s Ct 2.12; Ne 6.1   imp.3m.s Na 2.14; Ne 6.7
Ni.juss.3f.s Je 18.22   ptc.m.s Ps 19.4; Ne 6.6
Hi.imv.f.s+sfx Ct 2.14;8.13   ptc.m.s Na 2.1

שֵׁמַע = n.m   TIDINGS, SOUND   s.i.p Ps 150.5   s+sfx Na 3.19   *

שְׁמַעְיָה = n.pr.m   SHEMAIAH   Ne 6.10   *

שָׁמַר = vb   TO KEEP, WATCH, PRESERVE

Qal.pf	Qal.imp		Qal.juss
2m.s Dt 8.6	3m.s Ps 121.7,8	+sfx Ps 121.7	2m.s Gn 17.9
3m.pl Gn 18.19	2m.s Dt 8.2; 1Kg 3.6		2m.pl Dt 8.1
2m.pl Ne 1.9	3m.pl Pr 8.32		
1.pl Ne 1.7	2m.pl Gn 17.10		

Qal.inf.cs 1Kg 3.14; Ec 3.6   +sfx Gn 2.15; Ps 19.12
Qal.ptc.m.s.cs Ps 121.4; Ne 1.5;2.8   m.s+sfx Ps 121.3,5
Qal.ptc.m.pl Ps 130.6; Ct 3.3; Ne 13.22   m.pl.cs Je 20.10; Ct 5.7b
Ni.imv.m.s Gn 24.6; Dt 8.11   Pi.ptc.m.pl Jo 2.9

שְׁמָרִים = n.m   DREGS, LEES   pl+sfx Zp 1.12 Rl p87   *

שֹׁמְרוֹן = n.loc   SAMARIA   Ob 19; Ne 3.34   *

שֶׁמֶשׁ = n.m/f   SUN   s Gn 19.23; 2Sm 12.11; Jo 4.8; Na 3.17; Ps 19.5

שֵׁן = n.f   1. TOOTH   dual+sfx Ps 124.6; Ct 4.2; 6.6   *
                    2. IVORY   s Ct 5.14;7.5   *

שָׁנָה = 1. vb   TO REPEAT   Qal.imp.2m.pl Ne 13.21   *
                    2. n.f   YEAR   s Gn 17.1; Dt 8.2; 1Sm 4.15; 2Sm 11.1

שְׁנִי   s.cs Is 6.1; Je 11.23; Ne 1.1   pl Gn 1.14; Ru 1.4; Ec 11.8

שָׁנִי = n.m   SCARLET STUFF   s Ct 4.3   pl Is 1.18   *

שֵׁנִית/שֵׁנִי = ordinal number   SECOND   f Jo 3.1; Ru 1.4   *

שְׁנַיִם / = number   TWO   @24d   m Ne 6.15   f Is 6.2; Ne 13.6,20
שְׁתַּיִם   m.cs Gn 1.16; Ru 1.1; Es 2.21   f.cs Gn 19.8; 1Sm 5.4;6.7
m+sfx Is 1.31; Ru 1.5; Es 2.23   שְׁנֵים עָשָׂר = TWELVE Gn 17.20

שְׁתֵּים עֶשְׂרֵה = TWELVE Jo 4.11; Ne 5.14

שַׁעֲלִים = n.loc   SHAALIM   1Sm 9.4   *

שָׁעַן = vb   TO LEAN, REST   Ni.imv.m.pl Gn 18.4   *

שַׁעַר = n.m   GATE   s 1Sm 4.18   s.i.p 2Sm 11.23;15.2
s.cs Gn 19.1; Ob 13; Zp 1.10   pl Ps 24.7; Pr 8.3; Ne 6.1
pl+sfx Ex 20.10; Ob 11Q; Ps 100.4   pl.cs Na 2.7;3.13; Ne 2.8

שַׁעֲשֻׁעִים = n.m.pl.intensive   DELIGHT   Pr 8.30   +sfx Is 5.7; Pr 8.31   *

שָׁפַט = vb   TO JUDGE, GOVERN   Qal.pf.3m.s 1Sm 4.18; Is 2.4
Qal.imp.3m.s Gn 19.9; Ps 82.1   3m.pl Is 1.23   2m.pl Ps 82.2
Qal.imv.m.s Ps 82.8   m.pl Is 1.17;5.3; Ps 82.3   inf.abs Gn 19.9
Qal.inf.cs 1Kg 3.9; Ob 21; Ru 1.1   ptc.m.s Gn 18.25; 2Sm 15.4;
                                                                Je 11.20

Qal.ptc.m.pl Ru 1.1   +sfx Is 1.26; Zp 3.3
Qal.ptc.m.pl.cs Ps 2.10; Pr 8.16   *

שָׁפַךְ = vb   TO POUR OUT   Qal.inf.cs Zp 3.8
Ni.pf.1.s Ps 22.15   Pu.pf.3m.s Zp 1.17   *

שָׁפֵל = vb   TO BE LOW, ABASED   Qal.pf.3m.s Is 2.11,12,17
Qal.imp.3m.s Is 2.9   inf.cs Ec 12.4 G/K 45c   *

שְׁפֵלָה = n.loc   SHEPHELAH, LOWLAND   Ob 19   *

שָׁפַת = vb   TO SET, PUT, LAY   Qal.imp.2m.s+sfx Ps 22.16   *

שָׁקַד = vb   TO WATCH, BE VIGILANT   Qal.inf.cs Pr 8.34   *

שָׁקֵד = n.m   ALMOND-TREE   s Ec 12.5   *

שָׁקָה = vb   TO WATER, GIVE A DRINK   Hi.pf.3m.s Gn 2.6
Hi.imp.1.s+sfx Ct 8.2   3f.pl Gn 19.33,35   coh.pl Gn 19.32
Hi.coh.pl+sfx Gn 19.34   inf.cs Gn 2.10   ptc.m.s Ne 1.11   *

שִׁקּוּי = n.m   ?DRINK, REFRESHMENT   pl+sfx Hs 2.7   R1 p61   *

שֶׁקֶל = n.m   SHEKEL (unit of weight, later money)
s.cs 1Sm 9.8   pl Ne 5.15   *

שׁקף = vb   TO LOOK DOWN   Ni.ptc.f.s Ct 6.10
          Hi.imp.3m.s Gn 19.28   3m.pl Gn 18.16   *

שׁקץ = vb.denom   TO DETEST   Pi.pf.3m.s Ps 22.25   *

שׁקץ = n.m   DETESTED THING, SOMETHING UNCLEAN   pl Na 3.6   *

שׁקק = vb   TO HURTLE ABOUT   Hithpalpel.imp.3m.pl Na 2.5   *

שֶׁקֶר = n.m   DECEPTION, FALSEHOOD   s.i.p Ex 20.16   pl Ps 101.7   *

שׁר = n.m   NAVEL   s+sfx Ct 7.3   *

שׁרה = vb   TO LET LOOSE   Pi.pf.1.s+sfx Je 15.11Q   *
          K = root שׁרר. Text is difficult, see R2 p94

שׁרוֹן = n.loc   SHARON   Ct 2.1   *

שׁרירוּת = n.f   HARDNESS, STUBBORNNESS   s.cs Ps 81.13   *

שׁרץ = vb   TO SWARM, TEEM   Qal.pf.3m.pl Gn 1.21
          Qal.juss.3m.pl Gn 1.20   *

שֶׁרֶץ = n.m.coll   SWARMING THINGS   s.cs Gn 1.20   *

שׁרק = vb   TO WHISTLE, HISS   Qal.imp.3m.s Zp 2.15   *

שׁרר = vb   TO BE FIRM, STRONG   Qal.pf.1.s+sfx Je 15.11K   *
          Text dubious and unclear. See שׁרה and R2 p94

שׁרשׁ = vb.denom   TO TAKE ROOT   Po'al.pf.3m.pl Je 12.2   *

שֹׁרֶשׁ = n.m   ROOT   s Is 53.2   s.cs Jb 19.28   *

שׁרת = vb   TO MINISTER   Pi.imp.3m.s+sfx Ps 101.6
          Pi.ptc.m.s+sfx Ps 103.21   *

שׁשׁ = n.m   ALABASTER   s Ct 5.15   *

שׁשׁ/שׁשׁה = number   SIX   m Is 6.2; Ne 5.18   f.cs Ex 20.9,11   *

שׁשׁי = ordinal number   SIXTH   Gn 1.31   *

שׁשׁים = number   SIXTY   Ct 3.7;6.8   *

שׁתה = vb   TO DRINK   Qal.pf.1.s Ct 5.1   3m.pl Ob 16   2m.pl Ob 16
          Qal.imp.3m.s Ps 110.7   apoc 2Sm 11.13   3f.s 2Sm 12.3
          Qal.imp.3m.pl Ob 16; Zp 1.13   juss.3m.pl Jo 3.7
          Qal.imv.m.pl Pr 9.5; Ct 5.1   inf.cs 2Sm 11.11   *

שׁתל = vb   TO TRANSPLANT   Qal.ptc.pass.m.s Ps 1.3   *

שׁתק = vb   TO BE QUIET   Qal.juss.3m.s Jo 1.11,12   @13e   *

ת

תַאֲוָה = n.f   DESIRABLE THING, DELIGHT   s Gn 3.6   *

תְּאוֹמִים = n.m.pl   TWINS   cs Ct 4.5;7.4   *

תאם = vb   TO FORM TWINS   Hi.ptc.f.pl Ct 4.2;6.6 R2 p128   *

תְּאֵנָה = n.f   FIG TREE (s), FIGS (pl)   s Gn 3.7; Dt 8.8; Ct 2.13
        s+sfx Hs 2.14   pl @9e Na 3.12; Ne 13.15   *

תֹּאַר = n.m   FORM, APPEARANCE   s Is 53.2   +sfx Is 52.14   *

תְּבוּאָה = n.f   YIELD, PRODUCE   s+sfx Pr 8.19   *

תְּבוּנָה = n.f   INTELLIGENCE, UNDERSTANDING   s Ob 7,8; Pr 8.1   *

תֵּבֵל = n.f   WORLD   s Na 1.5; Ps 19.5;24.1;93.1; Pr 8.26
        s.cs Pr 8.31   *

תֵּבֵץ = n.loc   THEBEZ   2Sm 11.21   *

תֹּהוּ = n.m   CHAOS, EMPTINESS   s Gn 1.2   *

תְּהוֹם = n.f   PRIMEVAL OCEAN, ABYSS   s Gn 1.2; Jo 2.6; Pr 8.27,28
        pl Dt 8.7; Pr 8.24   *

תְּהִלָּה = n.f   PRAISE   s Zp 3.19,20; Ps 100.4
        s+sfx Je 17.14; Ps 22.26;48.11   pl.cs Ps 22.4   *

תַּהְפֻּכָה = n.f   PERVERSITY   pl Pr 8.13   *

תּוֹדָה = n.f   THANKSGIVING   s Jo 2.10; Ps 100.1,4   *

תָּוֶךְ = n.m   MIDDLE   s.cs Ne 6.10   +בְּ Gn 1.6; 1Kg 3.8; Ez 37.1
        s.cs+מִן Gn 19.29   s+sfx Is 5.2; Zp 2.14; Ct 3.10; Ne 4.5

תּוֹלְדוֹת = n.f.pl   ORIGINS   cs Gn 2.4   *

תּוֹלָע = n.m   SCARLET MATERIAL   s Is 1.18 B.D.B p1068   *

תּוֹלַעַת = n.f   WORM   s Jo 4.7; Ps 22.7   *

תּוֹעֵבָה = n.f   ABOMINATION   s Is 1.13   s.cs Pr 8.7   *

תּוֹעָה = n.f   CONFUSION   s Ne 4.2   *

תּוּר = vb   TO INVESTIGATE   Qal.inf.cs Ec 1.13   *

תּוֹר = n.m   1. PLAIT OF HAIR (N.E.B), or PENDANT (J.B)
        pl Ct 1.10   pl.cs Ct 1.11   *
        2. TURTLE-DOVE   s Ct 2.12   *

תּוֹרָה = n.f   LAW, INSTRUCTION   s Is 2.3; Je 18.18; Zp 3.4; Ne 13.3

        s.cs Is 1.10; Ps 1.2a;19.8   s+sfx Je 31.33; Ps 1.2b   *

תּוּרָק = n.m   ?TYPE OF OIL   s Ct 1.3   H.L

        So R2 p124, though many take as Ho of רִיק , eg R.S.V

תּוּשִׁיָּה = n.f   ABILITY, COMPETENCE   s Pr 8.14   *

תְּחִלָּה = n.f   BEGINNING   s+כְּבַ Is 1.26   s.cs Hs 1.2   *

תַּחֲלוּאִים = n.m.pl   DISEASES   +sfx כִי Ps 103.3 R1 p24   *

תְּחִנָּה = n.f   ENTREATY   s+sfx Ps 6.10   *

תַּחֲנוּן = n.m   SUPPLICATION   pl+sfx Ps 130.2   *

תַּחַת = adv & prep   1. UNDER   Gn 24.2; Ps 8.7; Ec 1.3; Ct 2.6;4.11

    +מִן Ex 20.4   +אֲשֶׁר Is 53.12   +sfx @14f Ob 7; Jo 4.5; Ne 2.14

              2. INSTEAD OF   1Kg 3.7; Je 18.20; Zp 2.10

+sfx @21e Gn 2.21   *

תַּחְתִּי = adj   LOWER, LOWEST   as subs.f.pl Ne 4.7   *

תֵּימָן = 1. n.f   SOUTH WIND   s Ct 4.16   *

        2. n.loc   TEMAN (In Edom)   Ob 9   *

תִּימָרָה = n.f   COLUMN (of smoke)   pl.cs Ct 3.6   *

תִּירוֹשׁ = n.m   WINE   s Hs 2.10,24; Ne 5.11;13.5,12   +sfx Hs 2.11   *

תְּכוּנָה = n.m   TREASURE, STORES   s Na 2.10   *

תָּלָה = vb   TO HANG   Qal.ptc.pass.m.s Ct 4.4

Qal.ptc.pass.m.pl Hs 11.7 (text difficult,   R1 p72)

Ni.imp.3m.pl Es 2.23   *

תלע = vb   TO BE CLOTHED IN SCARLET   Pu.ptc.m.pl Na 2.4   H.L

תַּלְפִּיּוֹת = n.f.pl   ?BUILT IN ROWS   Ct 4.4   H.L

Meaning very uncertain. G = place name, R.S.V = ARMAMENTS,
N.E.B = WINDING COURSES. R2 p128

תַּלְתַּלִּים = n.m.pl   CLUSTERS OF DATE PALM   Ct 5.11   H.L

Used in comparison with locks of hair R2 p130

תָּם = adj   COMPLETE   f.s+sfx Ct 5.2;6.9   *

תֹּם = n.m   COMPLETENESS, INTEGRITY   s.cs Ps 101.2   *

תָּמַהּ = vb   TO BE ASTOUNDED   Qal.pf.3m.pl Ps 48.6   *

תְּמוּנָה = n.f   LIKENESS, FORM   s Ex 20.4   *

תָּמִיד = adv   CONTINUOUSLY   Ob 16; Na 3.19   *

תָּמִים = adj   PERFECT, COMPLETE   m.s Gn 17.1; Ps 101.2,6

    m.s = INTEGRITY Ps 84.12   f.s Ps 19.8   *

תָּמַם = vb   TO BE WHOLE, COMPLETE   Qal.imp.1.s Ps 19.14   *

תָּמָר = n.m   PALM TREE   s Ct 7.8,9   *

תַּן = n.m   JACKAL   pl Ne 2.13 G/K 87e   *

    Could be read as   תַּנִּין R2 p49

תַּנִּין = n.m   SEA MONSTER   pl Gn 1.21   *

תָּעָה = vb   TO ERR   Qal.pf.1.pl Is 53.6   *

תַּעֲנוּג = n.m   DELIGHT   pl Ct 7.7   *

תֹּף = n.m   TAMBOURINE, HAND DRUM   s Ps 81.3;150.4   *

תַּפּוּחַ = n.m   APPLE TREE (s), APPLES (pl)

    s Ct 2.3;8.5   pl Ct 2.5;7.9   *

תְּפִלָּה = n.f   PRAYER   s Is 1.15   s.cs Ne 1.6,11

    s+sfx Jo 2.8; Ps 6.10;84.9   *

תָּפַף = vb.denom   TO BEAT, DRUM   Poel ptc.f.pl Na 2.8   *

תָּפַר = vb   TO SEW TOGETHER   Qal.imp.3m.pl Gn 3.7   inf.cs Ec 3.7   *

תִּקְוָה = n.f   HOPE   s Hs 2.17   +sfx Ez 37.11   *

תְּקוּפָה = n.f   CIRCUIT   s+sfx Ps 19.7   *

תָּקַן = vb   TO BE STRAIGHT (only Ec)   Qal.inf.cs Ec 1.15   *

תָּקַע = vb   TO BLOW (instrument), CLAP (hands)   Qal.pf.3m.pl Na 3.19

    Qal.imv.m.pl Ps 81.4   ptc.m.s Ne 4.12   *

תֵּקַע = n.m   BLAST (of ram's horn)   s.cs Ps 150.3   *

תַּרְדֵּמָה = n.f   DEEP SLEEP   s Gn 2.21   *

תְּרוּמָה = n.f   CONTRIBUTION, OFFERING   s.cs Ne 13.5   *

תְּרוּעָה = n.f   SHOUT OF ALARM/VICTORY

    s Je 20.16; Zp 1.16 ALARM 1Sm 4.5,6; Ps 150.5   ACCLAMATION   *

תַּרְמִית = n.f   CUNNING, DECEIT   s Zp 3.13   *

תְּרָפִים = n.m.pl   TERAPHIM (household idols)   Hs 3.4   *

    First mentioned in Gn 31; used in divination Zechariah 10.2

תִּרְצָה = n.loc   TIRZAH   Ct 6.4   *

תֶּרֶשׁ = n.pr.m   TERESH   Es 2.21   *

תַּרְשִׁישׁ = 1. n.m   PRECIOUS STONE (?TOPAZ, ?CHRYSOLITE)   s Ct 5.14   *

2. n.loc   TARSHISH   Jo 1.3   + ה loc Jo 4.2; Ps 48.8 R1 p33   *

תְּשׁוּבָה = n.f   RETURN   s.cs 2Sm 11.1   R2 p29   *

תְּשׁוּקָה = n.f   LONGING, URGE   s+sfx Gn 3.16; Ct 7.11   *

תְּשׁוּרָה = n.f   ?GIFT, PRESENT   s 1Sm 9.7   H.L

תֵּשַׁע/תִּשְׁעָה = number   NINE   @25d   m Gn 17.1,24   *

תִּשְׁעִים = number   NINETY   Gn 17.1,17,24; 1Sm 4.15   *

ADDITIONAL WORDS

from the title-pages and from the Songs and
Supplementary Readings of First Studies

אֲבִישַׁג = n.pr   ABISHAG   Text 7

אֲדֹנִיָּהוּ = n.pr   ADONIJAH   Text 7

אִיּוֹב = n.pr   JOB   Text 2

אֲלֻמָּה = m.f   SHEAF   Song 8

אָמוֹן = ptc   FAITHFUL   Song 10

אֹפֶן = n   (RIGHT) TIME   du+sfx Pro25.11

אָשֵׁם = vb   TO BE GUILTY   Text 8

בָּחִיר = n.m   CHOSEN ONE   Text 6

גְּדֻלָּה = n.f   GREATNESS   Song 9

זָן = ptc of זון @ 30e   TO FEED   Song 10

חָלַם = vb   TO DREAM, ? GET WELL   Song 8

לָבָן = adj   WHITE   Text 10

לָה = 'LA' in singing   Songs 2 and 5

מִיכָה = n.pr   MICAH   Text 4

מַשְׂכִּית = n.f   CARVING   pl מַשְׂכִּיֹּת   Pro 25.11

מִשְׂרָה = n.f   RULE   Text 5

נְמָלָה = n.f   ANT   Pro6.6

עוֹלָם = n.m   WORLD   Song 10

עוּץ = n.loc   UZ   Text 2

עָצֵל = adj as n.m   LAZY MAN   Pro6.6

סָכָל = n.m   FOOL   Text 10

סָכַן = vb   Qal   BE OF SERVICE   ptc.f Text 7
Hi   BE WONT TO   Text 9

פֶּלֶא = n.m   WONDER   Text 5

קְדֻשָׁה = n.f   HOLINESS   Song 9

רְגָלִים = n.f.pl of רֶגֶל   TIMES   Text 9

רָשַׁע = vb   TO BE WICKED   Text 10

שָׂטָן = n.m   ADVERSARY, SATAN   Text 2

שׁוּנַמִּית = adj. gent.f   WOMAN OF SHUNEM   Text 7

שָׁלַף = vb   TO DRAW OUT   Text 9

שֶׁמָּא = conj   LEST, PERHAPS   Pirke Aboth 2.5

שָׁנָה = vb   Qal   TO STUDY   Pirke Aboth 2.5

תִּפְאֶרֶת = n.f   GLORY, TURBAN   Song 9

בשם יי אלהי ישראל. מימיני מיכאל.
ומשמאלי גבריאל. ומלפני אוריאל.
ומאחורי רפאל. ועל ראשי שכינת אל.

A traditional prayer penned by H. St J. Hart.
(Words additional to the Glossary are the names
of the four archangels, שְׁכִינָה = Presence,
and יי = יהוה .)